Spreading the
AMERICAN DREAM

Spreading the
AMERICAN DREAM

★═★═★═★═★═★═★═★═★═

American Economic and Cultural
Expansion, 1890–1945

EMILY S. ROSENBERG

Consulting Editor ERIC FONER

AMERICAN CENTURY SERIES

HILL AND WANG · NEW YORK
A division of Farrar, Straus, and Giroux

Library of Congress Cataloguing in Publication Data
Rosenberg, Emily S.,
    Spreading the American dream.
    (American century series)
    Bibliography: p.
    Includes index.
    1. United States—Foreign relations—20th century.
2. United States—Foreign relations—1865–1921.
3. United States—Foreign economic relations. I. Foner,
Eric. II. Title.
E744.R82   1982   973.9   81-13250
                                         AACR2
ISBN 0-8090-8798-7   ISBN 0-8090-0146-2 pbk.

TO

★═══★═══★

NORM
SARAH
MOLLY
RUTH
JOSEPH

ACKNOWLEDGMENTS

MY greatest thanks go to Norman L. Rosenberg, with whom I have shared a disorganized life teaching, writing, and caring for children. His influence affected every page of this book. He deserves partial credit for any virtues the work may possess— and I'll gladly assign him partial blame for its faults.

A number of friends, colleagues, and acquaintances read and commented on my manuscript, and I deeply appreciate their time and effort. Special thanks should go to Frederick Adams, Richard J. Barnet, David Burner, Roberta Dayer, Eric Foner, Walter LaFeber, David Trask, and Richard Werking. My associates in American history at Macalester College, Ernest R. Sandeen and James B. Stewart, commented on portions of the manuscript and provided encouragement. A Mellon grant and other support from Macalester's administration and faculty activities committee eased the burden of preparing the manuscript. Kay Crawford and Jan Seashore were exceptionally skilled typists. Above all, Arthur Wang's patience and constructive suggestions were greatly appreciated.

Finally, I would like to thank my four children—Sarah, Molly, Ruth, and Joseph—for finding their mother better things to do than write books and my parents—Albert A. and Helen Griggs Schlaht—for their constant support.

CONTENTS

CONTENTS

Spreading the
AMERICAN DREAM

One
★ ═══ ★ ═══ ★

INTRODUCTION: THE AMERICAN DREAM

THE COLUMBIAN EXPOSITION OF 1893

A SPECTACULAR World's Fair, the Columbian Exposition, opened in Chicago in 1893. Acres of classical buildings, constructed especially for the fair, created an urban wonderland; it glittered with artistic splendor and burgeoned with America's latest technological achievements. After a visit to this White City, the French novelist and critic Paul Bourget wrote: "Chicago, the enormous town we see expanding, the gigantic plant which grows before our eyes seems now in this wonderfully new country to be in advance of the age. But is not this more or less true of all America?"

Bourget's comment was the kind Americans liked to quote; the exposition's exhibitors displayed their hopes for their country and for the world. Contrived and temporary, this Dream City flaunted America's faiths and glossed over its contradictions. Glamour triumphed over decay; time seemed suspended near the peak of perfection. From John Winthrop to Ralph Waldo Emerson to Josiah Strong, many Americans had thought, or hoped, that their country had escaped from history, that America was not just another power that would rise and then decline but that it was the quintessential civilization that would permanently culminate some long progression toward human betterment. Here, in rhetoric, iron, and stone, were the ideas and products that Americans prized and believed others would gratefully accept. In the Dream City, America's most significant gifts to the twentieth-century world were already apparent: advanced technology and mass culture.

The amazing scientific and technological innovations of America's farmers—displayed in Agriculture Hall—overwhelmed viewers and demonstrated the United States' importance as an exporter of primary products. Impressive displays of wheat, corn, and other crops from the prairie states bespoke opulence and plenty. In this pavilion, at least, there was no mention of the overproduction, the falling prices, and the crushing debts plaguing the Midwest and attracting converts to the populist revolt.

Perched on a platform in one section of Agriculture Hall was a huge globe with an array of farm machines, all American-made, revolving around its circumference. America's preeminence in agricultural machinery was unmistakable, and manufacturers looked toward potential markets in the new and still-expanding farming frontiers of Manchuria, Siberia, Australia, Mexico, and Argentina. America's leading food processors, some already well known abroad, also displayed their latest techniques and products: Cudahy and Swift proudly showed beef extract; Gail Borden lined up cans of condensed milk; sugar refiners and soapmakers touted their innovations.

Transportation Hall showed off the "engines of progress" that had opened the prairies to commercial cultivation. Railroad companies built massive Grecian-style pavilions and used full-size models to illustrate the historical development of locomotives. The Pullman Company escorted visitors through an entire train, to show its luxurious sleeping and dining quarters. The railroad's prominent place at Chicago seemed appropriate: promoters presented the railroad as a major civilizing force, one bringing prosperity, communication, and understanding to the world.

The Pullman Company treated fairgoers to a large model of its other proud creation—the industrial town of Pullman. The neat workers' quarters, company stores, and cultural centers depicted an idyllic scene of industrial contentment. Within a few months, the great Pullman labor strike would mar the picture, permanently associating the town with class violence instead of harmony. But labor discontent, like farmers' revolts, had no place at Chicago. At the fair, Pullman was the promise of the future.

Other transportation exhibits heralded America's new world-wide role. Pneumatic conveyors promised to revolutionize retailing by eliminating bottlenecks in the distribution of goods. Elevators effortlessly transported people and goods. A model of a canal across Nicaragua showed how modern technology might bisect Central America and stimulate American trade with Asia. The International Navigation Company erected a full-size section of an ocean steamer, showing the numerous decks and the different classes of staterooms and dining rooms. Twenty thousand people a day visited this lavishly outfitted "ship," absorbing the idea that comfort and luxury were now the rule in ocean travel. The day of the American tourist traversing the globe was still in its infancy, but the crowds at Chicago indicated tourism's potential.

The vehicle exhibit lacked steam-, electric-, or petroleum-driven carriages, but future trends were evident all the same. American carriages were lighter and cheaper than European models. Unlike their competitors, they were, in the words of one commentator, made by "modern machinery and the systematic methods of large manufactories." They contrasted with the fine British coaches, which, the same American commentator noted, were "interesting on account of their style, long since out of fashion." Even before the automobile age, advanced technology and mass appeal distinguished America's transportation industry.

Machinery Hall also emphasized technological wizardry. There, the White City's massive power plant, run by Westinghouse's huge engine-dynamo units, generated electrical power in quantities never before produced. Oil, rather than coal, was used for fuel, and Standard Oil built a forty-mile experimental pipeline that carried the fuel into the fair. Fifteen electric motors distributed the electricity throughout the fairgrounds, clearly demonstrating advanced techniques of power transmission. Half this power flowed to the most amazing exhibit of all—Westinghouse's incandescent lighting system. Illuminating the entire fairgrounds and its buildings, this system constituted the largest central power station in the United States. Not to be outdone, General Electric erected a ten-foot, 6,000-pound searchlight—the largest in the world—and powered the Edison Tower of Light, a seventy-eight-foot shaft glowing with thousands of colored flashing lights. Chicago's fair awesomely demonstrated the new electrical age.

At Electricity Hall, power set in motion a mechanical world that seemed as marvelous in 1893 as it would seem commonplace in 1945. Most visitors got their first look at electric trolleys, long-distance phones, and electrical heaters. Edison's new kinetograph, in conjunction with a phonograph, visually reproduced an orator's movements and then synchronized these movements with the sound of his voice. G.E.'s elevated electric railroad safely speeded the huge crowds around the grounds. Other machinery exhibits highlighted Americans' talent for substituting technology for labor. All the fair's restaurants used dishwashing machines, and there were laundry and pressing machines, soapmaking machines, steamrollers, automatic sprinklers, street cleaners, and a machine that quickly weighed and bagged several tons of ground coffee a day. American sewing-machine companies such as Singer displayed improved versions of the home sewing machine. The *Daily Columbian,* a special World's Fair newspaper, spun off the latest steam-powered presses at the rate of eight hundred copies a minute. For one souvenir issue, workers placed pulp in a machine to make paper, composed the text on a linotype, printed, and distributed a finished newspaper—all in sixty-three minutes.

Most startling in their diversity were the special machines for making boots and shoes. An expert operator using an improved sewing machine could sew nine hundred pairs of shoes a day; a "rivet and stud" machine inserted ninety rivets and studs per minute; a heeling machine drove three hundred nails per minute; a "burnishing and bottom-polishing and uppercleaning" machine finished the shoe for market. In all, more than a score of different processes contributed to making a single shoe.

In contrast to the fair's technological originality, its artistic styles were imitative and familiar. Ironically, exposition planners, who defined art as the statuary and painting of an elite European tradition, refused to give a place to one of America's most successful and unique "artistic" creations: Buffalo Bill's Wild West Show. But encamped outside the gates and across the street from the White City, the show attracted huge, enthusiastic crowds. An early yet fully developed expression of America's mass culture, Buffalo Bill's extravaganza became one of the Dream City's most popular exhibits. In Chicago, Americans flaunted the cheap mass products, the dazzling technology, and the alluring mass culture that, in the coming century, they would spread throughout the world.

THE IDEOLOGY OF LIBERAL-DEVELOPMENTALISM

This American dream of high technology and mass consumption was both promoted and accompanied by an ideology* that I shall call liberal-developmentalism. Reflected in partial form by some of the 3,817 lecturers who spoke in 1893 at the World Congress Auxiliary to the Columbian Exposition, this ideology matured during the twentieth century. Liberal-developmentalism merged nineteenth-century liberal tenets with the historical experience of America's own development, elevating the beliefs and experiences of America's unique historical time and circumstance into developmental laws thought to be applicable everywhere.

The ideology of liberal-developmentalism can be broken into five major features: (1) belief that other nations could and should replicate America's own developmental experience; (2) faith in private free enterprise; (3) support for free or open access for trade and investment; (4) promotion of free flow of information and culture; and (5) growing acceptance of governmental activity to protect private enterprise and to stimulate and regulate American participation in international economic and cultural exchange.

To many Americans, their country's economic and social history became a universal model. In order to become a modern society, a nation needed extensive capital investment generated by foreign borrowing and by exports; development of educational, transportation, communication, and banking institutions; a steady supply of cheap labor; maximization of individual initiative for people deemed most efficient; wide-open land use and freewheeling envi-

---

*The term "ideology" is here used to describe "the system of beliefs, values, fears, prejudices, reflexes, and commitments—in sum, the social consciousness" of the Americans—which generally dominated the expansion of America's influence into foreign lands. Ideology is also viewed as "a political weapon, manipulated consciously in ongoing struggles for legitimacy and power, as an instrument for creating and controlling organizations." These definitions are borrowed from historians Eric Foner and Robert D. Cuff, respectively. Ideology, as the term is employed here, both reflects and is used to affect the social organization from which it springs.

ronmental practices; and a robust private business sector solidly linked to capital-intensive, labor-saving technology. This blueprint, drawn from America's experience, became the creed of most Americans who dealt with foreign nations.

In the 1890s, this formula was closely related to a new sense of America's mission, one that had both religious and secular roots. Most Americans believed that Protestant Christianity was a spiritual precondition for modernization. The organizer of the Religious Congress at the exposition, for example, proclaimed that the sessions on religion would demonstrate the vigor of the new evangelical spirit in America and show that the divine purpose "of building up the Kingdom of Christ in America is to engage with fresh ardor in efforts to Christianize India and Africa, Turkey and China." Participants and spectators frequently called the World's Fair the Divine Exposition or the New Jerusalem, believing that its display of America's products and spiritual vigor presaged a new Christian age in which all peoples of the world would progress toward prosperity. Those heralding Christianity as a vehicle for both spiritual and material development also generally sounded themes of the "white man's burden." John Fiske, who spoke at the Congress on Evolution, extolled Anglo-Saxon productivity as he called for a worldwide extension of American institutions and industrial civilization. Religious duty and national destiny fused together. Other speakers, particularly at the Congress on Education, hailed new secular agents of progress. The trend toward technical education and professional specialization, observers believed, provided the expertise that would soon alleviate most social ills. Education in the new social sciences would enable people to eradicate poverty and build stronger social bonds at home and abroad.

The organizer of the World Congress, Charles C. Bonney, proclaimed that the purpose of the congress was the promotion of "the progress, prosperity, unity, peace, and happiness of the world." Deeply imbued with new theories that applied evolutionary principles to society, Bonney and other speakers clearly believed that American models provided guides to the earthly millennium. Whether speakers emphasized Protestant Christianity, Anglo-Saxonism, or professional expertise as the most important ingredient for global social and economic development, most did view America as the vanguard of world progress. Their faith in the ability of Americans to perfect and apply laws of progressive betterment and to uplift those lower on the evolutionary scale would reverberate throughout the twentieth century.

Belief in America's mission helped drive its internationalist impulse. As long as internationalists believed the world was destined to follow American patterns, they could remain confident that there was no fundamental conflict between national advancement and global progress. A strong internationalist spirit and an accompanying faith in American-led progress, the two most important themes of the Columbian Exposition, would recur again and again.

Central to the developmental process were tenets drawn from nineteenth-century liberalism. Seldom explicit in World's Fair speeches, which tended to explore specific elements of progress—such as new roles for women, industrial education, the spread of temperance, and scientific advance—liberal assumptions nevertheless underlay most Americans' views of progress. Many historians, such as Louis Hartz and N. Gordon Levin, have convincingly demonstrated how liberal beliefs drew the boundaries of significant public debate and have explored the content and consequences of the American liberal tradition.

Encouraging individual initiative through private enterprise was an important canon of nineteenth-century liberalism. Liberalism, of course, grew up in opposition to artificial, statist monopoly or government-conferred privilege. Freedom, in the American tradition, meant absence of the autocratic state and the full play of competing individual initiatives through private ownership. Private enterprise was free because it was not shackled by an overbearing governmental structure. And celebrants of the American system generally credited private business, above all, with producing rapid industrial development and increasing abundance. To be sure, nineteenth-century government, particularly states and localities, did not remain aloof from the process of economic growth. But government intervened in the economy primarily in order to release the energies of the private sector. Government kept the pump of American business in working order, but it did not raise and lower the handle.

Throughout the twentieth century, the national government adopted ever more elaborate ways of oiling and repairing the pump and of insuring a ready supply of water and pumpers. And while government became increasingly involved with the operation of the private sector, many businesses became so internationalized and so huge that they bore little resemblance to the enterprises America had known. Still, the mystique of the transforming qualities of private ownership remained intact and profoundly shaped American attitudes and policies toward others. Why should private entrepreneurs, unrestrained and encouraged by government—liberal-developmentalists asked—not duplicate their American success story in other parts of the world? Minimal interference by foreign governments in the supposedly free play of private initiatives became a fairly consistent American goal abroad.

Belief in free trade and investment accompanied the faith in private enterprise. The classical economists David Ricardo and Adam Smith and their popularizers bequeathed to American liberalism the law of comparative advantage: a division of labor in which specialization by each economic unit would result in increased efficiency within the worldwide system. The avid pursuit of *individual* gain, regulated by an "invisible hand," would promote the *general* welfare by enriching all those nations and people who participated in the free marketplace. To American entrepreneurs, comparative advantage translated into a practical article of faith: the gains of unregulated private business were synonymous with the advance of society as a whole. In an international setting, as at home, the invisible hand would convert the narrow self-interest of corporations (and nations) into general well-being and raise standards of living.

In practice, the faith in liberal rules of economic exchange had an important qualification. Throughout most of its history, the United States was a strongly protectionist nation. Those who favored protective tariffs on foreign goods expressed their liberalism in terms of equal access, or the open door. Nations, liberal protectionists argued, had a right to use tariffs to develop their own special endowments, as long as the duties did not discriminate in favor of certain trading partners and create privileged spheres of influence. For much of the twentieth century, both low-tariff and protectionist interests agreed that equal access for trade and investment, rather than the absolute doctrine of free trade, provided the fundamental ingredient of a liberal order.

In the twentieth century, Americans increasingly questioned the supposedly self-regulating nature of a liberal international order. Especially during the 1930s, international cartels and nationalistic restrictions distorted the free play of economic forces. The national government increasingly became a regulator, its visible hand replacing Adam Smith's mythical invisible one. But despite intervention in the economic system on both the national and the international levels, Americans retained the core of their liberal beliefs. The beneficence and fairness of the international division of labor, organized by private enterprise and maintained through policies promoting equal access for trade and investments, remained a fundamental faith for most policymakers.

The free flow of ideas related closely to free trade. In fact, liberal-developmentalists assumed that one free marketplace was a necessary condition for the other. Free flow was also largely defined as the absence of governmental control. Communications media were free if they were not servants of government; if private enterprise controlled communications, the cause of free expression was—almost by definition—advanced. Americans supported private ownership of broadcasting and news services abroad, and they championed the spread of the same advertiser-shaped mass culture developed at home.

Because the American government itself did not usually generate or severely censor information, liberal-developmentalists could not perceive American culture as either value-laden or ideological, because it was based on mass appeal and appeared inherently democratic. Was not America's own success story proof that the best ideas come to the fore in a liberal society? The notion that "the best idea wins" was the counterpart, in the realm of ideas, to the economic law of comparative advantage. Liberal-developmentalists thus saw America's free-flow doctrines as helping to spread truth and knowledge in an essentially democratic marketplace. Free flow, they argued, was nonideological and anti-authoritarian.

The marketplace metaphor permeated liberal-developmentalism. The ideal world was a great open market: each buyer and thinker had access to a separate stall and freedom to peddle his or her wares. But the buyer was sovereign, and because the buyer's decisions were critical in determining what goods or thoughts would be accepted, the marketplace was inherently democratic and anti-authoritarian. Because all met as equals, the marketplace eroded barriers that separated people; differences of class and nationality broke down, and all producers were judged solely by the merit of their products. Governments might arrange the marketing booths, keep the lanes of commerce open, and enforce minimal standards of fairness and safety, but the interaction of private buyers and sellers provided the dynamics of the system, bringing the best-quality products to the greatest number of people. The liberal marketplace (both economic and intellectual), then, was supposed to generate efficiency, abundance, democracy, wisdom, and social integration. It could be noisy and turbulent, but it was always, in the end, uplifting and fair. The ideology of the American Dream—both its domestic and its global versions—was a full rendition of this liberal marketplace utopia.

As the marketplace ideal implied, the role of private citizens was crucial. It is not surprising that in the late nineteenth and early twentieth centuries private Americans, more than government policymakers, tended to shape America's role in the world. As traders, investors, missionaries, philanthropists, international societies, and purveyors of mass communications pushed beyond America's continental frontiers, the private sector spearheaded American expansion. Even though private impulses have often had only peripheral status in traditional diplomatic histories, a study of America's foreign affairs must, to a large degree, focus upon these nongovernmental forces.

But during the course of the twentieth century, the federal government increasingly intervened to rationalize or extend contacts originated by private interests. Liberal-developmentalists gradually devised governmental structures to promote or guide American participation within the international system. The relationships between private initiatives and governmental structures thus became more complex. For each historical period, it is important to view American expansion within the context of both private and governmental activities and to try to understand the changing relationship between the two.

I have tried to characterize the general evolution of American economic and cultural expansion from the 1890s through 1945 and to trace the connection between expansionism and the state through three distinct periods. Although one period does not magically replace another, I believe it is useful to talk about the growth of the "promotional state" from the 1890s through World War I; the "cooperative state" during the 1920s; and the "regulatory state" growing out of the Depression of the 1930s and culminating in World War II. Each of these states represents a different phase of the political economy of expansion. In characterizing these different periods, I do not suggest that there have been no disagreements over American foreign policy or that policymakers and private citizens have always seen eye-to-eye. I am aware of the problems with either a "unitary state" or a simplified "power elite" model. Disputes have always existed in both public and private sectors and have often been bitter. On the other hand, most disagreements have not been over fundamental ideology. A broad consensus of liberal-developmentalism (free enterprise, free trade, free flow, and developmental laws) has generally provided the boundaries within which significant debate has occurred.

This book does not detail the effects of Americanization on others. Such an assessment would involve describing hundreds (if not thousands) of different cultural interchanges and social transitions. Obviously, the impact of the American Dream has varied widely. Some people have benefited; others have been none the better or worse off. Instead, this book narrows its focus to examine the process by which some Americans, guided and justified by the faiths of liberal-developmentalism, sought to extend their technology-based economy and mass culture to nearly every part of the world. It opens with the beginning of that process in the 1890s and ends with the formation, during World War II, of expansionist structures that would dominate the postwar world.

Two
★≡★≡★

CAPITALISTS, CHRISTIANS, COWBOYS: 1890–1912

ONE of the speakers who lectured at the Columbian Exposition's so-called World Congress was Frederick Jackson Turner, a young historian from the University of Wisconsin. Turner presented his famous "frontier thesis," a historical interpretation suggesting that westward expansion had been the formative influence on American life. Although Turner was primarily concerned with the past—the westward movement across the continent into territories once claimed by Native Americans, Mexicans, and various European nations—his message had implications for the future. Would Americans—thoroughly accustomed to seizing new lands, justifying their actions as inevitable or ordained, and having a frontier safety valve for social and economic problems—continue to seek new frontiers overseas? In "The Problem of the West" (*The Atlantic Monthly,* 1896) Turner himself suggested the answer: "For nearly three centuries the dominant fact in American life has been expansion . . . and the demands for a vigorous foreign policy . . . and for extension of American influence to outlying islands and adjoining countries, are indications that the movement will continue."

Expansion did continue. The outpouring of American economic and cultural influence, spearheaded by the efforts of private citizens and accelerating rapidly after 1890, provided the basis for America's global preeminence—a role dependent on advanced technology, surplus capital, and mass culture. And as Americans looked beyond their shores, they also refined their basic liberal beliefs to fit a global context. Traders, investors, missionaries, philanthropists, and entertainers: all contributed both to expansion and to the liberal-developmental paradigm that accompanied it.

TRADERS

Frank Norris, in "The Frontier Gone at Last" (*World's Work,* 1902), wrote that the close of the American frontier brought new ways of expending "our overplus energy":

> We are now come into a changed time and the great word of our century is no longer War but Trade . . . Had the Lion-Hearted Richard lived today he would have become a "leading representative of the Amalgamated Steel Companies" and doubt not for one moment, that he would have underbid his Manchester, England, rivals in the matter of bridge girders.

The year before, an Englishman, William T. Stead, described what he termed the "Americanization of the World":

> In the English domestic life we have got to this: The average man rises in the morning from his New England sheets, he shaves with "Williams" soap and a Yankee safety razor, pulls on his Boston boots over his socks from North Carolina, fastens his Connecticut braces, slips his Waltham or Waterbury watch in his pocket, and sits down to breakfast. There he congratulates his wife on the way her Illinois straight-front corset sets off her Massachusetts Blouse, and he tackles his breakfast, where he eats bread made from prairie flour . . . tinned oysters from Baltimore, and a little Kansas City bacon, while his wife plays with a slice of Chicago ox-tongue. The children are given "Quaker" oats. At the same time he read his morning paper, printed by American machines, on American paper, with American ink, and probably edited by a smart journalist from New York City.

Such observations reflected a statistical reality: the value of American exports surged from $800 million in 1895 to $2.3 billion in 1914, an increase of nearly 240 percent. The growth rate for manufactured goods alone was nearly 500 percent during that twenty-year period.

What lay behind the growth of American exports in the pre-World War I era? Although a definitive answer would include analysis of world demand and of the economies of leading competitors, the strengths of America's own domestic economy provided the foundation for its exportable surplus. These strengths included an efficient internal transportation system, a high degree of specialization and mechanization, rapid scientific advance, and innovative marketing techniques.

The activities of railroad baron James J. Hill nicely illustrate the link between the continental transportation revolution and the outreach overseas. In 1893, while the World's Fair attracted crowds to Chicago, St. Paul, Minnesota, held a three-day celebration to mark the completion of Hill's Great Northern railroad to the West Coast port of Tacoma, on Puget Sound. More important, Minnesotans and Hill celebrated because they realized the international possibilities of their venture. Hill had built his railroad empire on one cardinal rule—that lower rates and higher profits depended on two-way traffic. But Hill faced a problem: although the Great Northern carried large quantities of timber from the Pacific Northwest to the Midwest, most westward-bound boxcars were empty. Filling them with exports from the American interior bound for the Orient offered a solution. Hill printed and distributed wheat cookbooks written in various Asian languages, and he energetically tried to sign up customers, especially in Japan. Wheat was not all that Hill hoped to ship west. To encourage American rather than European steel exports, he obtained quotations on steel prices from European countries to Japan, compared them with American prices, and then adjusted his transportation charges so that the total cost of American steel would be less than the European. The wheat and steel sales he negotiated, Hill hoped, would be the first of many. In these activities, Hill reflected the mid-nineties optimism about trade with the Orient.

Hill's fascination with trade across the Pacific proved misplaced. American exports to the Orient never comprised more than a small fraction of total export trade; neither Hill nor most other traders found much profit in Asia. Nevertheless, Hill's efforts did highlight the connection between internal transportation and expansionist impulses. American transportation tycoons helped spread the idea of international destiny, just as they had once championed transcontinental expansion. They were accustomed to thinking of distance not as a barrier to commerce but as a problem amenable to technological solution. Distance merely enhanced the possibility for profit, if problems were solved. Furthermore, the transportation barons' outspoken advocacy of foreign commerce helped popularize the liberal economic tenet that increased trade brought greater wealth for all. In order to dangle the prospect of huge profits before American agricultural and industrial exporters, Hill used the fanciful arithmetic so commonly employed by those fascinated with the China market. "If the Chinese should spend only one cent per day per capita," Hill wrote, "it would amount to $4,000,000 a day . . ." Railroad builders such as Hill, Edward H. Harriman, Collis P. Huntington, and Jay Gould were the advance agents and the propagandists for America's new commercial might.

In their efforts to crisscross the American continent and then to connect America to the rest of the world, railroad entrepreneurs believed that a benign providence supported their cause. The title of Hill's book, *Highways to Progress,* epitomized his message. One speaker at the World's Fair's Railway Conference further embellished the theme, hailing railroad-building around the globe as

the largest human calling . . . We blow the whistle that's heard round the world, and all peoples stop to heed and welcome it. Its resonance is the diplomacy of peace. The locomotive bell is the true Liberty bell, proclaiming commercial freedom. Its boilers and the reservoirs are the forces of civilization. Its wheels are the wheels of progress, and its headlight is the illumination of dark countries.

Thus, the same railway entrepreneurs who had helped to provoke a populist revolt and a host of governmental regulations at home proclaimed that, if given access to the world, they would usher in an era of peace, freedom, civilization, and development abroad. Railroad profits, world trade, and global progress were to go hand in hand. The practical experience and liberal-developmental vision of late-nineteenth-century moguls eased America's transition from continentalism to globalism.

The promotional activities of railroad builders also illustrated that private, rather than governmental, initiatives provided the basic force behind turn-of-the-century economic expansion. President Grover Cleveland, after a discussion with Hill, said that the railroad baron knew more about Oriental needs than any other person he had met, a fact he found less surprising when he discovered that Hill "had spent more money than the government in sending competent men to Japan and China to study the need of those countries."

The growth of American exports also rested upon technological sophistication and specialization. The productivity of the agricultural sector, which until 1914 generated over half of America's total exports, leaped ahead throughout the late nineteenth century, as farmers used improved machinery to cultivate more extensively than ever before. Human ingenuity and governmental encouragement through the Morrill Act of 1862 promoted scientific advances in irrigation, farm mechanization, crop management, seed variety, and food processing. Scarcity of labor, aridity of land, barriers of distance were all overcome, and land once thought to be a Great American Desert was transformed into the Great American Breadbasket, spilling out its plenty to the world. Cotton production doubled between the early 1880s and about 1900, and America's wheat crop increased by about one-third.

Because nearly twenty percent of America's total agricultural production was exported, farmers depended heavily on foreign markets. In 1900, two-thirds of America's cotton crop was exported, and in some years forty percent of its wheat went abroad. Europe, especially Great Britain, was the primary purchaser of those two major exports. But as production increased and oversupply depressed prices, farmers clamored for the opening of other markets. The historian William A. Williams has written that in the latter half of the nineteenth century "the farmer's export-dominated relationship with the world marketplace led him to develop and advocate a vigorously assertive and expansionist foreign policy" and "to defend and justify such expansionism on the grounds that it extended the freedom of all men." Although the farmer and the railroad baron often clashed over domestic issues, both agreed that America's great productivity could supply large new markets. And they both identified expanding exports with world progress.

American agriculture was so productive that the world studied and borrowed its methods. As early as 1875, for example, experts from Massachusetts Agricultural College established, at the request of the Japanese government, an agricultural college and experimental farm at Sapporo. In addition to agricultural science, the school promoted American-style Christianity, field sports, military drill, white frame houses, and the Yankee slogan "Be Ambitious." The school farm introduced cultivation of American specialties—wheat, corn, oats, sugar beets—and imported dairy cattle, farm machinery, and barbed wire from the United States. By 1893, an all-Japanese faculty headed by a graduate of Johns Hopkins ran the school, but American methods and an American atmosphere prevailed. Such agricultural missions, like most other forms of late-nineteenth-century expansion, were arranged and run by private citizens with little or no involvement by the American government.

Advanced technology also contributed to what some Europeans called the American export invasion. Though exports were not as great as the word "invasion" implied, the impact came from the sudden appearance of American products abroad and their surprisingly low cost and high quality. In addition to its great agricultural capacity, America had created—overnight, it seemed—a formidable industrial plant so modern its products could often undersell European-made goods despite higher transportation costs. The growth of the farming and food-processing sectors continued, but exports of manufactured goods increased even faster, overtaking those of agriculture in 1914.

American industrialists pioneered mass-production techniques. The lowering of unit costs by using interchangeable parts, mechanization, and specialization at each stage of production promised greater availability of goods for all. Mass production, first applied in making firearms, spread after the Civil War into other industries. The same man who developed Remington's breech-loading rifle, for example, perfected the company's new mass-produced typewriter, and Remington's products for both war and peace found ready overseas markets in the late nineteenth century. The boot and shoe industry provided another conspicuous example of mechanization and specialization. Relying on machines rather than individual craftsmen, American firms lowered labor costs until their products competed well even in European markets. Ready-made into standardized sizes, high-quality footwear became available to large numbers of people, not simply to the upper class. The threat of the American export invasion forced Europeans to revamp their own methods of production. Throughout the twentieth century, America's industrial techniques would often follow closely upon its exports, Americanizing the world in the name of modernization.

Around the turn of the century, the rapid spread of Frederick Taylor's ideas of efficiency refined the techniques of mass production and revolutionized factory labor. "Taylorization," a system of rationalized movement and rigorous work discipline, lowered production costs still further, thereby improving the American competitive edge. By "mechanizing" people, as it were, and making human labor an extension of machine technology, Taylorism heightened class tensions between owners and laborers and produced a rash of strikes against the speedup of the assembly lines and the layoffs that came with increased productivity. American manufacturers, basking in the accomplishment of producing more for less, did not focus their attention on the social stratification and strife created by their *processes*. They were more aware of the potentially wide markets for cheaper *products*.

The democratic promise of mass production was also present in many American marketing techniques. For example, the Singer Sewing Machine Company, the first American industry to seek a large worldwide market, took pride in spreading the income-producing potential of the home sewing machine. Singer was able to tap a large market not only because of mass production but through the technique of installment buying. The company allowed purchasers to make a small down payment and, sometimes with the income generated by the machine itself, to pay the balance over a long period. Installment buying would become a major feature of American marketing in the twentieth century, but Singer employed it in the 1860s at home and, soon after, in foreign countries. In the late nineteenth century, Singer sold over half of its machines abroad.

Singer's marketing techniques differed from European practices in another way that would become characteristically American. European exporting firms usually sold their products through large commission houses, businesses that retailed a variety of products on commission. Singer tried and then discarded this technique; its executives felt that commission houses had no incentive to service their machines reliably and lacked loyalty to their brand. Singer established direct sales outlets that specialized only in Singer products, provided careful service, marketed aggressively, and responded directly to the guidelines of the central office in the United States. These outlets, which also partially masked Singer's foreign identity, gave the company a good reputation in host countries.

Products that sold well overseas were also often scientifically advanced. Thomas Edison's electrical inventions and Alexander Graham Bell's telephone patents made America a pioneer in communications and electrification. Establishment of national telephone systems abroad, some even initially owned by American companies, provided ready markets for telephone parts manufactured by American Bell, Edison Electric, and Western Electric. In electrical equipment, General Electric (formed in 1892) and Westinghouse (1886) were the giants, supplying many areas of the world. Other pathbreaking American exports included National Cash Registers, Otis Elevators, Columbia Gramophones, Kodak cameras, Heinz ketchup, Colgate tooth powder, Borden condensed milk, Ford and General Motors cars, New York Life Insurance policies, McCormick reapers, and business machines sold by forerunners of IBM and Burroughs. These innovative products, largely aimed at middle-class consumers, contributed to America's international image as the nation on the cutting edge of the future. In 1901 an Englishman, Fred A. McKenzie—in his book *The American Invaders*—claimed that "these newcomers have acquired control of almost every new industry created during the past fifteen years . . ."

The major characteristics of American exports, then, were established by 1900. American trade advantages were based on an extensive transportation network, technological advances, aggressive marketing, and scientific innovation. Americans enlarged existing markets by making products (such as sewing machines) available on a mass basis, and they created new markets by developing new products (such as electrical equipment).

As traders cultivated markets, they also developed a rationale for rapid overseas expansion and for the benevolent impact of their goods. Foreign critics might charge that an American export invasion could harm native industries, cause unemployment, or force the spread of Taylor's harsh industrial discipline, stirring labor violence; but American exporters saw their activities as inevitable, efficient, and highly moral.

Most trade expansionists viewed American commercial supremacy as an evolutionary necessity. They saw export expansion as simply an inexorable part of America's economic development. Albert Beveridge bragged in 1898 that "American factories are making more than the American people can use; American soil is producing more than they can consume. Fate has written our policy for us; the trade of the world must and shall be ours." Similarly, J. G. Kitchell's book *American Supremacy* (1901) predicted: "Commercially we are breaking into every market in the world. It is a part of our economic development. We are marching fast to the economic supremacy of the world." The State Department's primary economic adviser, Charles Conant, described overseas commercial expansion as "a natural law of economic and race development."

The very nature of America's exports—food grains, agricultural machinery, manufactured goods aimed at a mass market, and public improvements such as electricity—suggested the moral justification. Because they did not grow or manufacture for a small, elite market, American traders claimed that their impact uplifted their customers; they linked mass production, mass marketing, and technological improvement to an enlightened democratic spirit. According to the historian Robert Davies, for example, "Singer management concluded that poverty could be removed from society by self-help, and that the company was placing in the hands of hundreds of thousands a technological device by which the masses could improve their station in life as well as their material rewards."

By enlarging the world marketplace, American producers believed they leveled barriers of country and class; by lowering costs, they moved the world closer to an age without scarcity. To its celebrants, liberal capitalism would bring a rising level of abundance, and the means of consumption, not the means of production, would govern feelings of status and social contentment. In the emerging litany of the American dream, what the historian Daniel Boorstin later termed a "democracy of things" would disprove both Malthus's predictions of scarcity and Marx's of class conflict.

Farm and industrial exporters linked this vision of global social progress with their own freedom to penetrate any market. Increasing America's exports would presumably contribute to a general increase in living standards, to greater equality, and to personal freedom. If government barriers or monopolies closed access to America's products, class privilege and scarcity would remain unassaulted. Free enterprise, free trade, free men: these liberal tenets, embedded in mid-nineteenth-century domestic politics, matured and ripened in the service of overseas commercial expansion and bolstered the myth of American exceptionalism. America's economic extension abroad was unique; it was not exploitative or restrictive (as was the economic expansion of other powers) but liberating and democratic. International advancement, expansion of American trade, and personal freedom became indistinguishable.

INVESTORS

The export invasion paralleled an outflow of investment capital. Some of this money went for the purchase of foreign government bonds or foreign-owned corporations, but most of the capital that Americans sent overseas took the form of "direct investment," a situation in which the investor holds managerial control (usually a branch business). The acceleration of American direct investment during the 1890s formed the basis of many of today's huge international corporations.

A number of circumstances encouraged American companies to establish branches in foreign lands at the turn of the century: the domestic merger movement and new forms of large-scale corporate organization, efforts at vertical integration, the need to vault foreign tariff walls, and the interest in moving closer to raw materials or markets.

Mergers, accelerating after the mid-1890s, provided the organizational and financial basis for international expansion. Assembling many small businesses into giant combinations required new patterns of finance and management as well as entrepreneurial skill and daring. Most of America's early direct investors—such as Standard Oil, the Guggenheim interests, International Nickel, and various railroad trusts—gained power and perfected new managerial techniques during the domestic competitive struggle of the late nineteenth century.

To reap the benefits of vertical integration, large traders often became direct investors in the goods they traded. W. R. Grace and Company, which had become important as a shipping company in the Peruvian guano trade of the 1870s, later acquired sugar estates as payment for a debt, and finally formed the Cartavio Sugar Company in 1891. Before World War I, Grace also diversified into textile production. United Fruit Company, organized in 1899, expanded its banana plantations in Central America with the encouragement of a railroad builder, Minor C. Keith, who hoped to augment his company's cargoes. The interlocking interests of Keith and United Fruit—which ultimately included railroads, shipping lines, plantations, and livestock—gave them enormous leverage in Central America, especially in Costa Rica.

Some firms dealing in raw materials also began to integrate foreign sources into their corporate domains. Before the nineties, most American companies simply exported American minerals; they traded, distributed, and perhaps maintained sales outlets in foreign lands, but they controlled few foreign supplies. The American continent, after all, produced enormous quantities of raw materials. Standard Oil was almost exclusively a distributor of American oil overseas; during the 1890s it searched for oil in China and the Dutch East Indies, but eventually decided against investing there. The Guggenheim interests developed some diamond mines in the Belgian Congo and purchased copper-rich territory in Chile, but before World War I their only really significant foreign holding was American Smelting and Refining in Mexico. America exported about one half of its domestic production of oil and copper. But as American firms consolidated and moved into the world, foreign sources of supply became increasingly attractive. Many of the major primary producers of the 1920s—firms such as Amalgamated Copper, Guggenheim Brothers, Alcoa Aluminum, Du Pont, Standard Oil, Doheny Oil, United Fruit, Atlantic and Pacific Tea, and the Havemeyer sugar interests—invested in some foreign raw materials before World War I; these small prewar holdings foreshadowed the great influx of American investment during the 1920s.

Market-oriented manufacturers were the most important of the early American investors abroad. High tariffs imposed in many countries in the late nineteenth century, or the threat of imperial restrictions, forced American exporters either to produce their goods within the restricted market or to face exclusion. Even when tariffs posed no barriers, the decision to manufacture near an overseas market, especially the lucrative ones in Europe, reduced shipping costs. Singer established a huge plant in Scotland, producing machines there for Europe, and set up smaller branches in Canada and Australia. American Tobacco moved into Australia, Japan, and Germany to avoid being shut out by tariffs. Western Electric manufactured equipment in Japan after the termination of the unequal treaties in 1899 and the adoption of a protective tariff in 1911. General Electric established associates or subsidiaries in Europe, South Africa, Canada, and Mexico. Westinghouse built huge plants in Russia and Western Europe. Food companies and meat-packers such as J. F. Heinz, Armour, Swift, and American Tobacco increasingly processed abroad—closer to potential markets—thereby avoiding spoilage, breakage, and shipping costs. After America's Pure Food and Drug Act, which required labeling of the contents of patent medicines, Parke Davis and other drug companies established plants abroad in order to supply foreign markets unhampered by domestic regulation.

Before World War I, then, many American businesses expanded into foreign lands; from 1897 to 1914, American direct investments abroad more than quadrupled, rising from an estimated $634 million to $2.6 billion. Investment patterns varied. China received little direct investment, except for the Duke Tobacco interests, which converted large numbers of Chinese to chain-smoking and became one of the country's largest industrial employers. Africa attracted almost no American capital. Investments in Latin America tended to be in transportation or in raw materials. Investors in Europe, Canada, and Japan were usually market-oriented manu-

facturing firms. Between 1901 and 1914, United States manufacturers established no fewer than seventy subsidiaries or joint ventures in Great Britain alone. Except for America's neighbors—
Canada, Mexico, and Cuba—Britain became the most important
area for American direct investment.

A farsighted English analyst, Benjamin Kidd, recognized that
such direct investment by Americans was the most potent part of
the American invasion. "The great danger with which British trade
was threatened from the United States at the present time," he
wrote in 1903, "was not so much from an invasion of American
manufacturers, but it was that of our industries being drawn deeply
into the organization of trade and production now proceeding
outwards from the United States." As Kidd suggested, integration
into the American production system, through direct investment,
posed a major challenge to foreign economic systems. It promised
economic growth, but especially for nations with weak national
economic structures, direct investment could also bring varying
degrees of economic, cultural, and political dependence on America, the ultimate source of capital and management decisions.

Yet American investors argued that they offered not dependence
but development. They viewed their activities as modernizing
rather than exploitative. Generalizing from their country's historical experience, they argued that private foreign investment was a
first step in a process that would transform a host country, just as
the United States had been transformed in the nineteenth century.
Elihu Root, Secretary of State under Theodore Roosevelt from
1905 to 1909, offered in 1907 a typical invocation of developmen-
talism; like many others, he linked America's historical experience
with its future global mission:

> During the period now past, the energy of our people . . . has been
> devoted to the internal development of our own country. The sur-
> plus wealth produced by our labors has been applied immediately
> to reproduction in our own land . . . We have been drawing on the
> resources of the world in capital and labor to aid us in our work.
> We have gathered strength from every rich and powerful nation and
> expended it upon these home undertakings; into them we have
> poured hundreds of millions of money attracted from the investors

of Europe. We have been always a debtor nation, borrowing from the rest of the world, drawing all possible energy towards us and concentrating it with our own energy upon our own enterprises . . .

Since the first election of President McKinley, the people of the United States have for the first time accumulated a surplus of capital beyond the requirements of internal development . . . Our surplus energy is beginning to look beyond our own borders, throughout the world, to find opportunity for the profitable use of our surplus capital, foreign markets for our manufactures, foreign mines to be developed, foreign bridges and railroads and public works to be built, foreign rivers to be turned into electric power and light. As in their several ways England and France and Germany have stood, so we in our own way are beginning to stand and must continue to stand towards the industrial enterprise of the world.

To develop the world's industrial enterprises, investors from the United States offered not only capital but the gospel of technology as well. The benevolence of technology and the transferability of technological solutions formed a major part of the new credo. Some critics warned that machines might degrade labor, produce unemployment, induce social distress or wreak environmental havoc, but these views had few adherents among overseas investors. So self-confident and messianic were technology's missionaries that Mark Twain tried to puncture their self-assurance. In his popular fantasy, *A Connecticut Yankee in King Arthur's Court,* the well-intentioned introduction of Yankee ingenuity and technique into a pre-industrial setting ended not in the triumph of progress but in an orgy of annihilation. Mark Twain's fictional Yankee, Hank Morgan, like some of his counterparts in history, literally destroyed a people in order to convert them to "progress," and advanced technology eased the task of destruction more than it facilitated the effort of conversion. But Twain, the perceptive and skeptical nonconformist, scarcely dented American optimism; in fact, most contemporary reviewers of *Connecticut Yankee* took from it a message about how noble—if sometimes futile—was the effort to modernize a backward people. At any rate, the ambivalence that some Americans did have about technological transfer hardly showed to foreigners. The majority of those American pub-

licists and promoters who reached the outside world projected a
faith that technology, introduced by American investors, would
elevate anyone that embraced it.

MISSIONARIES

As American traders and investors of the 1890s developed a
world view that linked their own expansionist interests to the
general improvement of mankind, other private groups also sought
to provide uplift to the world. The conspicuous outpouring of
American Protestant missionary activity during the 1890s provided a cultural counterpart to the American economic invasion,
although missionaries, unlike businessmen, tended to concentrate
primarily on Asia, Africa, and the Middle East. Oscar E. Brown,
a professor at Vanderbilt University, wrote after a trip around the
world in 1914 that there were six global powers: "The British
Empire, the Russian Empire, the Japanese Empire, the Chinese
Republic, the American Republic, and the Young Men's Christian
Association." This dramatic overstatement did reflect the vigor of
missionary groups such as the YMCA's Student Volunteers. Rush-
ing to convert the world to American-style Christianity within
their lifetimes, Protestant missionaries became some of the most
zealous and conspicuous overseas carriers of the American Dream;
they provided Americans' first substantial personal contacts with
people of many nations.

Protestant missionaries of the 1890s mixed the Christian concept
of stewardship and a faith in the new social sciences with the
evangelical impulses of popular preachers such as Dwight Moody.
Notions of racial destiny and Anglo-Saxon superiority saturated
missionary writings, but these coexisted with buoyant optimism
that racial and cultural virtues were transferable. Often challenging
the grim racial determinism that denied the possibility of reforming
"backward" people, missionaries argued that transforming foreign
cultures was not only possible but was the duty of any true Christian. An article in *Mission News* (1901) in Yokohama, Japan, called
for "a reconstruction of our theories of ethnic psychology. The
power of a new thought, a new moral impulse, to radically change
the social environment, will have to be given a freer recognition
than most modern psychologists have been wont to give it." Trans-

forming ideas (Christianity), then, could alter environment, lift people above their genetic heritage and into the realm of "civilization." The symbolism of a parent-child relationship recurred in missionaries' arguments: it connoted utter dependence and domination at present, but promised eventual self-sufficiency if the "parents" performed their Christian duty and if the "children" learned their lessons.

The Student Volunteer Movement (SVM) of the YMCA epitomized the crusading spirit of the 1890s. The SVM, formed at Dwight Moody's birthplace, Northfield, Massachusetts, in the late 1880s by students from two hundred colleges, enthusiastically extended American cultural influence. Using Moody as their inspiration and model, the SVM dedicated its members to rapid, worldwide conversion and, in 1891, pledged to accomplish the "evangelization of the world in one generation." "Don't stay in this country theorizing, when a hundred thousand heathen a day are dying without hope because we are not there teaching the Gospel to them . . ." urged the SVM's traveling secretary. To the Y's youthful evangelists, the SVM's commitment was not overblown rhetoric. In 1891, six thousand students signed pledge cards to become foreign missionaries, and in the next decade the movement became larger and larger. Although other missionary groups existed, the SVM was probably the most important missionary arm of American Protestantism.

The SVM made the Far East, particularly China, a major target. Yet despite the volunteers' numbers and dedication, conversion progressed slowly. The first groups of young missionaries felt that a thorough knowledge of the Gospel would bring success, and they entered China with little sensitivity toward its language or culture. Why learn the values of a heathen civilization that would shortly be transformed? Inevitably, there was confusion of cultural symbols. Did a serpent represent evil, as it did to missionaries, or wisdom, as it did to the Chinese? Cultural chauvinism and racial superiority obstructed communication, and most Chinese considered missionaries eccentric rather than inspired. Moreover, the SVM's early emphasis on individual salvation as a solution to China's problems was much too simplistic. China's social disintegration, after all, had less to do with the heathen state of individual souls than with rigid class structure, appalling poverty, and the deleterious influence of foreign businessmen, especially those in the opium trade. And, in the early years, the SVM's efforts also floundered because its prescriptions for regeneration, based primarily on models of reform in American cities, had little relevance to a land of peasants. The SVM found it difficult to extend its influence beyond the treaty ports into the interior of China. The governing circles of the Chinese elite were uninfluenced by missionaries in the early years, and conversions had little cumulative impact as long as converts tended to be lower-class people who commanded little respect among their countrymen. (Catholic missionaries generally displayed greater cultural sensitivity and had more success, but American Catholic missions were very few during this period. America itself was still designated as a Catholic mission field.)

Initial failure soon made Protestant missionaries reassess their tactics. Few gave up on God's message, but many discovered more ingenious ways of packaging it. The SVM and other missionary groups began to spread Christianity as part of a broader Westernizing influence, one that many younger Chinese—especially after the humiliating defeat in the Sino-Japanese War of 1894–95—were anxious to embrace. As the demand for education in Western languages and science grew, missionary schools responded eagerly, pressing conversion less as a necessary first step toward Westernization (as in early days) than as a beneficial by-product of it. John R. Mott, the head of the YMCA, wrote:

> It is Western education that the Chinese are clamoring for, and will have. If the Church can give it to them, plus Christianity, they will take it; otherwise they will get it elsewhere, without Christianity—and that speedily!

The change in tactics paid off. The Y's English language schools were enormously popular in Japan, where they became known for their active sports programs, and in China missionaries used language schools and public science lectures to gain the audience—and the converts—they had desired. Following the fall of the Ch'ing dynasty in 1912, most young Chinese intellectuals viewed Westernization less as a repudiation of national traditions than as the only way to combat Western power and preserve their country's sovereignty. Enrollment in Chinese mission schools rose from

17,000 in 1889 to nearly 170,000 in 1915, and the estimated number of converts in China increased from about 96,000 in 1900 to 366,000 in 1920.

Although the SVM and other missionaries targeted the Far East, they were active all around the world. From 1895 to 1897, for example, the head of the YMCA, John Mott, toured Y branches in France, Switzerland, Bulgaria, Turkey, Egypt, Ceylon, India, Japan, and China. Among YMCA leaders, Mott's accomplishments assumed heroic dimensions. In India he was credited with facilitating completion of a YMCA building program that had been stalled because the Y refused to pay an exorbitant price to purchase two bazaars that occupied the proposed building site. Mott suggested that the Y's workers pray over the problem. "Within a few weeks," according to the legend, "the answer came in the shape of a cyclone, which knocked down the bazaars, and likewise the price." A large donation from department store mogul John Wanamaker financed completion of the building project. After the turn of the century, the Y experienced even more rapid growth, moving into Latin America and Africa. The Y especially flourished in the Philippines and Cuba, countries dominated by American military power after 1898.

Missionary activities had broad and often unexpected results. In the 1890s and later, those who advocated extending American culture abroad generally assumed that what they called cultural exchange (really a one-way process) gained friends, promoted understanding, and shaped the world in America's image. Some foreigners gained an enduring affection for things American, but others reacted against Americanization by turning—sometimes violently—to traditional ways and religions, as in the Boxer Uprising in China. Despite missionaries' efforts at the grass-roots level, they seldom became part of the host country, but remained an external force acting upon it, often creating social dislocation. As Mark Twain's *Connecticut Yankee* suggested, America's cultural expansion was not a simple process that would replace a "degenerate" culture with a "superior" one. Contrary to the expectation of late-nineteenth-century missionaries, their activities did not necessarily promote goodwill toward the United States.

Cultural expansionists were probably even less effective in bringing international understanding back home. Missionaries hoped to enlighten Americans about different parts of the world, but as they became bureaucratized and professionalized, promotional techniques crowded out educational functions. Samuel Capen, president of the American Board, did the most to wed missionary work to business concepts of organization and advertising. Appropriately, his slogan for missionary work was "organization, efficiency, and power." In 1906 he founded the Laymen's Missionary Movement, an organization located on Madison Avenue in New York City, which sponsored and organized fund-raising efforts for missionary groups around the country. Although Capen insisted that contributions to missionary work represented simple acts of Christian stewardship, he also argued that modern business techniques were needed to induce stewardship in Christians.

Inevitably, promotional techniques distorted cultural reality. Fund raisers focused on the desperate plight of the foreigner—the filth, the hunger, the disease—and flattered American donors with fantasies of selfless gifts and grateful natives. The scenario included the foreign beggar, robbed of imagination and self-respect, and the American savior, anointed with benevolence. Showing other lands as one-dimensional backdrops to American rescue efforts, fund raisers seldom enlightened prospective donors. In 1911, for example, a spectacular Pageant of Darkness, showing the exotic horrors of the heathen world, attracted huge crowds at the World in Boston Exposition and then toured the country. It shocked audiences and brought in money. In such extravaganzas, other societies and cultures were trivialized.

Finally, the results of the early missionary movements illustrated another trend: the tendency of cultural expansionists to become involved with economic expansionists and, ultimately, to link both causes together. Although some missionaries had initially disdained the "godless materialism" that traders sometimes brought overseas, most believed that America's commercial presence would assist their efforts. Missionaries, after all, flourished in port cities and had their greatest success in converting foreigners employed by, or trading with, American businesses. In appealing for business support, missionaries claimed that their work would open potential markets. Samuel Capen, for example, wrote: "When a heathen man becomes a child of God and is changed within he wants his external life and surroundings to correspond: he wants the Christian dress and the Christian home and a Christian plow and all the other things which distinguish Christian civilization from the narrow and degraded life of the heathen." Self-interest, Capen argued, demanded that businessmen contribute to the missionary effort. Under Capen's influence, large donations from wealthy business-men, rather than solicitations from congregations, increasingly be-came the mainstay of missionary finance. From a fund raiser's point of view, it was easier to concentrate on collecting a few big contributions than to coax small change out of individual church-goers. Eventually this growing dependence on the country's finan-cial elite helped shape the missionaries' social and political policies.

PHILANTHROPISTS

Like the missionary movement, organized philanthropy also began to reach overseas during the 1890s. The Russian famine of 1891 produced America's first large-scale effort to send philan-thropic relief to a foreign country. An enterprising Minnesota newspaper, seeking shocking stories to build circulation, mounted a crusade to alleviate the famine. As a public-relations gesture, Minnesota millers, whose elevators were glutted by overproduc-tion, donated excess grain. Finally, Minnesota's governor spon-sored a fund-raising commission to publicize the problem. From these beginnings in the farm belt, which reflected both humanitari-anism and an aggressive strategy to develop foreign grain markets, the campaign to alleviate Russia's famine took on national propor-tions. Philanthropists marshaled the new promotional and organi-zational techniques to stir up public enthusiasm, and humanitarian groups and commercial interests around the country donated their products and their time. (Iowa not only sent large quantities of corn to wheat-eating Russia but also dispatched housewives to demonstrate how to prepare and cook it.)

Mobilization of public opinion on behalf of Russian relief soon created questions about the government's role in foreign aid. One of Minnesota's senators introduced a bill in Congress to charter ships to take the grain to Russia at government expense. But despite substantial public support, the House balked. Representatives argued that government involvement would serve to support the world's most tyrannical and corrupt regime—that of the Czar —and would also be unconstitutional. Even though Russian relief remained a wholly private venture, there was, for the first time, a full-scale debate over the proper relationship between government and private overseas relief. Philanthropists lost this initial fight for government support in 1891, but they would win others in the near future.

After 1891, Americans seemed never to be without a foreign crisis to relieve: attention turned quickly to the massacres of Armenians, to famine in India, and then to the Spanish suppression of Cuba's independence movement. With these crises, the limits of private philanthropy became clear. The country could be marshaled to support only one emergency at a time. In a world full of disasters, the question of which would get the most attention turned more on who controlled the organizational and propaganda networks in the United States than on the objective need. The Russian famines of 1893 and 1897 were probably more severe than that of 1891, yet Americans were by then concentrating on other parts of the world and hardly heard about them. In the late nineties, the Hearst papers and other "yellow journals" were directing public attention to atrocities in Cuba.

More important, there was no effective supervision of overseas relief. How could people distinguish a legitimate philanthropist from an opportunist? And even had there been only bona-fide relief committees, which surely was not the case, duplication of effort and organizational feuding confounded humanitarian intentions.

The problems of fund raising also caught philanthropists in the same traps as missionaries. They accentuated the helplessness and deprivation of foreign people, while inflating American egos, and they cemented ties to the business community in order to ensure large donations. The connection between benevolence and business made fund raising easier but undercut the myth of apolitical assistance. During the Mexican Revolution of 1910, for example, efforts to relieve suffering were spearheaded by Joseph Cudahy, the Guggenheims, and other large investors friendly to the old, prerevolutionary order; their philanthropy was neither politically neutral nor purely humanitarian.

MASS CULTURE

Initially, missionaries and philanthropists were the most active groups involved in America's cultural expansion. But, by the turn of the century, purveyors of mass culture began to employ the techniques they would soon use to flood the world. Buffalo Bill's Wild West Show was one of the first examples of the export of popular culture.

Building its appeal on a mixture of nostalgia and promotional hype, Buffalo Bill's show displayed little of the originality and technical accomplishment associated with "elite" art. Instead, it repetitively presented archetypal themes that later analysts of popular culture would call "formula." Buffalo Bill's successful formula consisted of a simplified presentation of conflict between good and evil, between the forces of civilization and barbarism. The cowboy-hero of the American frontier became a mythic creature of extraordinary virtue and skill with whom the audience identified. (Buffalo Bill never missed a shot; in fact, he really could not miss, since he used buckshot.) The cowboy exemplified popular values: he stood above man-made law, but always followed a higher law; he was close to nature, yet a foe of savagery; he was civilized and gentlemanly, yet an enemy of contrivance or corruption. The inevitable triumph of nature's nobleman, after a series of predictable trials, provided ritualistic catharsis.

In the early 1890s, Buffalo Bill's show circled the world, introduced huge crowds of foreigners to American popular entertainment, and demonstrated that the American Western formula had universal appeal. In some countries the protagonists and villains changed to fit the locality (Indians cued their hair to become the Chinese Boxers, who were then defeated by civilized forces), but the formula remained the same: the skill and heroism of the forces of progress pushed back the legions of darkness. And crowds throughout the world identified with the victors and loved it. The Wild West Show revealed a virtually insatiable worldwide demand for mass-produced formula art—art based on ritual and value confirmation.

Although the Wild West Show's nostalgia and structural predictability offered a conservative message, its production techniques were revolutionary. Nate Salsbury, Buffalo Bill's promoter, advanced the arts of nineteenth-century advertising and public relations by building larger-than-life images, arranging publicity stunts, and pandering to popular stereotypes. Moreover, to reach widely scattered audiences, the show adopted the latest technology. Specially equipped trains efficiently transported the troupe from destination to destination. So quickly could the Wild West Show set up and break camp that German military officials, who followed the show in Europe, used it as a model for their armies, the most mobile in the world.

American journalism of the late nineteenth century also wedded advanced techniques to formulas for mass appeal. In the 1890s, American journalistic trends became popular, especially in Europe. The export of the Hoe rotary presses, which produced 20,000 impressions an hour, lowered the cost of newspapers and spread America's graphic revolution abroad. Trying to expand circulation to match the new possibilities of production, a few European newspapers moved toward sensational formats modeled on the American yellow press. American editors were themselves sometimes imported to apply the methods and energy of mass journalism. For example, the halfpenny morning *Daily Mail,* established in London in 1896, hired one of William Randolph Hearst's editors to Americanize the paper. Some Europeans decried the inroads of American-style journalism, then a pejorative term for sloppy sensationalism; they saw popularized features and flashy headlines as a threat to truth and even to social stability. But the profits from mass-circulation papers could not be ignored, and the graphic revolution spread. American news services were not yet internationally prominent, but American newspaper technology and mass-circulation methods preceded them.

The Wild West Show and mass journalism pointed the way toward the American-dominated, globalized mass culture of the twentieth century. America's mass culture, like its mass-produced exports, was democratic in that it appealed to a broad social spectrum, but oligarchic in that it was carefully contrived and narrowly controlled. Appealing to the masses, it could appear revolutionary, yet by its ritualistic, escapist, and standardized nature, it could also prove profoundly conservative.

The nature of American expansion and its ideological justification crystallized during the 1890s. American traders would bring better products to greater numbers of people; American investors would assist in the development of native potentialities; American reformers—missionaries and philanthropists—would eradicate barbarous cultures and generate international understanding; American mass culture, bringing entertainment and information to the masses, would homogenize tastes and break down class and geographical barriers. A world open to the benevolence of American influences seemed a world on the path of progress. The three liberal pillars—unrestricted trade and investment, free enterprise, and free flow of cultural exchange—became the intellectual rationale for American expansion.

Three
★ ≡ ★ ≡ ★

THE PROMOTIONAL STATE: 1890–1912

PRIVATE impulses, more than government policies, laid the basis for America's enormous global influence in the twentieth century, an influence based on advanced technology, surplus capital, and mass culture. Yet from the 1890s on, as Americans sought wider and easier access to foreign lands, the government had necessarily to define its relationship to these overseas activities. Operating on the assumption that the growing influence of private groups abroad would enhance the nation's strategic and economic position, the government gradually erected a promotional state; it developed techniques to assist citizens who operated abroad and mechanisms to reduce foreign restrictions against American penetration.

EXPANSIONISM—NATIONAL INTEREST AND INTERNATIONAL MISSION

For a number of reasons, the government began to take an active interest in overseas expansion during the 1890s. As American traders and investors enlarged their international stakes, many people argued that the national welfare depended, in part, on continued access to global opportunities. It would, of course, be a mistake to exaggerate the extent of American overseas economic expansion prior to World War I. Compared to Britain's foreign activity, America's efforts seemed slight (except in Mexico and Cuba); by today's standards, the absolute value of exports and investment seems minuscule—export trade and foreign investment comprised only a fraction of domestic economic activity. Yet overseas trade and investment comprised about the same percentages of the United States' GNP at the turn of the century as in recent years, a time when foreign economic activity has certainly been a major governmental concern.

For a variety of reasons, most policymakers of the late nineteenth century, like their more recent counterparts, *did* believe that free participation in international trade and open access to investment opportunities were vital to the nation's well-being. Early multinational companies and the many American firms with international aspirations pressed for greater governmental assistance. Certain important industries, then as later, derived a substantial portion of their profits abroad. By the early twentieth century, Standard Oil, International Harvester, and New York Life—to name only three giant firms—already depended heavily on foreign earnings.

The expansive outlook of these new and powerful international companies gained additional strength from the formation of trade associations. In the late nineteenth and early twentieth centuries most industries developed associations designed to transcend intra-industry rivalry and operate on behalf of the group as a whole. The National Association of Manufacturers (formed in 1895), the American Asiatic Association (1898), the United States Chamber of Commerce (1912), and the American Manufacturers' Export Association (1913) were just a few of the influential offspring of the trade-association movement that urged more governmental support and promoted the identification between foreign commerce and national interest.

But government's new interest in commercial promotion did not stem simply from special pleading. Especially during and after the severe depression that began in 1893, business leaders and policymakers alike became convinced that expansion was needed to avoid overproduction and to maintain prosperity and social cohesion at home.

The reality of overproduction in the 1890s—that is, the validity of any particular ratio placing production higher than consumption—is of little historical importance in assessing the motives behind government's new commercial activism. The so-called crisis of overproduction of the 1890s was rooted less in empirical data than in contemporary attitudes. Twentieth-century Americans have witnessed a process that nineteenth-century analysts could not have imagined: the expansion of domestic demand through techniques such as planned obsolescence, mass advertising, and annual model change. To most American businessmen and policymakers of the 1890s, however, it was domestic production, rather than consumption, that seemed almost infinitely expandable.

Foreign commercial expansion and national prosperity seemed intertwined. The National Association of Manufacturers resolved in 1903: "If, as is claimed, the capacity of our mills and factories is one-third greater than is necessary to supply the home demand, it is obvious that the time is near at hand when we must obtain a broader foreign market, in order to keep the wheels of the factories moving." The *Forum* was more direct: "It is the duty of our government in order to supply remunerative employment to the greatest number of our citizens to take every step possible towards the extension of foreign trade." And farmers also echoed the call for greater governmental assistance. In 1899, the National Grange argued that government had begun to spend "very large sums of money . . . to widen the market for our manufacturing industries in foreign countries" and demanded that it devote "the same energies and efforts" to agricultural marketing. Thus, the overproduction thesis (which mistakenly presumed a fairly inelastic domestic demand) did provoke a reassessment of government's role. Accepting the proposition that government had new responsibilities to enlarge foreign markets, a State Department memo of 1898 stated that the "enlargement of foreign consumption of the products of our mills and workshops has, therefore, become a serious problem of statesmanship as well as of commerce . . . and we can no longer afford to disregard international rivalries now that we ourselves have become a competitor in the world-wide struggle for trade."

Policymakers' social attitudes were also easily compatible with a new role for government. Drawing support from the ideas of Social Darwinism and "scientific" racism, America's dominant groups felt confident of their own superiority. Moreover, they had grown accustomed in domestic affairs to calling upon government to enforce and maintain their prerogatives. In the late nineteenth century, governmental power crushed those ethnic groups that were perceived as threats to social stability. On the frontier, federal troops quashed the last great Indian resistance at Wounded Knee in 1890; in the South, state governments enforced Jim Crow apartheid against blacks, and the Supreme Court buttressed the system with the separate-but-equal doctrine of *Plessy* v. *Ferguson;* in Northern cities, governmental power clashed with strikers branded as radical "new immigrants"; in the Far West, immigrant restriction laws were enforced against the Chinese.

Concepts of racial mission, so well rehearsed at home, were easily transferred overseas. Editor Theodore Marburg argued: "We have brushed aside 275,000 Indians, and in place of them have this population of 70,000,000 of what we regard as the highest type of modern man . . . [W]e hold to the opinion that we have done more than any other race to conquer the world for civilization in the past few centuries, and we will probably go on holding to this opinion and go on with our conquests." And because governmental power had consistently supported Anglo-Saxon dominance at home in the name of advancing republicanism and progress, so it seemed natural for policymakers to adopt a similar activist role and rationale abroad. Senator Albert Beveridge urged President William McKinley not to shirk the white man's burden. God, he declaimed, "has made us adept in government that we may administer government among savage and senile peoples . . . He has marked the American people as His chosen nation to finally lead in the regeneration of the world." Theodore Roosevelt, who became President in 1901, agreed. Drawing on America's own history, he argued in 1901 that when the United States government fought "wars with barbarous or semi-barbarous peoples" it was not violating the peace but merely exercising "a most regrettable but necessary international police duty which must be performed for the sake of the welfare of mankind."

Crusades to dominate those who were not Anglo-Saxon also found support from the burgeoning Progressive movement, of which Roosevelt, Beveridge, and other imperialists considered themselves a part. Progressivism, a reform impulse that profoundly reshaped American domestic life and foreign relations from the 1890s through World War I, comprised a loose and often contradictory coalition of clean-government crusaders, conservationists, Anglo-Saxon supremacists, muckraking journalists, social-welfare workers, efficiency experts, middle-class professionals, and advocates of business regulation. Although people who adopted the "progressive" label could champion causes as diverse as prohibition, juvenile courts, national parks, and antitrust laws, almost all shared a fundamental faith in professional expertise. Progressives sought to guide the nation and the world away from the social disorders of the late nineteenth century by the scientific application of the problem-solving technique: define the problem, search out relevant facts, deduce a solution, carry it out. Progressives enshrined bureaucratic method and expertise, opening the way for greater governmental action while excluding "irresponsible elements" from decisionmaking. If only they could take charge and attack social problems in a scientific way, the new professionals believed, they would bring order and progress at home and abroad. Such elevation of expertise easily became paternalistic: "expert" and "efficient" people had to dominate lesser breeds in order to uplift them, and, as at home, the force of government might be needed to support, indeed to institutionalize, this effort.

Thus, the entire rationale for overseas expansion was shaped in a domestic crucible. Economic need, Anglo-Saxon mission, and the progressive impulse joined together nicely to justify a more active role for government in promoting foreign expansion.

To say that perceived economic conditions and dominant values supported greater governmental involvement in expansion is not to argue that all, or even most, people favored militant colonialism. Americans differed profoundly over *how* to spread civilization. At home, "undercivilized" peoples were made to conform to Anglo-Saxon standards by many means, ranging from violence to educational persuasion. So, in dealing with foreigners, some believed that "backward nations" could be brought into civilization only by means of force, while others sought to conquer the world peacefully, armed with sewing machines, Bibles, schools, or insights from the new social sciences. Whether the government would promote expansion by brutal domination or peaceful reform (or a mixture of the two) presented a tactical question within a broader consensus that accepted the necessity and ultimate benevolence of American expansion.

COLONIALISM

Cuban rebellion against Spanish rule stirred Americans into a crusade to free Cuba and, ultimately, to seize an empire at Spain's expense. In 1898 the Republican Administration of William McKinley annexed Hawaii, defeated Spain in a quick war, and acquired Puerto Rico, the Philippines, and Guam as fruits of victory. (Cuba could not be annexed, because Congress had passed the Teller Amendment promising the island independence, but American military occupation dragged on after the war until Cuba agreed to accept protectorate status.) To some people, acquisition of these overseas colonies seemed to offer a way in which the government could both advance its economic interests and fulfill its mission of improving mankind.

The debate over colonialism centered on the issue of acquiring the Philippines. The economic arguments in support of keeping those islands as a possession stressed their importance as a stepping-stone to China. Both farmers and industrialists hoped to open Oriental markets, and yet, after China's defeat in the Sino-Japanese War in 1895, China seemed in imminent danger of being closed off to Americans. A military and political presence in the Philippines, trade expansionists hoped, would give the United States more leverage in dealing with the big-power scramble for concessions and spheres of influence in China. By serving as a coaling station and base for America's newly strengthened navy and as a relay point for an infant communications system, the Philippines would become, one business publication predicted, America's Hong Kong—its gateway to the Orient. McKinley's Assistant Secretary to the Treasury, the prominent banker Frank Vanderlip, stated that the islands would be "pickets of the Pacific, standing guard at the entrances to trade with the millions of China and Korea, French Indo-China, the Malay Peninsula, and the islands of Indonesia."

Possession of the Philippines would also advance American Protestant missionary efforts, both in those Catholic islands and on the Asian mainland. "The Christian view of politics," explained one missionary in 1901, "emphasizes the burden of Government and the responsibility of dominion, and thereby transforms empire from an ambition to an opportunity. Blindly and unworthily, yet, under God, surely and steadily, the Christian nations are subduing the world, in order to make mankind free."

The classic formulation linking American expansion to a militant colonialism was found in Josiah Strong's *Expansion* (1900), written mainly to justify the subjugation of the Philippines. Strong expressed the views of most imperialists when he distinguished between independence and freedom. Because real freedom was possible only under the rule of law, and Anglo-Saxons were the most effective law bringers, spreading freedom into non-Western lands could necessitate violating national independence and imposing Anglo-Saxon colonial governments. Because national independence movements generally supported anarchy or tyranny, America's superior "free" culture probably could be imported only through outright governance. In addition, Strong stressed, the resources of the tropics were underused by their owners, and the well-being of all mankind required interposition by efficient "producer" races. Thus, Strong emphatically defended American suppression of the Filipino independence movement; he believed that the war reflected God's will and furthered the spiritual and economic evolution of mankind. Republican Senator Orville H. Platt advanced the same view when he described Admiral Dewey's warship in Manila Bay as "a new Mayflower . . . the harbinger and agent of a new civilization." And after investigating America's policy, the first Philippine Commission reported: "Only through American occupation, therefore, is the idea of a free, self-governing, and united Philippine commonwealth at all conceivable. And the indispensable need, from the Filipino point of view, of maintaining American sovereignty over the archipelago is recognized by all intelligent Filipinos . . . "

After the seizure of the Philippines, however, the taste for imposing colonial status on an alien people turned sour for most Americans. The costs of colonialism seemed to outstrip potential advantages. The Filipino independence movement, led by Emilio Aguinaldo, allied itself with the United States in the victory over Spain, but when McKinley's imperial policy became clear, Aguinaldo resumed warfare against the United States. By the time American troops had quelled the nationalist resistance, one of every five Filipinos was dead from war or disease, and America's own casualties reached 4,300 men. The American commander in southern Luzon admitted, "it has been necessary to adopt what in other countries would probably be thought harsh measures." Such slaughter in the name of "freedom" fueled the anti-imperialist movement by making humanitarian arguments for colonialism appear ridiculous. Even Dr. Jacob Gould Schurman, president of the Philippine Commission that had so strongly defended American subjugation of the Philippines, publicly confessed his error after touring the battlefields and seeing the horrors there. By 1902, Schurman had become outspoken in denouncing the brutality of the war and in calling for a government based on Filipino consent.

The anti-imperialists also turned concepts of national mission and economic advantage against colonialism. John W. Burgess, the widely read advocate of Anglo-Saxon supremacy, opposed colonialism on the grounds that it incorporated "inferior" people into the American system. Upper-class reformer Carl Schurz and others suggested that the militarism that would inevitably accompany the seizure of colonies would undermine America's best traditions of representative government and equality under the law. Joining the imperial game would tarnish, not spread, the American dream. Even staunch expansionists such as Theodore Roosevelt and Alfred Thayer Mahan supported acquisition of naval bases but felt grave reservations about annexing large populations of alien peoples. And the prominent anti-imperialist businessman Edward Atkinson attacked the economic argument: "We may not compute the cost of our military control over the Philippine Islands at anything less than 75,000 dollars a day . . . I leave to the advocates . . . to compute how much our export trade must be increased from last year's amount, to cover even the cost of occupation." The expense of empire, Atkinson argued, would always outweigh the benefits.

As the Philippine insurrection demonstrated the moral ambiguity and expense of colonialism, domestic divisions over the issue doomed any further attempts to accumulate an empire. Although most Americans continued to favor expansion, a national consensus never formed to support more acquisition of territory.

The new relationship developed with Cuba—the protectorate—presented fewer problems. After the defeat of Spain, American military officials set up an occupation government in Cuba; in late 1899, General Leonard Wood became military commander and vowed to create a polity "modeled closely upon lines of our great Republic." Wood brought in a host of experts to reshape Cuba. Americans assumed direction of the customhouses (the major source of government revenue), controlled the country's finances, organized a postal service, established telephone and telegraph lines, encouraged railroad and shipping facilities, built roads, carried out sanitation projects (Wood even included "before and after" photos of public toilets in his reports to Washington), established schools (the new Cuban school law closely resembled Ohio's), and invited New York City police to organize their counterparts in Havana. Mark Twain's Connecticut Yankee could not have done more. These measures superficially Americanized and "developed" the island, but Wood bowed to the pressure of the native elite and American landowners and avoided basic changes in land tenure or tax structure—important changes that would have accorded with a liberal, Americanized model. Wood's program further entrenched Cuba's foreign-dominated, export-oriented monoculture of sugar.

America refused to terminate its occupation of Cuba until Cubans accepted the Platt Amendment, which made their country a protectorate. Reluctantly voted by Cubans into their constitution in 1901, the Platt Amendment and its economic counterpart—the Reciprocity Treaty of 1902—gave the United States the right to establish a naval base in Cuba, to intervene against internal or external threats to the country's stability, and to maintain a privileged trading relationship. Under the Platt Amendment, Cuba was independent, but only nominally so.

The protectorate relationship seemed to work economic magic. Trade boomed; American investment in sugar and tobacco shot up; manufacturing sales outlets opened by the score. Integration into America's economy was labeled "development." In 1918, the head of the Latin American Division in the State Department drew this happy conclusion:

> The total trade of Cuba with the United States just prior to the end of the Spanish rule over that island (1897) amounted to about twenty-seven million dollars per annum. During the decade following the termination of our war with Spain the island of Cuba, guided by American influence, increased her trade with us over four hun-

dred and thirty million dollars. This unprecedented *development* of Cuba may serve as an illustration of what probably would take place in the Central American countries provided this government extended to them aid of a practical character as it did to Cuba. [My emphasis.]

Cuba thus became a laboratory for methods of influence that fell short of outright colonialism. Using the Platt Amendment as a model, American Presidents negotiated protectorate treaties with other nations in the strategically and economically important canal area: Panama (1903), Dominican Republic (1905), Nicaragua (1916), Haiti (1916). These protectorates also received a dose of military-directed Americanization. Moreover, the American military and many of the technical advisers who worked to "develop" and Americanize protectorates continued to offer their skills to other foreigners, seldom doubting the universal applicability of their expertise. After a great earthquake in Messina, Italy, in 1909, for example, the navy supervised construction of three thousand new cottages (unfortunately, choosing building materials and styles totally inappropriate to the region). And a great number of American technical and financial missions during the 1920s were staffed by personnel who received their initial foreign experience in Cuba.

With outright colonialism out of fashion, the expansionist debate revolved around other means of control: tutelage under theoretically independent protectorates, or more important, governmental encouragement of private connections, especially economic ones. Increasingly, Americans understood that the extension of American know-how and the expansion of trade and investment could best proceed without formal colonialism. William Graham Sumner, for example, wrote: "What private individuals want is free access, under order and security, to any part of the earth's surface, in order that they may avail themselves of its natural resources for their use, either by investment or commerce." Colonialism was not necessary, or even desirable, to Sumner's ends. If Americans, Sumner added, could have open access to foreign countries but let others actually run the foreign governments, "we should gain all the advantages and escape all the burdens" of colonialism. One exporter, ridiculing the notion that American political control was vital to commercial expansion, confidently proclaimed: "Trade follows the flag is the slogan of laziness!"

ERECTING THE PROMOTIONAL STATE

During the 1890s the government laid the foundations of a promotional state that employed new ways of stimulating America's foreign expansion. The promotional state developed in two directions: its architects gave more active assistance to American entrepreneurs who wished to export or invest abroad; and they formed economic policies designed to reduce foreign barriers against American trade or capital.

Devising a more active role for government raised difficulties. Americans remained wedded to the nineteenth-century liberal theory that government involvement in the private economic sphere would subvert individual freedom and distort the self-regulating nature of economic processes. Clearly, the creators of the promotional state had to present their programs as compatible with the tradition of limited government and as necessary for the preservation of a free marketplace.

There were several ways to fit a promotional apparatus into a liberal framework. New forms of assistance could be linked to older examples of government's role in stimulating the economy. During the nineteenth century, protective tariffs, general incorporation laws, antimonopoly legislation, land policy, prohibitions on labor union activity, and subsidies for canal and railroad builders had all been justified as measures by which government could help to release the energies of the private sector. Thus, Americans had always used certain kinds of government intervention to pump vitality into the liberal marketplace. The extension of government regulatory powers at the turn of the twentieth century was also justified as being compatible with a liberal order, protecting the marketplace from unscrupulous operators and monopolistic practices. When these domestic precedents of government activity were translated into the foreign arena, they provided considerable room for maneuver. If government helped American businessmen gain access to opportunities for growth abroad, it was not very different from what it had been doing at home.

Both farmers and industrialists expected, in fact demanded, such help. Government should not dominate their participation in the world economy, they argued, but it should actively remove obstacles against it. The Master of the Grange nicely articulated prevailing views as he argued for greater trade expansion:

> Commerce and trade, like water, flow along the route offering the least resistance, and it now becomes the mission of our lawmakers to clear away every obstacle or impediment . . . The downfall of our country will date from the hour that we fail to make the occupation of the farmer and laborer profitable in this nation.

Such demands augured a government policy of continual involvement in world economic and political affairs.

There were other arguments. European governments were heavily involved in foreign economic activity; they encouraged, subsidized, and even sometimes partially owned the international companies or cartels operated by their citizens. For those Americans who believed their expansionism to be both economically and morally imperative, European practices were threatening. Businessmen repeatedly complained about Americans' unequal participation in world economic competition and urged the government to do more to support them. Fair competition, after all, implied a relative equality of players and consistency of rules. In order to be able to compete, Americans would have to emulate their rivals. There would have to be a new partnership between government and the private sector, although the partnership would always be limited by the canons of liberalism. Government could assist business within the competitive international environment, but not dominate or control it.

The promotional state that developed after 1890 was a preliminary effort to shape that partnership. In this early stage, it consisted of a modern navy, new tariff strategies, efforts to spread acceptance of the gold standard, and greater cooperation between the government bureaucracy and the business community.

Many who believed that government action was necessary to promote economic access to foreign markets became strong supporters of an enlarged navy. The economist and State Department adviser Charles Conant explained in 1900 the connection between commercial promotion and military power. He began with the familiar overproduction thesis:

> The United States have actually reached, or are approaching, the economic state where . . . outlets are required outside their own boundaries, in order to prevent business depression, idleness, and suffering at home. Such outlets might be found without the exercise of political and military power, if commercial freedom was the policy of all nations. As such a policy has not been adopted by more than one important power of western Europe, and as the opportunities for the sale of the products of American labor . . . under conditions of equality of opportunity are seriously threatened by the policy of some of these powers, the United States are compelled, by the instinct of self-preservation, to enter, however reluctantly, upon the field of international politics.

International engagement and military power, according to Conant, were forced on the United States by a world that was not sufficiently enlightened to have adopted the policies of free trade and open access. Lurking in Conant's analysis was a proposition that Woodrow Wilson would elevate into a national article of faith: that creation of a liberal international order would ultimately foster the conditions for world peace. As long as restrictionism and spheres of influence prevailed, however, militarism—particularly the construction of a larger navy—would seem a necessary part of the promotional state.

After taking office in 1889, President Benjamin Harrison and his Secretary of the Navy, Benjamin F. Tracy, spearheaded an ambitious naval program. Both men were influenced by Alfred Thayer Mahan, whose *The Influence of Sea Power upon History* (1890) associated great national power with naval supremacy. Mahan's views fused all the expansionist impulses of the late nineteenth century: Protestant evangelism, Anglo-Saxon destiny, fear of overproduction, confidence in commercial supremacy. The key to all, he argued, was control of the seas. Tracy pressed upon Congress the need for a large navy to give force to America's new involvement in international politics and global commerce. And Congress responded by authorizing construction of three large battleships in

1890, the first of many similar appropriations. Gradually, America built a naval capability to match its growing economic power.

The connection between naval power and the promotion of commerce emerged clearly during the Administration of Theodore Roosevelt. After years of inconclusive negotiations with Nicaragua and Colombia for the right to build a canal across the Isthmus of Panama, Roosevelt decided the United States could wait no longer. In 1901 he cooperated with a separatist movement in Colombia and helped to establish the new country of Panama, with whose leaders he then promptly signed a treaty granting the United States the right to build a canal and to intervene militarily if stability were threatened. Proponents of the canal argued that it would strengthen America's strategic position, by easing the difficulties of a two-ocean defense, and also provide a commercial shortcut to Asia and the western coast of South America. Roosevelt's brash action to assure a United States-owned canal showed how the expansion of military capabilities and the needs of a burgeoning commerce reinforced each other.

The drive to open more foreign markets also led the government to pursue various strategies aimed at converting tariff policies into instruments of commercial expansion. Before the 1890s, tariffs had served primarily two functions: set moderately high, they could bring in revenue to finance the federal government; set even higher, they could make foreign goods too expensive in the American market and thereby protect producers against foreign competition. But the promotional state began to employ tariffs for a purpose beyond revenue and protection. Bargaining tariffs, customs unions, and the open-door policy were all strategies for widening the access for American trade.

A bargaining tariff employed a simple principle: to force other countries to reduce their barriers against American commerce, Congress could pass tariff legislation that would permit the President to threaten higher rates or promise lower ones on certain commodities. Although the precise bargaining mechanism took different forms at different times, in general a bargaining tariff allowed the President some discretionary power over rates in order to enhance his ability to bargain for freer access for American products.

The McKinley Tariff Act of 1890, passed during the Presidency of Benjamin Harrison, contained the first bargaining, or reciprocity, provision. It passed Congress largely through the efforts of James G. Blaine, the Secretary of State. A fervent advocate of increased trade with Latin America, Blaine was the organizer of the first Pan-American Congress of 1889, devoted to strengthening hemispheric economic bonds. He saw tariff reciprocity as one way of gaining greater access to Latin-American markets and raw materials. This initial bargaining provision permitted sugar, molasses, coffee, tea, and hides to enter duty free, but it authorized the President to penalize goods imported from a country levying unreasonable duties on American products. Presidents Harrison and Cleveland subsequently effected ten agreements for tariff reduction against American exports and announced penalties against three countries. Although the reciprocity clause was repealed in the tariff of 1894, Congress authorized a slightly different bargaining provision three years later.

Then, in the Payne–Aldrich Tariff Act of 1909, Congress established a range of minimum and maximum duties for certain commodities and granted the President authority to set rates within that range. In addition, the Payne–Aldrich bill set up a permanent tariff commission to study world economic conditions and recommend how the Executive might use the flexible rates to enhance trade in a "scientific" way, removed from the play of special interests in Congress.

Protectionists split over the issue of bargaining tariffs. Some stalwart protectionists opposed reciprocity provisions, fearing they might sacrifice the protection of those producing for the domestic market in order to advance the opportunities for exporters. They also viewed the tariff commission suspiciously, seeing the "scientific" tariff as one that would undercut Congress's rate-setting authority and, thus, undermine the power of those who cared less for foreign trade than for domestic protection. But many high-tariff industrialists, even some of those not interested in exporting, were won over to reciprocity because it could mean cheaper imported raw materials. President Cleveland made this argument in 1894, concluding that "when we give to our manufacturers free raw materials we unshackle American enterprise and ingenuity, and these will open the doors of foreign markets . . . and give opportunity for the continuous and remunerative employment of American labor."

Despite domestic divisions, after 1911 tariff bargaining conducted by the Executive and based upon recommendations from trade experts became part of the structure of the promotional state. Foreign policy and trade issues became integrated as never before, and tariffs took on the new function of expanding the export trade. The bargaining tariff began a trend that would accelerate rapidly in the twentieth century: Congress's delegation of more and more direct power over commercial matters to the executive branch.

Some policymakers hoped to go beyond reciprocity and eliminate trade barriers altogether through customs unions. During the late nineteenth century many Americans, such as Secretary of State Blaine, dreamed of a customs union for the Western Hemisphere, a free-trading sphere that would become an economic counterpart to the Monroe Doctrine by effectively excluding European competitors and giving the United States a huge protected market. The reciprocity treaty with Cuba in 1902 was a first step; and the United States also brought its colonies of Puerto Rico and the Philippines into free-trade relationships. President William Howard Taft negotiated a similar treaty with Canada in 1911. Writing to Theodore Roosevelt in 1911, Taft argued that the agreement with Canada

> would produce a current of business between western Canada and the United States that would make Canada only an adjunct of the United States. It would transfer all their important business to Chicago and New York, with their bank credits and everything else, and it would increase greatly the demand of Canada for our manufactures.

Clearly, a customs union had lopsided benefits, and the Canadians rejected the treaty, realizing that it would strengthen American economic and political dominance.

After Canada's refusal, the idea of a Western Hemispheric customs union largely died out. Total elimination of customs duties was never popular with domestic agricultural interests that would have suffered from the competition of duty-free Latin American commodities; selective reduction of barriers through reciprocity was more satisfactory to everyone, because duties could be reduced on only those products that the United States really needed to import. In addition, despite the claims of Americans that a free-trade zone would benefit all within it, most Canadians and Latin Americans viewed economic integration as another manifestation of Yankee hegemony. America's free-trading relationship with its colonies and with Cuba boosted commerce with those areas, but Americans ceased to pursue similar arrangements elsewhere.

Ironically, as Americans sought to bargain for special tariff privileges in the Western Hemisphere, they championed the open door in Asia. In 1899, McKinley's Secretary of State, John Hay, sent his first Open Door Note, asking all nations to respect the principle of equal commercial opportunity in China. A year later, fearing that the Boxer Rebellion might lead to outright European colonization, he sent a second note requesting nations to respect Chinese territorial integrity. The principle of the Open Door—noncolonization and equal access—became the foundations of American economic diplomacy in the Far East.

Europeans noted the inconsistency in America's attempt to preserve equal commercial access in areas where other powers were stronger (the Far East and Middle East), while attempting to forge a privileged trading position in its own hemisphere. John Hay, the architect of the open door in Asia, had himself convinced Brazil to repudiate the open-door principle and grant special tariff rates to United States goods. How could American diplomats denounce other nations' spheres of influence at the same time that they assumed the right to dominate one of their own? For a time, the rhetoric of American liberalism could paper over such a paradox. Policymakers talked of *equal access* in Asia; they talked of *freer trade*—through special privileges—in the Western Hemisphere. In both cases, the policy meant more markets for Americans and hence seemed perfectly compatible with their view of world progress. Selling American products, after all, would help spread the American dream.

The tariff policy in these early years was more inconsistent than it would become in the 1920s, when Americans began to recognize that they no longer needed special privilege to become economically dominant in the Western Hemisphere. Feeling secure in their own superior trading position throughout the world, policymakers of the 1920s began to adopt the principle of equal access, or the open door, everywhere (except Cuba).

The currency question—one of the major political and economic issues of the 1890s—was also related to expansion and promotion of trade. Those who argued that the United States should resume coinage of silver and make America's currency bimetallic stressed closer trading ties with Asia and Latin America. (China, Japan, India, Mexico, and Brazil all employed a silver standard in the 1890s.) Bimetallism, they claimed, would make the United States more competitive with European countries in these potentially large new markets. The case for bimetallism became identified with William Jennings Bryan, the Democratic and Populist candidate for President in 1896.

Advocates of the gold standard, led by Republican Presidential candidate William McKinley in 1896, argued that the United States could never join the ranks of the major commercial nations unless its dollar was made as sound as the British pound. They identified gold with development and economic leadership and silver with underdevelopment and economic subservience. They proposed that the United States maintain the gold standard and urged less-advanced nations to do the same.

Following Bryan's defeat in 1896, America seemed permanently committed to gold, and the government tried to convince silver-standard nations to switch to the "civilized" standard. Basing all currencies in the world on the same international standard—gold —would make the international environment for trade and investment more predictable and less risky. Mexico and Brazil responded to pressure from the United States and Great Britain and moved on to gold. Following the recommendations of Charles A. Conant, a private banking adviser who assumed a quasi-official role, the American-run military government in the Philippines also carried out currency reorganization. Conant realized that abandoning silver currency would be psychologically difficult for Filipinos, and he established new silver coins, which came to be called "conants." But he pegged their value tightly to the United States gold dollar, in effect giving the Philippines a gold standard. In 1903, Conant tried to introduce a scheme calling for gold-based currency reorganization and American financial advisers in China as well, but the plan ran afoul of Chinese and European opposition. Until his death in 1915, Conant also advised the government on currency reforms in America's Caribbean protectorates.

In addition to tariff and currency policies, the promotional state included new bureaus and procedures specifically designed to encourage commerce. As early as the mid-nineteenth century, the State Department had regularly published reports from consular officials on business opportunities abroad. In 1897, Secretary of State John Sherman created a Bureau of Foreign Commerce that published daily reports and sent a circular instruction to all American consuls to "give special attention to the question of extending the sales of American manufacturers." In 1903 Congress further strengthened the government's promotional capacity by moving the Bureau of Foreign Commerce into a newly created Department of Commerce and Labor and assigning four "special agents" to it. Unlike the State Department's consuls, each in charge of one particular foreign district, these special agents traveled to report on worldwide markets for specific American goods. And as the Commerce Department increased its promotional capabilities, the State Department reorganized its consular office to make it more effective. The (Henry Cabot) Lodge Bill of 1906 and an executive decree by Theodore Roosevelt reformed the consular service by giving agents higher salaries, placing restrictions on the hiring of foreigners, and introducing the civil-service merit system. These reforms helped to convert the consular service from a dumping ground for patronage appointments into a professionalized foreign-trade bureaucracy. In addition, the State Department created a Bureau of Trade Relations (abolished in 1912 and superseded by an Office of Trade Advisors).

The State Department also began to authorize diplomats to aid American business directly. This marked an important reversal of policy. In the late 1880s, for example, the department required that its minister to China, Charles Denby, obtain specific authorization before assisting any United States businessman, and Washington often withheld its approval. In 1896, however, Secretary of State Richard Olney reversed this policy and granted Denby permission to use all personal and official influence on behalf of any reputable American businessman. Noting that European competitors constituted a serious threat to American production, State Department officials increasingly issued instructions such as a 1906 message to the minister in Chile that "the Department is not likely to disapprove of your showing considerable energy in behalf of American trade . . ."

In the early twentieth century the Commerce and State Departments vied with one another to be the most vigorous promoter of foreign trade. Indeed, the intense rivalry between the two departments fueled their aggressiveness. Finally, in 1912, the Commerce Department and its allies in the business community succeeded in making Commerce, rather than State, the focus of trade promotion when Congress established the Bureau of Foreign and Domestic Commerce (BFDC) within the Commerce Department. Commerce Secretary Charles Nagel said that the new BFDC "will be in a position to provide for industrial and commercial interests governmental assistance similar to that which the commerce of foreign countries has enjoyed for many years."

Although promotion of economic expansion increased, the government did not assist every private economic advance. Theodore Roosevelt, who succeeded McKinley as President in 1901, held back because of his firm geopolitical notions about spheres of interest. Roosevelt believed that America should dominate the Western Hemisphere but that its primary role elsewhere should be to contribute to a balance of power. In Asia, Roosevelt wanted to offset Russian power with Japanese, even at the expense of the strong American position in Korea.

In the late nineteenth century, Horace Allen, a missionary, an adviser to the Korean government and then American minister to Korea, helped American businessmen obtain concessions to run Seoul's trolley line, lighting plant, water supply, and telephone system. Allen also convinced Americans to develop Korea's first railroad and its gold mine. In none of these endeavors did he receive backing from the United States government. In fact, fearful that Allen was involving the United States too heavily in an area fraught with Japanese-Russian rivalry, the Roosevelt Administration repeatedly advised Allen to restrain his concession hunting. In the Treaty of Portsmouth of 1905, a settlement mediated by Roosevelt to end the Russo-Japanese War, Roosevelt acquiesced to a Japanese sphere of influence in Korea. The United States government subsequently withdrew its legation from Seoul, making diplomatic support for American interests virtually impossible, and

Japanese entrepreneurs easily crowded out Americans. Allen wrote that once "in Korea everything seemed to be American," but to Allen's dismay, Roosevelt turned the land into a Japanese protectorate. During Roosevelt's Presidency, American loans for railroad-building in Manchuria (another prime area of Russian-Japanese rivalry) also faced the State Department's declaration that it had "no wish or authority to involve the United States in any obligation either legal or moral with reference to such a loan." Roosevelt's balance of power politics prevailed over the wishes of economic interests.

Roosevelt showed great support for economic stakes primarily when he perceived larger issues of national honor. In 1905, China canceled a concession for an uncompleted railroad financed by J. P. Morgan. The Chinese government agreed to pay Morgan enormous damages for the loss of potential profits on the unfinished line. Morgan, under fire for having completed only twenty-eight miles of a proposed 840-mile track in five years and for certain contract violations, quickly snapped up the generous settlement. But Roosevelt was furious at the Chinese cancellation. America's credibility, he believed, depended upon preventing the Chinese government from voiding a contract held by Americans. If China canceled Morgan's contract with impunity, he fulminated, Americans would look weak and their competitive position vis-à-vis the Europeans would suffer. He arranged personal meetings with Morgan, and repeatedly urged him not to accept the Chinese settlement and to stand firm, with the United States government behind him. Morgan ultimately refused the President's request, but the President told a friend that, had Morgan decided to fight cancellation, "I would have put the power of the government behind them, so far as the executive was concerned, in every shape and way."

Roosevelt's geopolitical calculations and obsession with national honor changed under his successor, William Howard Taft. Taft was a globalist who saw world politics primarily in commercial terms; his Administration pressed economic expansion everywhere, not just in the Western Hemisphere. Taft's approach, which he called "dollar diplomacy," was based on the theory that the growth of private economic ties internationally would increase both the strategic position and the economic prosperity of the United States. In 1912 Taft explained that his policy was one of substituting dollars for bullets . . . It is an effort frankly directed to the increase of American trade upon the axiomatic principle that the Government of the United States shall extend all proper support to every legitimate and beneficial enterprise abroad . . . If this Government is really to preserve to the American people that free opportunity in foreign markets which will soon be indispensable to our prosperity, even greater efforts must be made . . . The absolute essential is the spirit of united effort and singleness of purpose.

Taft's dollar diplomacy expanded on promotional techniques and pioneered new ones. His Administration supported the passage of the Payne–Aldrich Tariff of 1909, and it created the Bureau of Foreign and Domestic Commerce. It also helped begin the United States Chamber of Commerce, a private association that became an important advocate of economic expansion, and gave official blessing to the international building campaign of the YMCA. More importantly, Taft developed a practice that his successors of both parties would use later. He encouraged syndicates of private bankers to extend loans and financial advice to countries needing economic stabilization. Taft and Secretary of State Philander Knox, a successful corporation lawyer, believed that large loans to shaky regimes, accompanied by some degree of financial guidance to secure the banker's investment, would create governments that would attract further American investment, develop strong political ties to the United States, and withstand foreign threats to their territorial integrity.

This decision, by which the government encouraged specific private concerns to carry out a particular policy deemed in the national interest, might be called the chosen-instrument policy (to borrow a phrase used in the 1920s). In three particularly troublesome places—China, Nicaragua, and Liberia—Taft, in effect, anointed certain private bankers with foreign-policy functions.

CHOSEN INSTRUMENTS

In Far Eastern matters, Taft relied heavily on the advice of Willard Straight, who had been consul at Mukden in 1906–07. Straight had then pressed the idea that American-built railroads in Manchuria would develop resources, create a market for American goods, and stabilize the area against absorption by Russia or Japan. He began to work with railroad entrepreneur Edward Harriman and bankers Kuhn, Loeb and Company on his Manchurian plans, but his efforts stalled for lack of governmental support during the Roosevelt Presidency. But when Taft took office, Straight became acting head of the State Department's Far Eastern Division and vigorously argued that unless American investors plunged quickly into Asia, the United States would lose the potentially great Oriental trade. At that time, a consortium of European bankers was negotiating to grant loans to China. Taft and Knox, encouraged by Straight, became alarmed that the lack of American participation in those loans might ultimately mean the exclusion of American commerce from the area. As a result, they elbowed America's way into the consortium and convinced the House of Morgan to organize a syndicate of banks to represent America's interests. Willard Straight then resigned his government post to become the American syndicate's principal representative to the consortium.

Negotiations between China and the consortium became increasingly complex. Under Knox's and Straight's influence, the bankers expanded proposals to include railroad loans, loans for the development of Manchuria, and currency reorganization. Knox even hoped, at one point, that the bankers might, as part of a comprehensive loan program, insist that China appoint an American financial adviser with substantial authority over the Chinese treasury. After the toppling of the Ch'ing dynasty in 1911, Taft made it clear that American recognition of the new Chinese government depended on its acceptance of the consortium's loans and financial supervision. But China delayed, and the election of Woodrow Wilson in 1912 brought the Taft Administration's plans for China to an abrupt end. Wilson extended recognition to China and advised the bankers that their proposed loans for China no longer had governmental support.

Taft's China policy was not followed, but the consortium did demonstrate how bankers could serve as instruments of foreign policy. And despite Wilson's initial opposition to this kind of dollar diplomacy, he too would eventually embrace it.

Nicaragua provided another example of foreign policy conducted through the agency of private bankers. In 1910, Secretary of State Knox assisted a Nicaraguan opposition group into power and then negotiated a protectorate treaty with the new leader. Under the treaty, Nicaragua promised to refund its debt through an American bank and to allow the bankers and the United States government to select an administrator of the customhouses, the country's major source of revenue. Reluctant to have the United States assume direction of yet another foreign territory, the United States Senate rejected the agreement. Then, with Knox's support, the bankers (Brown Brothers and Seligman) advanced the funds and designated a collector of customs anyway. Brown Brothers simultaneously purchased controlling interest in Nicaragua's Pacific Railroad and national bank. So Americans had firm control over Nicaragua without official governmental involvement or the need for congressional approval (though Congress did ratify a protectorate treaty during the Wilson Administration).

Under Taft, dollar diplomacy even extended into Africa. Although the United States had few interests in Africa and tried to remain aloof from European rivalries there, Americans held a strong beachhead in Liberia, a country settled in the nineteenth century by former American slaves. Internal turmoil in Liberia, prompted by the threat that Britain might turn the debt-ridden country into a colony, convinced Taft to send a fact-finding commission there. The commission recommended that Liberia become a United States protectorate: America should guarantee independence, grant technical aid, and institute a customs receivership.

Congress once again balked at any official commitment, and the State Department once again turned to private bankers. In 1912 State Department officials put together a plan with American, British, and French bankers to extend a private loan to Liberia in return for a customs receivership directed by an American. Tripartite control proved awkward, and the arrangement broke down after the American receiver general, a Georgian, kicked Liberia's Minister of Finance down the steps of a government building and had to be smuggled out of the country.

In each case—China, Nicaragua, and Liberia—Taft substituted dollars for bullets by using private bankers as instruments of public policy. That none of these attempts at dollar diplomacy succeeded did not dampen the appeal of a chosen-instrument approach to foreign policy. Through designated private enterprises, architects of the promotional state hoped to encourage a favorable foreign business climate yet limit their own direct responsibility for the day-to-day administration of foreign economies. The relationship between government and a chosen instrument seemed fitting for a liberal state: it gave the United States government-backed financial houses that could more ably compete with European banks; yet, because the relationship was informal, it also preserved liberalism's important distinction between public and private spheres.

Expansion became a prominent feature of American life between 1890 and 1912; it was evident in commerce and investment, in cultural outreach, and in government policy. Whether Americans favored formal territorial colonialism or simply an expansion of private economic and cultural ties (sometimes called neocolonialism), most believed in America's superiority and the urgent need to spread its products and messages to the world. Gradually, the balance swung away from formal colonialism toward the belief that private institutions—especially businesses and voluntary associations—would spread the American dream more effectively than conquering armies.

An increasingly activist government—a promotional state—accompanied and nurtured America's business abroad. Gradually, government developed policies to assist the private sector: a big navy, bargaining tariffs, the open-door policy, currency advisers, and new executive-branch bureaucracies. Taft even turned private banks into instruments of public policy, hoping that their stabilization loans would increase the possibilities of trade. Compared to European practices, the American government's role still seemed limited, and most American businessmen complained that they received too little direct governmental assistance. But in the United States the new partnership between government and business had to develop within a liberal tradition that frowned on excessive government interference. Government's enlarged powers after 1890, then, were designed to assist private businesses indirectly, being careful not to dominate them.

Four

★═══★═══★

WORLD WAR I AND THE TRIUMPH OF THE PROMOTIONAL STATE

WOODROW WILSON, President from 1913 to 1921, accelerated the growth of America's power in the world, increased its moralistic zeal, and enlarged government's role in spreading economic and cultural influence. Especially during World War I, the Wilson Administration expanded the scope of the promotional state in order to usher in a reformed and liberalized international order. As the historian N. Gordon Levin's work suggests, Wilson believed that a postwar world of open economic access, growing American economic might, and international cooperation led by the United States would ultimately bring prosperity and development, peace and liberal democracy to most people. To Wilson, as to his predecessors, America's influence and global progress went hand in hand.

ECONOMIC EXPANSION

Woodrow Wilson and his advisers, like their predecessors, continued to view strategic and economic concerns as inseparable. In 1915, Wilson's second Secretary of State, Robert Lansing, wrote that "commercial expansion and success are closely interwoven with political domination over the territory which is being exploited." He suggested the extension of economic influence over Latin America as the best way to strengthen America's strategic posture. Lansing's assumption, previously espoused by Taft—that economic penetration contributed to political dominance and strategic security—remained a premise of Wilson's promotional state. Although committed to commercial expansion, Wilson harbored a deep-seated suspicion of any business that violated his notion of an open, liberal order. He encouraged American entrepreneurs less to promote private profits than to secure areas against exclusive domination by anyone, thus keeping them open to greater numbers of Americans. His failure to support American businesses overseas in a few celebrated cases, especially in China, Mexico, and Costa Rica, mislead some observers into thinking that Wilson was not an economic expansionist. Yet, in each case, Wilson believed that he was upholding a liberal economic order that advanced American interests in the long run.

Shortly after taking office, the President withdrew government support of American participation in the international banking consortium for China that Taft had encouraged. Wilson viewed the consortium as a vehicle of special privilege; he feared that the agreements the bankers sought might violate the principle of the open door. And, because only a few New York-based banks comprised the American contingent, it also discriminated against other American banks that might have wished to be involved in Chinese ventures. (By the time of Wilson's decision, the bankers' enthusiasm over China loans may have cooled to the point that they actually welcomed a clear-cut termination of negotiations.)

Wilson also refused to grant the strong governmental backing demanded by American oil and mining interests that were adversely affected by the Mexican revolution. In 1914 Wilson ordered military occupation of Mexico's major seaport, Veracruz, but refused to take into protective custody the American-owned oil fields just to the north of the port. The purpose of the occupation, Wilson explained, was not to protect oil investments but, by assisting the Mexicans in overthrowing an unconstitutional president, Victoriano Huerta, to show Mexico the necessity for following constitutional procedures. Learning to elect good men, the American President avowed, would create a stable, law-abiding society that would, in the long run, ensure a favorable climate for trade and investment. Similarly, in 1918, when the oil companies requested military intervention to secure their holdings against possible nationalization under Mexico's revolutionary constitution of 1917, Wilson refused and sought more peaceful ways of bringing Mexicans to accept American principles regarding private property.

In Costa Rica, Wilson similarly denied United Fruit's request that he recognize a new government which the company had apparently sponsored in a military coup. Wilson lectured United Fruit officials, just as he had Mexicans, on the importance of constitutional procedures. Contrary to the recommendations of many advisers (such as young John Foster Dulles, Lansing's nephew), Wilson steadfastly refused to recognize the new government. Moreover, he used wartime economic controls to slap an embargo on exports to Costa Rica. The economic distress that Wilson's measures induced finally forced collapse of the unconstitutional regime, despite United Fruit's attempts to save it.

As these examples suggest, Wilson drew a sharp distinction between advancing the *nation's* economic interests and advancing *particular* businesses. Businesses could get government support, but only if their actions accorded with Wilson's definition of the public good within a liberal framework. Wilson's first Secretary of State, William Jennings Bryan, said it best: "It is our intention to employ every agency of the Department of State to extend and safeguard American commerce and legitimate American enterprises in foreign lands . . . But this Government will . . . know no favorites."

In line with this policy, Wilson enlarged the structure of the promotional state and expanded its services. Secretary Bryan announced in 1914 that "the government, while it cannot create trade, can give to trade an environment in which it can develop." The outbreak of war in Europe that year, however, threatened stability. American exports and investors rushed into Latin America to fill the need brought about by the withdrawal of European goods and capital. But, despite easy gains in Latin America, Wilson was pessimistic about the long-term prospects for America's continued peace and prosperity in a world at war. For two years, Wilson tried to mediate a peace, but he gradually became convinced that to secure a stable, open international environment, the United States had to join the war, help defeat Germany, and then become a prominent force in the postwar settlement. After April

1917, when the United States declared war, Congress granted the Executive emergency powers that further strengthened the promotional apparatus of Wilson's bureaucracy. Building on old powers and taking advantage of wartime authority, Wilson launched America's most ambitious attempt to globalize liberal values and American influence.

During the Wilson Administration, the Cabinet offices responsible for foreign trade and investment—Commerce, Treasury, and State—all improved their services to business. Wilson appointed William C. Redfield—a prominent member, and future head, of the American Manufacturers' Export Association—Secretary of Commerce. Redfield enlarged the Bureau of Foreign and Domestic Commerce (BFDC), placed commercial attachés in leading centers of the world, and expanded the number of special agents gathering data on the automobile market and the paper industry. Other services of the BFDC included *Commerce Reports,* a daily journal on trade opportunities; a sample room, containing products of foreign competitors; and an exporter's index, listing firms that desired confidential bulletins on specific opportunities. This government-sponsored market research amounted to a substantial subsidy for businesses engaged in foreign commerce.

The Treasury Department, headed by Wilson's son-in-law William Gibbs McAdoo, also played an active role in economic expansion. McAdoo championed a Pan-American financial conference, held in Washington in May 1915, at which he proposed creation of an International High Commission that would seek uniform laws and practices regarding the gold standard, commercial paper, customs regulations, and postage. Standardization of commercial rules would stimulate trade and investment with Latin America. The Treasury also helped overturn Secretary of State Bryan's ban against private loans to Allied nations. In late 1914, Bryan had announced that loans to warring nations would violate the "spirit of neutrality" because more would be extended to Britain and France than to Germany. But McAdoo argued that Allied purchases of American goods would drastically diminish if Americans could not lend money to finance the buyers. Besides jeopardizing American prosperity, McAdoo argued, a ban on otherwise-legal financial transactions was an essentially unneutral act, even though loans really benefited only one side in the war. Wilson backed McAdoo's recommendations; Robert

Lansing replaced Bryan as Secretary of State; and, by April 1917, private bankers had lent $2.3 billion to the Allies. (Germany had borrowed only $27 million.) By late 1916, the American stake in Allied successes had become so great that the Treasury Department and the Federal Reserve Board grew alarmed. The loans, financing a brisk trade in war matériel with Britain and France, stimulated American industry, but made continued prosperity dependent on an Allied victory.

With America's entry into the war in April 1917, Congress granted the Treasury Department emergency powers: authority to extend government loans to Allied nations and to control the shipment of bullion out of the country. Treasury officials used these both to prosecute the war more effectively and to enhance America's economic position overseas. For the first time, government had the power to decide how much to lend to foreign governments that sought to purchase American exports. And, of course, the power to grant or withhold credits implied considerable political and economic leverage. The Wilson Administration, for example, delayed loans to the Allied government in Cuba until it agreed to accept a certain price—established in Washington—for its sugar exports. It also embargoed bullion to Mexico as a warning to the neutral, nationalist government there not to move against American-owned oil companies.

The State Department likewise increased its efforts to promote economic expansion. At a conference in Paris in the summer of 1916, English and French delegates adopted resolutions that favored protection and imperial preference. Secretary of State Robert Lansing feared that these Paris resolutions "could create trade restrictions in the post-war world which would cause a serious situation for nations outside the union." In attempting to respond to the danger of economic restrictionism, however, the government found information on worldwide economic conditions gravely inadequate. Early in 1917, the State Department consequently issued the first of a series of wartime fact-finding circulars, requesting consular officials all over the world to describe local economic conditions and to forecast the United States' commercial position at the end of the war. Consuls were to send trade figures and describe changes or opportunities, particularly in industry, banking, railroads, and strategic raw materials. This information was then sent on to appropriate American businesses.

Ministers and ambassadors also received instructions to assist reputable American enterprises, especially in the Western Hemisphere. Lansing, for example, gave oil interests in Colombia full support on the grounds that "only approved Americans should possess oil concessions in the neighbourhood of the Panama Canal." American diplomats interceded with the governments of Argentina and Brazil on behalf of the Central and South American Telegraph Company, a firm working to break the British monopoly on cable communications in South America. Before the war, the president of the company had complained about a total lack of governmental interest in the extension of his business; toward the end of the war, however, he told the State Department: "We rejoice to know that you appreciate . . . the urgent necessity to do everything possible now and hereafter to safeguard American commercial supremacy in Central and South America."

In addition to the new activities of these Cabinet departments, several newly created agencies fostered trade and investment. The Tariff Commission, which had begun under Taft, continued its compilation of worldwide trade practices in order to advise the President how best to bargain for increased access to markets. The Federal Trade Commission (FTC), an agency created in 1914 to enhance cooperation between business and government, assisted exporters by collecting information on trade and tariffs for their use and worked closely with business associations to provide a strong and successful lobby in favor of legislation designed to legalize monopolistic combinations in the export trade. The Tariff Commission, the FTC, and the BFDC all issued reports outlining how European governments organized banking, shipping, and manufacturing sectors in a cooperative effort to conquer foreign markets, and they recommended that America adopt similar coordination—especially by developing a foreign banking capability.

The Federal Reserve Act of 1913 provided the statutory basis for American banks to establish branches in foreign countries. And the outbreak of war the next year, by closing off traditional English channels of financing, gave added incentive. After promises from American companies such as U.S. Steel, the Du Pont interests, International Harvester, and Swift that they would conduct their trade through its foreign branches, First National City Bank of

New York became the most enthusiastic promoter of overseas commercial banking and started an affiliate, the American International Corporation (AIC). AIC's board of directors, reflecting the emerging ties between international businessmen and foreign commercial banking, consisted of the chief executives of Armour, General Electric, Great Northern Railway, W. R. Grace, International Nickel, Anaconda, Westinghouse, American Telephone and Telegraph, and Standard Oil, plus several other leading bankers. Similar new banking networks—the American Foreign Banking Corporation and the Mercantile Bank of the Americas—also contributed to America's new economic presence abroad. Before the war, America had few branch banks abroad; the historian Carl Parrini estimates that by 1920 Americans had established 180 branches and affiliates in foreign countries.

The War Trade Board, established in 1917, became the most important war emergency agency, and it, too, promoted economic expansion. The State Department urged the WTB to "collect information that will be useful in our fight for foreign trade after the war," and the WTB's Statistical Division provided the government with its first comprehensive data on world economic conditions. More important, the WTB exercised complete control over imports and exports and employed a blacklist of enemy-controlled businesses abroad. Occasionally, it wielded authority in matters only marginally related to the war: it sought to use embargoes on food and gold to force Mexico to modify revolutionary legislation that adversely affected American enterprises; it banned imports of Ecuadoran cacao until Ecuador began paying off an American railroad company's bonds. In other cases, the WTB's actions did hit German overseas investment, but these moves neatly dovetailed with American economic interests. The Commerce Department recommended that "a good method for the development of American commerce would be the purchase of some enemy firms by American interests," and the State Department instructed consuls to report such opportunities. Some gains were made, especially in Latin America. American capital bought out the German firm G. Amsinck and Company and the German interest in American Metals. American dominance replaced German in Guatemala City's electrical system and Honduras's major Pacific port. The United States government also attempted, though with less success, to assist W. R. Grace in purchasing extensive German-owned cacao plantations in Ecuador and large sugar estates in Peru.

Although the Wilson Administration effectively improved America's international economic position, there was growing economic concern toward the end of the war that the loss of war orders might bring about depression and unemployment. Moreover, Americans feared that Britain and France would institute economic restrictions after the war and greatly reduce America's overseas markets. Before the war, nearly three-quarters of America's total foreign trade was conducted with European belligerents and their colonies. When Wilson presented his Fourteen Points for peace to Congress in January 1918, he advocated "the removal, so far as possible, of all economic barriers and the establishment of an equality of trade conditions," but this American peace aim was not shared by the Allies, who believed they needed certain mercantile restrictions to rebuild their own war-torn economies. In 1918 and 1919, pressure mounted in Congress to pass new promotional legislation to help Americans increase their competitive edge internationally. More overseas customers would put more Americans to work. The export-oriented legislation passed toward the end of the war once again extended the promotional state.

Two significant pieces of legislation related to the issue of business monopoly, one of the most perplexing problems for a liberal state bent on foreign expansion. In 1890, to prevent combinations in restraint of trade and to help ensure healthy competition at home, Congress had passed the Sherman Antitrust Act. During the next two decades of foreign-trade expansion, however, American exporters and financiers realized that they could not compete effectively with powerful European interests unless they could occasionally create monopolies to operate outside the United States. Their argument was simple: in the world economy, nations, rather than individual companies, were competing, and other nations not only permitted but encouraged cartels; combinations that at home might restrain competition were necessary to ensure America's competitive place abroad. By this reasoning, a law permitting combinations in overseas business activity was not illiberal but was the vehicle for a fairer international marketplace.

Using such thinking, in 1918 Congress passed the Webb–Pomerene Act. It allowed monopolistic business combinations in the export trade; similar companies could join to bid on a foreign project, or through export associations, firms could jointly offer products at agreed prices to foreign buyers. Then, in late 1919, Congress passed the Edge Act, an amendment to the Federal Reserve Act, which allowed national banks to buy shares in corporations engaged in foreign investment, opening the way for large investment trusts. Congressmen hoped that the Edge Act would marshal large sums of American capital, increase American loans abroad, and enhance the ability of foreigners to purchase American exports. Edge Act corporations, supporters argued, would provide the coordination between banking and trade that Europeans had long practiced. Both of these laws helped establish the legal basis and the justifications for government encouragement of American-owned international cartels.

Other important legislative proposals designed to help exporters raised the issue of the proper role of government in overseas lending. Most policymakers realized that American credits abroad would be desperately needed in the postwar period to provide foreign purchasing power for American exports. During the war, Congress had granted to the executive branch the power to make government loans to foreign countries, but this emergency authority expired when the war ended. Some businessmen and officials urged Wilson to back legislation that would continue the government's foreign lending in the postwar period. Wilson, however, insisted that government should only assist private banks (as in the Edge Act), not take over their functions as lending agencies. He was heir to a nineteenth-century liberal tradition and, in contrast to policymakers after World War II, believed that postwar world economic recovery and stabilization should be accomplished by private, not government, capital. Although the President was adamantly opposed to governmental foreign lending in peacetime, Congress overrode the President's veto of a measure allowing the War Finance Corporation to extend, on a limited basis, short-term loans to American agricultural exporters who were unable to obtain funds through regular banking channels after the war. This small program of government assistance in financing the export trade would be revived in the 1930s and become a lasting part of the government's function. In 1919, however, it reflected not so much a new direction of state power as a reminder of the constraints that a liberal tradition imposed upon the government's ability to act directly in the international economy.

Because government foreign lending did not continue after the war, encouragement of private foreign loans became all the more urgent if export trade was to thrive. Wilson hoped the Edge Act would help (actually, it accomplished little in its early years, because bankers were wary of long-term foreign investment). But he also revived Taft's chosen-instrument strategy of asking private banks, especially the House of Morgan, to embark upon large foreign lending and stabilization programs—programs he felt the government itself had no authority to undertake. Wilson targeted two important countries as particularly unstable and important to American interests: Mexico and China.

In August 1918, the Wilson Administration completed plans for creation of two international consortia of bankers, one to offer loans to China and one to deal with Mexico. In exchange for the loans, the bankers were to request financial supervision of the countries. Presumably, such agreements would bring economic stability to these nations and advance the investment opportunities of American entrepreneurs. The Morgan interests, representing the United States, dominated both consortia, and Thomas Lamont— Morgan's talented alter ego and "ambassador to the world"— became the bankers' principal negotiator. In China, Wilson hoped that the inclusion of Japan in the consortium would head off an exclusive Japanese loan that might restrict the products of other nations from the China market. A new China consortium would also block any further expansion of European interests in China, because, unlike the one that Taft had supported earlier, American capital would dominate this group. To avoid the appearance of favoring special privilege (the reason he had given for cancelling participation in Taft's consortium five years earlier), Wilson made sure that financing would come from a large group of bankers representing all sections of the country rather than a few New York banks. In Mexico, Wilson hoped to use the bankers' offer of a loan to secure repeal of the nationalization clause in the Mexican constitution of 1917, a clause that was causing American oil and mining interests, backed by prominent Republican senators, to clamor for military intervention. Supervision of Mexican finances by American bankers, Wilson reasoned, would not bring the visibility, the ill will, or the expense of military action.

Negotiations between the bankers' groups and the Mexican and Chinese governments dragged on inconclusively for years, and these negotiations became powerful forces in Chinese and Mexican affairs during the 1920s. Eventually, Lamont's discussions with Mexico led to an overall financial agreement, although the final settlement did not include direct foreign supervision. In China, no comprehensive loan agreement was ever reached. But Wilson's Mexican and Chinese policies clearly illustrated the President's desire to encourage private capital to serve official foreign-policy objectives at the end of the war. Wilson's chosen-instrument strategy, which had its roots in Taft's dollar diplomacy, would find its greatest champion in Herbert Hoover during the 1920s.

Wilson's dedication to economic expansion, coupled with the growth of wartime bureaucracies, extended the apparatus of the promotional state. New techniques, new war agencies, and new legislation all pointed toward a new era for American trade and investment. In an address before the United States Chamber of Commerce in 1915, Wilson had summarized his view of the government's promotional role:

> The Government of the United States is very properly a great instrumentality of inquiry and information . . . We are just beginning to do, systematically and scientifically, what we ought long ago to have done, to employ the Government of the United States to survey the world in order that American commerce might be guided . . . Here in these departments are quiet men, trained to the highest degree of skill, serving for a petty remuneration along lines that are infinitely useful to mankind.

The President's vision of bureaucratic expertise, of government as efficient servant of the public good, of order and rationality, of harmony between public and private endeavors, captured the essence of the progressive movement and the promotional state.

In some ways, the justifications for this dedicated effort to expand America's economic influence sounded familiar. Wilson and his appointees, like their predecessors, stressed the need for closer cooperation between business and government in order to compete effectively with European rivals. They also sounded the alarm against domestic overproduction, talked of "efficient, producer races" (meaning themselves), and exuded faith that American economic influence would stimulate development both at home and abroad. Wilson, however, infused this expansionist litany with fresh fervor. His enthusiasm derived from his deeply held Calvinist beliefs in "duty" and "calling" and from the crusading atmosphere of war. During the struggle against Germany, Wilson always emphasized the special benevolence of America's war aims, as compared to those of either the enemy or the "associate powers." (Wilson, in fact, refused to call the United States an "ally" in order to emphasize America's separateness and disinterested concerns; the United States was an "associated power.")

Such a view conditioned the Wilson Administration's peace terms: only a postwar world dominated by Americans would be just and peaceful, because only America, supposedly, had participated in the war in a disinterested way. Edward N. Hurley, head of the United States Shipping Board, for example, revealed the very common identification between American expansion and international justice when he wrote this memo to Bernard Baruch, head of the War Industries Board, after a meeting with Wilson to consider postwar economic strategy:

> The more we study world conditions, with respect to commerce, the more convinced I am becoming that world peace in the future, as well as total leadership, will swing upon the pivot of raw materials . . . Whatever nation does control them (unless it be America) will make other nations pay a heavy toll. Great power may be used either for good will or for evil. If possessed by the United States we may be sure it will be used for good. The nation, under President Wilson, has given ample proof of this in the present war . . . I doubt whether any other nation is in a position to put the same moral force behind trade-leadership.
>
> If America would invest substantially in the essential raw materials of all foreign countries . . . America would then be in a position to say to the rest of the world, that these commodities would be sold at a fair price . . . In what better way could we be of real service than by the use of our financial strength to control the raw materials for the benefit of humanity . . .

Hurley's hopes revealed how Wilson's war effort heightened Americans' sense of mission and dovetailed with the growth of the promotional state. The bureaucratic revolution, brought by Wilson and the war, both built upon Taft's efforts to forge cooperation between business and government and provided an infrastructure for continued economic expansion during the 1920s

FOREIGN ASSISTANCE

The war also transformed the government's relationship to international relief and technical assistance. Even before Wilson became President, public interest in foreign philanthropy had forced the government to break its tradition of noninvolvement. Only six years after Congress refused to subsidize grain shipments to alleviate the Russian famine of 1891, it easily passed a similar bill authorizing grain sent to India at government expense. And as foreign philanthropy increased, duplicate effort and some fraudulent practices created a need for the government to rationalize foreign-aid efforts and certify legitimate groups. To end misrepresentations and squabbling among different organizations involved in Cuban relief before and during the Spanish-American War, the government officially delegated Clara Barton's Red Cross to supervise all private philanthropic efforts. It then worked closely with this private group, and the arrangement was so successful that in 1905 the Red Cross was reorganized to incorporate government officials into its governing body. Claiming to be nonpartisan, the Red Cross nonetheless became a semi-official relief agency—a chosen instrument for disbursement of foreign aid—which coordinated the activities of the government and various private relief groups.

After the German invasion of Belgium in 1914, American relief became even more closely associated with the government. The story of American aid during World War I largely involved the activities of the successful mining engineer Herbert Hoover.

Hoover had a knack for organizing and directing people. When the outbreak of war stranded 200,000 American tourists in Europe in 1914, Hoover efficiently arranged their orderly return home, no mean feat when most were stranded without funds. (Alfred Vanderbilt reportedly borrowed two shillings from his porter for a shave.) Building on this success, Hoover then accepted a position as Commissioner of Belgium Relief. During the war, the Commission on Relief in Belgium became a semi-official body, directing food supplies to Belgium and France, and Hoover's reputation as a humanitarian soared. In August 1917, Wilson appointed him head of the Food Administration, a wartime agency. The position gave him high public visibility, and he came to symbolize to many the technocrat-humanitarian, the expert engineer who employed his administrative skills for social betterment.

After the Armistice in November 1918, Hoover became head of the American Relief Administration (ARA), an official organization charged with disbursing Congress's $100 million appropriation for postwar relief and handling loans made directly from the U.S. Treasury to certain newly established governments. These funds for direct foreign aid were small, however, and with the signing of the Treaty of Versailles, Congress terminated all official relief. But Hoover remained in Europe and recast the ARA into a chosen instrument; that is, it became a private organization disbursing private charitable contributions but operating in coordination with government policy. Hoover's postwar ARA, like Lamont's banking consortia, fulfilled a foreign-policy function that Congress did not permit the government to undertake directly.

Beyond question, Hoover's relief agencies helped millions avert malnutrition and starvation, but in the immediate postwar period, relief had political as well as humanitarian purposes. Hoover wrote that "after peace, over one-half of the whole export food supplies of the world will come from the United States," and that the United States government should therefore avoid any cooperative distribution plan. Inter-Allied distribution of wheat, he wrote to Wilson, "fills me with complete horror." By keeping national resources under tight rein, Hoover skillfully coordinated their use with the nation's diplomatic goals. A contemporary observer wrote in 1919: "Food and politics have had an inevitable and inseparable connection ever since the beginning of the war; and they have it still." Hoover even created a minor stir at the Paris Peace Conference in 1919 by openly advocating the use of food for political ends.

Hoover's political goal in the rapid movement of food and medical supplies into Central Europe after the war's end was to stabilize the new parliamentary governments against the influence of Bolshevism. American policymakers feared that governments modeled on the radical new Soviet regime, which had come to power in November 1917, might spring up in the uncertain political climate of Central Europe and perhaps spread to Western Europe as well. When a Bolshevik government led by Béla Kun came to power in Hungary in March 1919, most American officials realized the futility of a military campaign against Hungary, a solution that French general Marshal Ferdinand Foch advocated. Wilson argued that "to try to stop a revolutionary movement by a line of armies is to employ a broom to stop a flood." Instead, Hoover suggested using food as a weapon in Hungary, just as, he argued, it had been used successfully in Austria. Hoover wrote Wilson:

> We have clear proof of the value of feeding in the maintenance of order in the case of German-Austria where any action of the Bolshevik element is, on statement of their own leaders, being withheld until harvest, because of their dependence upon us for their daily supply of food.

Hoover consequently sent no supplies to Hungary and announced that food aid would begin only after a non-Bolshevik group came to power. The strategy worked. By August 1919, the food blockade and other internal difficulties had destabilized Kun's regime, and he fled the country. In Poland, the threat of a food embargo helped secure a Conservative regime in power until the departure of the Hoover mission in late 1919. Commenting on postwar Eastern Europe, one of Hoover's assistants said: "Bread is mightier than the sword."

If offers of food could assist American diplomacy, offers of American know-how might also be effective. Hoover's belief in self-help, mixed with his engineering background, inclined him to favor sending technical missions as a most practical means to foster European reconstruction. Helping people reorganize and rehabilitate their own production would have greater long-range consequences than a temporary handout, and the impoverishment of immediate postwar Europe offered a splendid opportunity to spread the American way. Hoover strongly urged Czechoslovakia, Poland, Yugoslavia, and Austria to accept American technical missions, especially since those governments, they were told, would "probably be in need of railway material and finance from the United States," and such advisers would be "of the greatest possible use in negotiations for such finance." All four governments accepted. Hoover's suggestion that hiring American advisers would increase the chances for receiving private American loans became a standard way of promoting economic expansion during the 1920s, when Hoover was Secretary of Commerce.

Throughout the war, other private relief agencies also became agents of government policy. Russia itself provided the best illustration. In the chaotic period after the overthrow of the Czar in March 1917, a Red Cross mission headed by Wall Street financier William Boyce Thompson became America's most energetic representative in Russia. America's aging ambassador, David Francis, seemed ineffectual, and Thompson began to direct his own version of American foreign policy by spending over one million dollars of his personal fortune urging the Russians to stay in the war and trying to bolster Alexander Kerensky's unstable provisional government. Thompson's blatant political meddling became an embarrassment for Kerensky and for the United States. When Lenin's Bolshevik regime replaced Kerensky in the November 1917 revolution, Raymond Robins replaced Thompson. Robins, however, continued to use the Red Cross primarily as a political agency. He first tried to negotiate an arrangement with Lenin that would keep Russia in the war against Germany, but when it became apparent that no amount of aid or exhortation would stop Lenin from suing for peace, Robins drew the Red Cross closer to the White Russian counterrevolutionary commander, General Kolchak. Kolchak, on whom the Wilson Administration also pinned its hopes for an anti-Bolshevik, liberal Russia, kept his armies in the field partly because of the medical care, supplies, and other support that came from the supposedly apolitical American Red Cross.

Other private groups also became antirevolutionary instruments in Russia. The YMCA carried on anti-Bolshevik activities throughout the country, and Samuel Gompers, the moderate head of the American Federation of Labor, traveled to Russia to appeal to Russian workers. Wilson hoped that Gompers's visit, which was extended to Western Europe, might dampen the working class's revolutionary potential by attracting laborers to American-style unionism. Such "private" activities, paralleling Wilson's official policy of joining the Allied military intervention in Siberia on behalf of anti-Bolshevik forces, convinced the Soviet regime of America's determination to destroy it.

Major philanthropic efforts, then, became wedded to governmental policy during the war. The Y, for example, diminished its evangelical religious emphasis and became a service organization working closely with the military to provide canteens for servicemen. The distribution of food, relief, and technical assistance, made more efficient under the influence of progressivism and brought into closer alignment with government policy during the war, helped to spread American influence.

CULTURAL EXPANSION

Spreading American culture and values also came under greater government direction. The Committee on Public Information (CPI), created by Congress shortly after America entered the war, constituted the first thoroughgoing official effort to convert the world to what its director, newspaperman George Creel, fervently called "the Gospel of Americanism." Creel's committee rationalized and accelerated the export of American "information." "We did not call it propaganda . . ." wrote Creel. "Our effort was educational and informative throughout."

Using the techniques and exuding the zeal of progressivism, Creel and his lieutenants conducted what he called "a vast enterprise in salesmanship, the world's greatest adventure in advertising." The private economic and cultural expansion of the previous quarter century greatly facilitated Creel's campaign. The CPI commandeered window displays in 650 American businesses abroad and filled them with posters and photos touting the American war effort; its "export service" inserted copies of war aims into business catalogues; it arranged for wounded Americans of Italian descent to convalesce in Italy and "[preach] the gospel of democracy" in that country; it organized speaking tours of "patriotic American socialists" to sell the war among foreign leftists. In Mexico City, Creel's committee established reading rooms that provided American books and magazines. It also sponsored free classes in English, borrowing from the missionary experience the technique of using language to sell an ideological message. Every one of the "English-language students in Mexico became an understanding champion of the United States," Creel proudly claimed. In China, the CPI called on the YMCA, missionary groups, and employees of Standard Oil to distribute government information into even the smallest interior settlement.

Throughout the war, the CPI churned out an array of educational pamphlets, for distribution at home and abroad, publicizing America's war aims and way of life. Throughout this campaign, Creel sold America, in part, as a model for modernization. Creel worked to project America's image as a powerful, industrialized, free, and just society that others should emulate. "What was needed were short descriptives of our development as a nation and a people," he wrote, "our social and industrial progress; our schools; our laws; our treatment of workers, women and children . . ." Explaining the American dream, Creel assumed, would promote converts and imitators and accelerate global acceptance of an international order based on American values.

Creel used a wide variety of strategies to convince foreign newspaper editors to cover American news and viewpoints on a regular basis. First, he began a government-run newspaper wire service (Compub) which supplied stories to foreign subscribers free of charge. Because the Associated Press and the United Press, America's largest domestic news agencies, had little foreign business before World War I, Creel's service provided many countries with their first news coverage directly from the United States. Some editors gladly accepted CPI stories. To the satisfaction of the committee, for example, the official Japanese news service, Kokusai, translated and distributed Creel's service throughout Japan. For China, where the United States wished to counter the rapidly expanding influence of Japan's Kokusai, Creel created a new press service that sent American news to some three hundred vernacular papers. In some countries, editors needed special prodding. In 1918 the CPI brought a delegation of Mexican editors to the United States and treated them to a whirlwind tour of national and industrial monuments. After this visit, long articles praising America and its war effort appeared in Mexico, a neutral country, and throughout the rest of Latin America. Foreign editors not naturally sympathetic to the United States, or attracted by the carrot of special attention, sometimes felt the stick of American economic power. As a result of Creel's prodding, the WTB embargoed shipments of newsprint to foreign papers reluctant to publish his stories. (Many nations, particularly in the Western Hemisphere, relied on United States paper supplies.)

Creel unceasingly sought innovative methods of spreading America's message. Even though film had only recently emerged from the nickelodeon days, he quickly grasped its potential. His film division began making documentaries on the "wholesome" features of American life—"model farms, welfare work in factories, etc."—and then moved into the production of feature-length films such as *America's Answer* and *Pershing's Crusades.* But Creel also realized that allying with private movie producers was more fruitful than attempting to usurp their empire. Foreign audiences were more anxious to see Mary Pickford and Douglas Fairbanks than to see General John Pershing, and Creel knew that he would reach a vast audience if he could simply attach his messages to entertainment films starring the new celluloid heroes and heroines. The WTB, which licensed all exports, allowed Creel's committee to approve Hollywood's films, and Creel attached the following conditions for export: every film shipment had to contain 20 percent of his "educational matter"; foreign exhibitors would get American entertainment films only if they also showed the CPI's war pictures and refused to screen German films. And thrillers portraying "false" (according to Creel) impressions of America, such as *Jesse James,* were denied a license.

Where ordinary channels of movie distribution seemed inadequate, Creel called on the private organizations that had been America's advance cultural agents since the nineteenth century. Assisting the anti-Bolshevik campaign throughout Russia, the YMCA and Red Cross showed CPI films in peasant villages. American mining companies in Chile showed Creel's products and sent them into nearby cities as well. In Peru, the Red Cross brought American films to every backcountry settlement in which it had a chapter.

After the war, Creel's committee and its Compub service shut down, but this first effort at using a government-sponsored information agency provided experience for the future. Because of Creel, American books, movies, and press dispatches by 1920 were becoming as familiar around the world as Gillette razors and Heinz ketchup. And the job of opening the world to American information and entertainment had taken on a new importance. Creel proved that America could be "advertised" through the mass media, and his efforts had lasting effects on America's position in international communications, as the next chapter will show.

LABOR MOVEMENTS

Wilson's wartime Administration was the first to forge close ties with the American trade-union movement and actively to assist the extension of its influence into foreign lands. As part of the government's effort to promote economic expansion and to marshal international support for its war effort, Wilson naturally sought to head off radical, anticapitalist labor movements abroad. He used the less threatening pattern of industrial relationships represented in the "business unionism" of Samuel Gompers's American Federation of Labor.

American labor leaders made their first formal efforts at internationalism after the Pan-American Financial Conference of 1915. John Murray, a wealthy Quaker and socialist who led many causes on behalf of the Mexican poor in California and strongly supported the Mexican revolution, joined Santiago Iglesias Pantín, the AF of L's general organizer for Puerto Rico and close confidant of Samuel Gompers, to call for formation of a Pan American Labor Federation (PALF). Murray and Iglesias convinced Gompers that the effort to extend American capital into Latin America necessitated a similar effort on behalf of labor solidarity. In February 1917, after months of planning, Gompers issued a manifesto inviting hemispheric participation in a conference to form the PALF.

But the rupture of relations between the United States and Germany in the same month caused Gompers to postpone the conference and devote his energies elsewhere. A fervent supporter of Wilson's views, Gompers began to see his major international mission as rallying support for an American victory. Although Murray and Iglesias had been socialists, and much of Gompers's early appeal in Latin America was due to his own supposedly socialistic views, his patriotic position on the war led him into direct conflict with socialist labor movements elsewhere. In Mexico, the radical labor organizations born in the Mexican revolution supported Venustiano Carranza's policy of neutrality; socialist and anarchist labor movements in the rest of Latin America and in Europe either opposed the war or, at least, gave it little active support. Despite the prewar direction of the PALF, during the war Gompers steered the organization in a strictly nonsocialist direction. Like the Wilson Administration itself, the AF of L came to equate the spread of moderate, pro-war trade unionism with the strategic national interest.

Work on behalf of the PALF thus became indistinguishable from efforts to garner support for America's war policy. Gompers backed Wilson and the war; Wilson supported Gompers and his organization. Murray and Iglesias traveled to Mexico ostensibly to organize for PALF, but their major task was to urge Carranza to abandon neutrality. Wilson approved of their trip, advising, however, that its connection with government policy be carefully concealed. Wilson also agreed to channel government money through the Creel Committee to bankroll a newspaper published by PALF in San Antonio. The President pledged an initial contribution of $50,000 and expenses thereafter, though Wilson and Gompers both agreed that the government's sponsorship of PALF publications should not be made public. Gompers's organization subsequently distributed Spanish-language newspapers and pamphlets in Latin America designed to counteract the anarchist and socialist influence in Latin-American labor circles. And in 1918, when the PALF's long-planned first convention finally took place, it clearly reflected Gompers's pro-war, moderate views. After displaying its close connection to official United States policy (though the details of financing were little known at the time), PALF largely lost credibility. One critic called its efforts *monroismo obrero.*

While supporting PALF in the Western Hemisphere, Wilson and Creel encouraged Gompers to form another organization to spread the values of American trade unionism elsewhere. As in the case of PALF, Wilson secretly committed discretionary funds to support creation of the Alliance for Labor and Democracy (AALD), channeling the money through the Creel Committee. The purpose of the AALD was to draw workers into pro-war activity at home and to appeal to workers' groups abroad, especially in Europe, on behalf of American war aims.

After the Bolsheviks seized power in Russia and withdrew from the war, Gompers and the prominent pro-war socialist William English Walling urged the Wilson Administration to adopt a strongly anti-Bolshevik policy and to engage in labor diplomacy to counter the Bolshevik threat. Gompers, Walling, and Wilson were all concerned about the antiwar mood in European labor circles and decided that the A F of L should send missions to Britain and France in 1918. Samuel Gompers headed the second labor mission; he lectured European workers on patriotism and preached the virtues of American trade unionism. Although the Gompers mission, with its self-righteous tone and often unpopular view of organized labor's proper role, probably antagonized more European workers than it persuaded, Gompers nevertheless returned home celebrating his patriotic deeds. He proclaimed his wartime philosophy: "America is more than a country. America is more than a continent. America is . . . an ideal, America is the apotheosis of all that is right."

After the war, the influence of the PALF and the AALD waned; they never became significant international bodies. But the relationship between these AF of L-dominated labor organizations and the Wilson Administration illustrated the government's new activism in spreading American values through cooperation with private groups. Wilson's use of moderate labor organizations as chosen instruments of policy would be revived during and after World War II.

THE LEGACY OF THE NEW PROFESSIONALS

With the end of the war, the government's direct involvement in economic and cultural expansion ended abruptly. Executive powers over trade and loans, granted under the Trading with the Enemy Act, lapsed. The American Relief Administration ceased to be an official agency of the government and became an umbrella for a number of private charities, though Hoover remained in command. Congressmen, many of whom distrusted George Creel, terminated his committee, and official propaganda efforts ceased. The alliance between the government and the AF of L dissipated in the Republican twenties. But the war left some lasting legacies: a growing professionalization of government agencies staffed with trained experts, and a firmer conviction of the connection between American expansion and world well-being.

Under the influence of progressivism and wartime emergency, the national government increasingly became a professionalized bureaucracy. Randolph Bourne, at thirty-one a perceptive critic of

America's participation in World War I, in 1917 described the new professionals in this way:

> The war has revealed a younger intelligentsia, trained up in the pragmatic dispensation, immensely ready for the executive ordering of events, pitifully unprepared for the intellectual interpretation or the idealistic focusing of ends . . . They are a wholly new force in American life, the product of the swing in the colleges from a training that emphasized classical studies to one that emphasized political and economic values. Practically all this element, one would say, is lined up in service of the war-technique. There seems to have been a peculiar congeniality between the war and these men. It is as if the war and they had been waiting for each other.

But marshaling expertise to expand American influence abroad, even if done in the name of the common man, posed difficult dilemmas. What if foreigners' views of progress and the future differed from those of the American experts, as they did in Mexico, Haiti, and the Soviet Union? What if foreigners did not agree that American influence always brought progress? The new professionals' faith in a harmony of interests allowed them to disregard discrepancies between their professional expertise and foreign opinion. Woodrow Wilson, for example, had a favorite story that he liked to tell at querulous Cabinet meetings. It concerned a gathering at Princeton that contained men of such diverse viewpoints that agreement seemed impossible. Yet, Wilson marveled, after a lengthy and rationally conducted discussion in which all perspectives were aired, the group arrived at a common viewpoint. To Wilson, Princeton might have been the country or the world. Its conference rooms offered realistic lessons about conflict: consensus was possible if rationality prevailed. And in an international context, the new professionals surely viewed themselves as the carriers of the rational solutions around which others would eventually rally. Believing that liberal republicanism on the American model would soon spread worldwide, they could not see how an intelligent, unilateral policy, if properly understood, would be incompatible with a rational, multilateral one. Foreign dissenters were just insufficiently enlightened. National and international interests could be harmonized as thoroughly as the different academic factions in Wilson's Princeton anecdote. (Wilson's use of this anecdote further illustrated his capacity for self-deception; his inflexible style as Princeton's president produced discord and dissent, not consensus.)

The new professionals believed in a harmony of interests, in part, because they believed in the objective application of scientific principles to society's problems. Fact-gathering and social-problem-solving by properly trained experts was a science that transcended cultural values or subjectivity. George Creel, for example, believed that his efforts differed from those of publicists in other nations because they were not self-serving or slanted. Professional journalists like himself, he confidently asserted, could present objective and value-free "facts." The notion that America's journalism, unlike that of other nations, was value-free—a conviction that would again strongly affect America's cultural diplomacy after World War II—provided a sturdy building block in America's imperial ideology. "At no time," wrote Creel, "did Compub depart from its original purpose—*the presentation of facts.*" Such a claim seemed especially spurious in view of Creel's censorship of materials, his one-sided glorification of America, and his calculated dissemination of the forged Sisson Papers, documents that discredited Lenin by purporting to show collusion between Germany and the new Bolshevik government. Creel was an expert propagandist, but he —like too many other Wilsonians—refused to admit that his "facts" could have a subjective quality or be self-serving.

The new professionals, such as William Redfield, Herbert Hoover, and Creel, brought greater efficiency to expanding America's influence. By helping American investment, products, and culture reach more people, they claimed to combat injustice, poverty, and ignorance. But they often offered ethnocentric solutions disguised as internationalist ones and subjective judgments dignified by the name of rationality and fact. Inspired yet blinded by faith in expertise, most of the new professionals failed to see that a foreign policy based on the exportation of American-style liberalism might itself be illiberal.

Five

★═★═★

INTERNATIONAL COMMUNICATIONS: 1912–1932

SCHOLARS representing vastly different ideological viewpoints—from Herbert Schiller to Zbigniew Brzezinski to Lucian Pye—agree that America's dominance in mass communications has been vital to its global influence in this century. Before World War I, American-owned communications industries had hardly ventured abroad. As George Creel put it, Americans were "at once the best-known and least-known people in the world." During World War I and throughout the 1920s, Americans rapidly expanded their global position in cable communications, wireless telegraphy, news services, motion pictures, and airline services. Though American communications industries differed from those of many other countries because of the government's commitment to private—rather than state—ownership, political officials were hardly disinterested in international communications. The promotional state worked for the expansion of American-dominated communications networks, and the government repeatedly used the chosen-instrument policy in an effort to shape private initiative to public policy.

Even before the outbreak of World War I, Woodrow Wilson pressed for the expansion of American-owned communications facilities. He not only supported vigorous private efforts but threatened more direct action should private companies not move quickly enough into the international arena. "If private capital cannot soon enter upon the adventure of establishing these physical means of communication, the government must undertake to do so," Wilson announced before a Pan-American commercial conference in 1915. And during the war Wilson made communications an urgent national priority, one that required governmental attention and, in the case of radio, temporary nationalization of privately owned outlets. Echoing arguments that representatives of the industry had pressed since the 1890s, Wilson justified the growth of an American communications network on strategic, economic, and moral grounds.

World War I accentuated the hazards of foreign-dominated communications. In the period of United States neutrality, from 1914 to 1917, governmental officials who had to send sensitive dispatches over British-owned and monitored cable lines began to wish they had an independent, nationally owned system. Once the United States joined the conflict, policymakers realized some advantages of an American-controlled communications network. United States government censors in Panama monitored dispatches sent over American-owned cables in the Western Hemisphere and reported on the correspondence among neutral Latin American nations. A wider American communications network, officials realized, would enable them to eavesdrop and deal even more effectively with wartime diplomatic problems. At the same time, the lack of American news services abroad, which was closely related to the availability of affordable cable facilities, hampered the Wilson Administration's effort to publicize its war aims and foreign policy goals. After the experience of World War I, independence in communications became a prime concern of the 1920s.

As American property holding and trading interests expanded globally, the commercial benefits of an independent, American-owned communications network also became evident. Businessmen repeatedly complained about having to send details of confidential negotiations over British lines, especially when British firms were often their prime competitors. And businessmen uniformly agreed that greater familiarity with American life, through news or motion pictures, enhanced the marketability of their products in foreign lands. The government's strong interest in promoting

American commerce overseas fed its desire to assist American-dominated communications.

Wilson and his successors related communications to the causes of international peace and freedom. Americans tended to view the government-owned communication systems of other nations as partisan instruments; they pictured their own privately owned enterprises as impartial channels. If American-owned networks could be created, enlightened international policies and impartial rate structures presumably might emerge; ignorance, prejudice, and national discrimination in rates might be swept away.

Because foreign restrictions and monopolies impeded American expansion in many areas of the world, Wilson and his successors championed the doctrines of free flow and equal access to the communications media. The American position at the Paris Peace Conference in 1919 was that "civilization depends upon open communication among nations, [just as] the economic stability of the world depends upon the open door." Yet the government often applied free flow in selective ways, as it did the open-door policy. Where Americans were not dominant, policymakers decried state-supported monopolies and championed a free marketplace of ideas; but in areas of American preeminence, they assumed that freedom, in the form of privately controlled systems, had already triumphed and did not worry about monopolization. The contradiction between advocating open access and yet supporting American monopolies, where advantageous, surfaced in the government's attempt to define a policy toward communications. It was a contradiction that was never resolved, as a closer look at cable and radio policy reveals.

CABLES

Cable lines carrying telegraph messages were the major means of international communication in the early twentieth century, and Great Britain dominated cables in the Atlantic, the Far East, and Latin America. Before World War I, America's pioneers in communication, especially James A. Scrymser, challenged British supremacy and tried to construct an American system. Backed by the Morgan banking interests, Scrymser established All-America Cables and, in the 1880s and 1890s, extended lines from Galveston through Mexico City and Central America and then down the Pacific coast of South America. At that point, British monopolistic concessions blocked further American advance. Scrymser also tried to promote a trans-Pacific cable. In fact, the need for Pacific relay stations provided one argument for acquiring insular territories, especially Wake Island and the Philippines, during the Spanish-American War. In 1903 a nominally American company, Commercial Pacific, completed a ten-thousand-mile Pacific cable; but the company actually operated under the thumb of British capital and was constrained by interlocking agreements with British interests.

Clearly, expansion of an independent American cable system depended on breaking the British monopolies. During the war, All-America Cables, then headed by John Merrill, and the Wilson Administration carried out a persistent antimonopoly campaign against the British company, Western Telegraph, that was blocking construction of American cable lines from Buenos Aires through Uruguay and up the Brazilian coast. The government gave All-America Cables the official support that Scrymser had unsuccessfully sought earlier. All-America became a chosen instrument, a company that received special treatment from the government in return for carrying out a designated policy function—in this case, building an independent cable system in the Western Hemisphere. The Secretary of State, Robert Lansing, repeatedly instructed American ambassadors in South America to assist All-America in its legal maneuvers against Western. The government also put direct pressure on British interests by refusing to grant a British-dominated cable company landing rights at Miami until its parent renounced monopolistic concessions in South America. (A naval vessel actually patrolled the coast of Florida to make sure the British-connected cable was not landed.)

The battle for cable-landing rights was, from the start, cast in terms of a struggle on behalf of liberal principles. American officials urged Argentina and Brazil to renounce the monopolistic concessions they had granted to British companies and embrace the tenets of free enterprise, free competition, and free flow of ideas. The antimonopoly campaign begun during the Wilson Administration continued under his Republican successors, Warren G. Harding and Calvin Coolidge. In 1922, for example, the United States ambassador to Argentina thanked the Argentine government for its action "looking to the removal of restrictive monopolies in cable communications" and expressed "the hope that the way is now open for free and beneficial competition for cable facilities between North America and South America and between the countries of South America resulting in closer business relations, free exchange of ideas and more intimate association of the people of the Western Hemisphere."

Persistence and government support enabled All-America Cables to complete an independent network throughout the Western Hemisphere in a few years. In late 1919, crucial court tests, especially in Brazil, broke the British monopoly, and within six months American-owned lines carried messages from the United States to Rio de Janeiro. All-America then laid cables from northern Brazil into the Caribbean, completing the circle of cable lines around the continent. By 1926 the company had 31,800 miles of cable in the Western Hemisphere, double its mileage in 1914. And in 1927, International Telephone and Telegraph (ITT) bought out All-America, merging it with many smaller companies to create an international giant.

In other areas, the United States government also pressed for acceptance of an antimonopoly position and searched for American-owned companies that would work with it to build an independent, wholly American cable network. But America's major companies operating in the Far East and the Atlantic—Commercial Cable and Western Union—found it more advantageous, indeed probably essential, to divide up routes and enter into cooperative business agreements with British firms.

In 1921, businessmen, newspaper interests, and various private associations dealing with the Far East mounted a broad campaign to convince Congress to subsidize an American-owned trans-Pacific cable. They argued that the high rates charged by the British-dominated Pacific cable impeded the spread of American trade and influence in the Far East and that some direct governmental involvement was necessary if Americans (particularly American news services) were to become competitive. The Harding Administration, however, resisted this congressional effort, insisting that communications should remain a wholly private enterprise.

But under such pressure the Harding Administration renewed its commitment to promote private expansion. Officials urged their antimonopoly position even more forcefully upon Western Union and Commercial Cable, trying to convince them to break ties with the British network and build a system of their own. Moreover, following the technique that had proved successful in the Western Hemisphere, the State Department tried to withhold cable-landing rights at Miami as a means of forcing both British companies and their American allies to break monopolistic practices along the trans-Atlantic lines. But neither appeals to nationalism nor overt pressure succeeded. In the Atlantic and in the Far East, American companies continued to integrate their services and rate structures into the British-dominated system.

In 1923 the State Department gave up and withdrew its active support from these American companies, arguing that they were not helping to create an American network and thus were not entitled to assistance. Concluding that British dominance in cables was impregnable outside the Western Hemisphere, American policymakers devoted more and more effort to insure U.S. dominance in a newer, alternative communications system—radio.

RADIO

Before World War I, the great pioneer in wireless communications, British Marconi, was trying to build a global position for Britain in radio that would match its preeminence in cables. Marconi controlled a large share of the United States radio industry through the American Marconi Company, planned a network of wireless stations throughout the Western Hemisphere, and held a competitive edge in much of the rest of the world. But the United States government always exhibited a strong and consistent interest in radio communications. As far back as the Presidency of Theodore Roosevelt, the White House had encouraged the navy to develop a radio network; and by 1914 the navy operated major wireless stations in Virginia, San Diego, the Canal Zone, Hawaii, Guam, and the Philippines. At this time, radio did not transmit voices but carried coded messages. From the start, then, wireless telegraphy in the United States was bound closely to strategic capabilities, and the radio system was in part privately owned and in part government-owned.

When America entered World War I, Congress nationalized the radio industry and greatly expanded its transmission capabilities. Providing extensive service for point-to-point telegraphic communication, particularly from naval vessels to shore, was initially the network's primary function. But President Wilson saw even greater potential for radio through use of new developments— voice transmission and broadcasting.

Wilson believed that voice broadcasting could revolutionize world order by providing the means for beaming truth directly to the people, over the barriers of government censorship and propaganda. Radio broadcasting seemed the perfect liberal democratic medium: it was democratic in that it reached out to large numbers of people and was liberal because, once people had receivers, access was difficult to restrict. Confident of his ability to harmonize different interests by convincing others of the reasonableness of his point of view, Wilson employed radio as a tool of direct popular persuasion during the war. On January 8, 1918, Wilson became the first international figure to address "the world." His famous Fourteen Points speech was relayed simultaneously from transmitters in Brooklyn (to reach Europe), San Diego (to reach the Far East), and Darien in Panama (to reach Latin America). And in July 1918 a new transmitter in New Brunswick—the most powerful in the world—signaled Berlin in order to bring Wilson's appeal for peace directly to the German people. (A German operator, surprised at a direct message from the president of an enemy nation, radioed back in English, "Your signals are fine, old man.")

The potential of radio diplomacy to create an "enlightened" global community prompted the Wilson Administration to move decisively to improve America's postwar international position in this new medium. Some officials, especially the Secretary of the Navy, advocated that radio remain a permanent government monopoly, but Congress refused to begin the precedent of nationalized communications in peacetime (except for the network needed by the navy). Radio thus reverted to private hands after the war. But Wilson had been working behind the scenes toward a chosen-instrument approach to radio. First, he encouraged creation of a new company with which he could work.

Wilson took his request for a wholly American-owned radio industry to Owen D. Young of General Electric, and G.E. became the government's surrogate in masterminding the absorption of American Marconi into an independent American radio monopoly. Young recalled a meeting with a representative of President Wilson in April 1919:

> Admiral Bullard said that he had just come from Paris, at the direction of the President, to see me and talk with me about radio.
>
> He said that the President had reached the conclusion, as a result of his experience in Paris, that there were three dominating factors in international relations—international transportation, international communication, and petroleum—and that the influence which a country exercised in international affairs would be largely dependent upon their position of dominance in these three activities; that Britain obviously had the lead and the experience in international transportation—it would be difficult if not impossible to equal her position in that field; in international communications she had acquired the practical domination of the cable system of the world; but that there was an apparent opportunity for the United States to challenge her in international communications through the use of radio; of course as to petroleum we already held a position of dominance. The result of American dominance in radio would have been a fairly equal stand-off between the U.S. and Great Britain— the U.S. having the edge in petroleum, Britain in shipping, with communications divided—cables to Britain and wireless to the U.S.
>
> Admiral Bullard said that the President requested me to undertake the job of mobilizing the resources of the nation in radio.

The Administration took no liberal, antimonopoly line on radio, as it had with cable policy. In fact, Wilson's representative directly proposed that G.E. create an American-owned monopoly that could become a steady consumer of G.E.'s electrical equipment and could also serve the national interest in time of war and open the world to American ideas. In late 1919, G.E. announced its accomplishment: it bought out the British interest in American Marconi, and, together with American Telephone and Telegraph, Western Electric, and United Fruit, formed a new company—

Radio Corporation of America (RCA)—to handle all foreign expansion of radio communications. The government appointed one member to RCA's board of directors.

Under Owen Young, who left G.E. to direct the new company, RCA began to consolidate its empire. Although British Marconi had once held most of the rights and patents needed to create a network in the Western Hemisphere, Britain's shortage of capital during the war had forced Marconi to sell its Latin-American interests to Pan American Telegraph, one of the companies that then became a subsidiary of RCA in the 1919 agreement. (In 1918 the British Foreign Office and Admiralty, alarmed that control of radio in the Western Hemisphere was about to slip from British to American hands, argued that the British government should grant Marconi a large subsidy so it would not sell its rights, but the Treasury flatly refused to consider such an expenditure when the government was strained by wartime spending and, in fact, borrowing huge sums from the American government.) From its beginning in 1919, then, RCA had acquired Marconi's competitive edge in building a radio system for the Western Hemisphere.

Young, however, wanted no competition at all. He quickly began negotiations to organize all European-owned radio interests in Latin America into a cooperative system dominated by Americans, much as Britain had done elsewhere in cables. In 1921 representatives of German, French, and British companies joined RCA in granting all of their remaining South American rights to a board of trustees dominated and chaired by Americans. The cooperative agreement, which the American government firmly supported, limited competition, and as Young announced, it carried "the principle of the Monroe Doctrine into the field of Communications."

In China, RCA also tried to substitute cooperation for competition. Using the international consortium of banks that was trying to negotiate loans with China as a model, RCA tried to put together a radio consortium of European, Japanese, and American interests that would agree to divide up routes. Under RCA's plan, Americans would control the United States–China traffic. Japan, however, blocked any proposal that might curtail its own influence in Chinese radio communications. As a result, RCA simply expanded in the Far East on its own throughout the 1920s. By opening direct lines with Japan, Indochina, the East Indies, and the

Philippines, RCA came to dominate trans-Pacific radio communications (though some domestic critics charged that RCA's monopolistic character made its expansion less aggressive in the Far East than desirable).

Government policy supported RCA's cooperative and multinational approach to radio, even though its position was in striking contrast to cable policy, which stressed the need for free competition and independence. The reason for the divergence was clear: Britain dominated cables and would, therefore, dominate multilateral agreements; the United States perceived its own emerging preeminence in radio and saw multilateralism as a co-optive device in its own interests.

The government's contradictory attitudes also appeared in its relations with international regulatory bodies. The American government consistently refused to join the International Telegraph Union, a body formed in 1865 to promote consistent policies and rational rate schedules for cables. The government argued that it had no power to bind private cable companies to the ITU's rules and thus had no reason for membership. One company spokesman in the 1920s, for example, wrote that to compel compliance by American cable companies with ITU's regulations would "not only destroy the enterprise and competitive service but reduce the private companies to the conditions of government ownership." In fact, the government's failure to cooperate with this international body had less to do with the private nature of the industry than with the fear that the ITU's rules might hinder expansion of the American-based network that it was trying to encourage. The American companies and government believed that the ITU rules were "created more in the interests of the European Government-owned telegraph systems."

Americans felt differently about a similar regulatory agency for radio. The United States government joined the International Radio-telegraph Union, formed in 1906, and fought to keep it from merging with the ITU, an action many Europeans favored. The Radio-telegraph Union held one of its most significant conferences in Washington in 1927, a meeting that Secretary of Commerce Herbert Hoover dominated. Delegates to the radio conference divided the spectrum of frequencies according to types of usage, restricted certain designated harmful activities, and tried to set rate

guidelines (though the United States government would not participate in rate regulation, because its companies were privately
owned). In sharp contrast to their attitudes on international cable
policy, American policymakers led the movement for international
radio regulation.

NEWS SERVICES

The extension of American news services closely followed the
expansion of cables and radio, and this expansion fell into a similar
geographical pattern: rapid growth and dominance in Latin America; limited activity in Europe; slower extension into the Far East,
because of great-power rivalries.

In the late nineteenth century, the major news services of the
world agreed to divide up territories and eliminate competition.
The French agency Havas serviced France, Southern Europe, and
South America; the British agency Reuters took the British Empire, Turkey, and the Far East; the German agency Wolff controlled Austria, Germany, Netherlands, Scandinavia, the Balkans,
and Russia; and the American Associated Press operated in the
United States, Mexico, and Central America. For the AP, membership in this international cartel made worldwide expansion impossible, but it did protect it against interference from more powerful
foreign news services in its territory.

Although the AP cooperated in the cartel, it nonetheless styled
itself as the only truly democratic and objective news agency in the
world. European news services, AP's supporters argued, were gov-
ernment-linked; they sprang from an essentially statist and
monopolistic tradition. By contrast, the AP was an association
created not by government but by local newspapers. It was democratic, since its authority worked from the bottom up, not the top
down; it was presumably nonpartisan, because it had to satisfy all
its members, no matter what their political affiliation. The most
eloquent exponent of AP's exceptionality, Kent Cooper, displayed
an almost messianic vision of his association's work. Cooper dedicated his memoir, *Barriers Down,* to "True and Unbiased News—
the highest original moral concept ever developed in America and
given to the world."

Actually, AP's expansion was initially stimulated less by any commitment to a global mission than by its need to outdo an upstart competitor—the United Press (UP). During World War I, government officials and businessmen alike deplored the lack of American information in foreign lands; because the United States had no truly international news service, George Creel's CPI had to organize a government-run news bureau, Compub. But Compub was a temporary expedient, and the Wilson Administration sought a more permanent solution. As he had in finance and radio, Wilson used a chosen instrument. Because AP was tied down with restrictive agreements, government officials looked to AP's newer domestic rival, the United Press, to establish a global news service independent of the European-dominated cartel.

UP initially moved into the international arena in 1916, when it enrolled *La Nación* of Buenos Aires, one of the most prestigious papers in the hemisphere. (*La Nación* had desired to subscribe to AP, but was turned down because of AP's agreement with Havas.) Two years later, Roy Howard of the UP, armed with a letter of introduction from President Wilson and backed by official support from the United States diplomatic corps in Latin America, traveled the continent to sign up clients, particularly among those papers that had become Compub subscribers.

As the United Press began to reap the advantage of the prestige that World War I brought to America, AP grew restive. In 1918, Kent Cooper, a vigorous opponent of AP's restrictive covenants, finally convinced the association to terminate the agreement with Havas relating to South America. Cooper himself then went south to keep track of Howard's activities. In the closing days of the war, both Howard and Cooper traveled the southern continent together, "visiting many countries," Cooper recalled, "each not disclosing to the other what he was actually doing." And although UP had greater support from the government, AP—a much larger and more prominent association—enrolled more papers. (*La Nación* quickly switched allegiance.) By early 1919, Cooper had worked out a favorable rate structure for telegraphic service with his good friend John Merrill, president of All-America Cables, and inaugurated service to twenty-five Latin-American papers. During the 1920s, the AP, and to a much lesser extent the UP, continued to sign up Latin-American subscribers.

For another decade, practicality limited the AP's efforts to bring "barriers down." The association's leadership, like that of the cable companies, feared European competition; outside of the Western Hemisphere, they continued to seek the shelter of multinational, cooperative arrangements. The contract with Havas was revised to allow AP into South America, but the remainder of the old agreement remained intact. Reuters continued to have an exclusive arrangement with Japan's press service, Kokusai, and to service China. AP quelled any ambitions Cooper might have had for bringing America's "highest moral concept" to the Far East. As a result, George Creel's successful drive to place Compub news in hundreds of Chinese newspapers during the war had little lasting impact. AP could not pick up members without offending Reuters, and UP was initially stymied by high telegraphic charges on the trans-Pacific cable. In the early 1920s, Congress directed the navy to let American news services use its trans-Pacific radio circuits, because the private cable and radio companies were expensive, inadequate, or overloaded. UP consequently gained some ground in the Far East, but its progress was slow.

As UP moved into Asia, AP again began to rethink its relationship with the cartel. In 1927, AP began overt and vigorous expansion outside the Western Hemisphere, helping to set up "press associations" modeled on American organizations. Kokusai in Japan even adopted the associational structure and moved away from Reuters to form closer ties with AP. Finally, in 1932, AP forced the Europeans formally to recognize their right to provide news directly to foreign papers anywhere in the world. In 1934, AP and UP jointly and publicly endorsed the concepts of free access and free competition. They both promised to oppose exclusive arrangements such as had governed international news for the previous fifty years. The two major American press services, now powerful enough to compete worldwide, firmly embraced the open door.

MOTION PICTURES

Americans also worked to open the world to their motion pictures. Movies were by no means trivial in the international system of the 1920s. Movie stars could promote goodwill and create markets; moreover, films symbolized larger issues of national censorship and free flow.

In 1920, Douglas Fairbanks and Mary Pickford toured Europe on their honeymoon. In London, thousands spent the night crowded outside their hotel; in Paris, throngs tied up traffic for hours and made it difficult for the stars to move about. As though they were royalty themselves, Doug and Mary called on kings and queens and invited them to visit Hollywood. The couple's films had dominated the screens of Europe (and of the Soviet Union), and their honeymoon extravaganza dramatized the magnetism of the United States film industry.

European film studios had largely collapsed under the economic strain of World War I, while American movies became increasingly lavish. George Creel saw the value of well-financed productions and made sure that motion-picture producers received wartime allotments of scarce materials. In the 1920s, audiences worldwide grew dissatisfied with the poor technical quality of America's competitors and demanded Hollywood's stars and high-budget glitter. In 1925, American films comprised approximately 95 percent of the total shown in Britain and Canada, 70 percent of those in France, 80 percent in South America.

Movies of the 1920s constituted the latest link in a chain of American cultural exports. Like the Wild West shows, movies used predictable formulas with universal appeal. Motion pictures also improved on the work of the flagging missionary movement to spread the American dream. One perceptive French critic wrote during the 1920s:

> Formerly the preachers of Cincinnati or Baltimore deluged the world with pious brochures; their more cheerful offspring, who pursue the same ends, inundate it with blond movie stars; whether as missionaries loaded with Bibles or producers well supplied with films, the Americans are equally devoted to spreading the American way of life.

Filmmakers and government officials believed that this cultural export promoted democracy and understanding, in much the same way that American products or news services did. In contrast to Europe's elitist films, America's movies always appealed to mass audiences. Created not out of the traditions of elite art but designed to entertain a diverse, multi-ethnic patronage at home, early American films were perfectly suited to a world market. Silent films presented no language barriers, and the humor and appeal of stars such as Charlie Chaplin—probably the most popular actor abroad—were truly universal. Foreign audiences loved the Little Tramp, who burlesqued the ravages of modern life; at the same time, they flocked to see Hollywood's version of modernity. Many films of the 1920s emphasized sex and the lavish material consumption of America's leisure class. American filmmakers liked to think they were producing a universal, nonpolitical art form that was democratic in its impulses; in fact, they largely peddled formula art based on a distorted view of American tastes and manners. The American cinema was also touted as a vehicle for world peace. Will Hays, the powerful head of the Motion Picture Producers and Distributors Association (MPPDA), declared that film was promoting peace by destroying barriers between nations. A French critic accused Hays of assuming that "the only way to assure peace is to Americanize the thoughts, the language, and the souls of foreigners." But if Hays did, indeed, confuse international harmony with Americanization, he was articulating a view shared by most American politicians and businessmen.

The movies' appealing, highly sanitized version of American life was, in effect, an extended commercial for American products. "Trade Follows the Film" proclaimed a *Saturday Evening Post* article in 1925. According to popular beliefs, American movies stimulated the demand for mass-produced American goods such as cars, telephones, cameras. Inspired by the movies, people around the world began building California-style homes, whether or not the architecture suited their particular climate. The movie-equipment industry also flourished with the global expansion of American films in the 1920s: Kodak manufactured 75 percent of the film in the world; ITT monopolized the production of sound equipment; American companies directly owned over half the leading movie houses in the world and outfitted them with American wares.

As American movie entertainment spread, so did American newsreels, with their emphasis on quick visual impact rather than the complexity of events. Newsreel producers simplified issues and shaped them to entertain. Fox's Movietone News, begun in 1919, took its viewers "Around the World in Fifteen Minutes in Picture and Sound." Although it stationed cameramen and editors in many countries and claimed to be international, its most appealing and spectacular news usually came from America. Charles Lindbergh's takeoff to Paris, for example, became the subject of one of Fox's earliest and most ambitious sound newsreels. A competitor, Paramount News, begun in 1927, received diplomatic assistance from the State Department in gaining access to European countries to take news footage. On the first anniversary of Paramount News, Secretary of State Frank Kellogg sent his congratulations and expressed this commonly held opinion of the motion-picture industry: "I cannot help feeling that, in these days when the movie is so vitally important in the life of every country that it, more than anything else, can create good understanding."

As Kellogg implied, the United States government placed heavy emphasis on stimulating exports of film and newsreels. In 1926, Herbert Hoover's Department of Commerce established a special Motion Picture Section (characteristically, the bureau's first report was on the China market). And, like Paramount News, motion-picture producers regularly received diplomatic assistance to build and maintain their international position. A major diplomatic controversy of the late 1920s, in fact, involved European attempts to restrict the export of American movies to the Continent.

Many European politicians and intellectuals believed that American movies undermined their cultural traditions and national identity (one film showed only American troops marching under the Arc de Triomphe after World War I). The European film industries, of course, led the anti-American campaign, arguing that American ownership of theaters and the practice of block booking (American producers sold one or two feature films on the condition that a large number of lesser films also be screened) made it impossible for their domestic film companies to compete. In response, the German government became the first to effect a quota system (film imports were limited to the number of domestically produced films), and Britain followed.

But quotas only led to new strategies. American producers invested heavily in the German, and then in the British, film industry and cranked out "quota quickies." These films qualified as local products and enabled the Hollywood studios to expand their exports of American-made films. Quotas, thus, only contributed to the deterioration of national industries. When France attempted another solution, requiring Americans to import French films in return for their exports, Hollywood boycotted French movie houses, and the MPPDA sent Will Hays to France as a negotiator.

Under Hollywood's pressure, Hays convinced the French to soften restrictions so that American movies retained primacy in the French market.

In 1929, in response to the new nationalism in the film industry, the State Department sent a circular protesting all such restrictions. After recounting the attack made on the American motion-picture industry, "one of the leading industries of the United States," Secretary of State Henry Stimson wrote:

> the building up of this market has involved an investment of large proportions, and . . . the foreign regulations are often so subject to arbitrary and unpredictable change that they introduce an element of commercial uncertainty and industrial instability to which American motion picture producers and distributors find it difficult or impossible to adjust themselves . . . [T]his government has adopted no restrictive regulations similar in any way to those enforced in certain foreign countries. I believe firmly that the interests of the motion picture industry in all countries are best promoted by the freest possible interchange of films based solely on the quality of the product.

The rhetoric of liberalism and free flow only thinly veiled the government's attempt to perpetuate what was, in effect, a virtual monopoly. The "freest possible interchange," in fact, meant the continued global dominance by Hollywood.

American movies became so entrenched in the world market during the 1920s that, even after the advent of sound at the end of the decade, foreign receipts diminished only slightly. Subtitles and dubbing enabled movies to hurdle language barriers more easily than anyone had predicted. In one decade, American movies had become an immense worldwide cultural and economic influence. As one magazine article put it: "The sun, it now appears, never sets on the British empire and the American motion picture."

AVIATION

As Americans enlarged their communications empire, they also became interested in commercial aviation. Before the 1920s, most of the American enthusiasm centered in private groups such as the

Aero Club, a group seeking to promote air travel within the hemisphere. A few private Americans established training schools in Brazil, Argentina, and Peru; the Curtiss Company sold some equipment within the hemisphere; and a few American-owned airlines briefly operated in Mexico and the Caribbean. But government efforts to stimulate foreign air-transport operations were limited. Some of the naval missions in Latin America included aviation trainers, and U.S. Marines used planes against rebels in protectorates, but the U.S. Army's Air Service Division (unlike the European military planners) actually discouraged sale of surplus planes and engines, arguing that such sales did not enhance American security. Moreover, most government officials saw little strategic value in the establishment of commercial airline service. Even World War I did little to change the government's indifference to aviation.

By the mid-1920s, however, European governments were showing such great interest in airline routes in Latin America that some Americans began to show concern. In 1923, Secretary of War John W. Weeks warned that commercial planes could easily be fitted with bomb racks and that foreign airlines so equipped might threaten the Panama Canal Zone. Exporters predicted that they would lose a lucrative market in parts and service if airplanes used in Latin America were not American-made. These strategic and commercial arguments persuaded the Harding Administration to launch America's first major goodwill trip on behalf of aviation. In early 1924, three government aircraft, guided only by a standard Rand McNally map, took off from Panama and stopped at every Central American country but Honduras. The War Department, which planned the mission, hoped to promote better relations with the United States, aid the American aviation industry in establishing Central American markets, and map air routes for future airmail or commercial service.

The War Department also urged more direct ways of stimulating commercial air service, service they believed could be turned to military uses in time of war. Although the government lacked authority to go into commercial aviation, promoters in the War Department argued that the Post Office's authorization to deliver mail might justify operation of a national airline. A subsequent study for the Post Office concluded that an airmail service, even one limited to the Caribbean area, would not be cost efficient, but it did argue that a "broader viewpoint" might justify the expense of an airline on strategic and commercial grounds.

As government policymakers considered various options ranging from continued noninvolvement to a government-owned airline, the sensational court-martial of Brigadier General "Billy" Mitchell in 1925 dramatized the issue before the public. Mitchell had run afoul of his superiors for charging that the government's failure to move faster in developing an airway to South America amounted to criminal neglect of the country's security interests. Although Mitchell was convicted, his trial raised fears about America's lethargy in promoting international aviation. Responding to pressure, in late 1926, the Administration of Calvin Coolidge sent a second and more elaborate air mission to Latin America. Landing in almost every country, this ambitious mission sought to demonstrate the practicality of airline service throughout the continent. (To the embarrassment of its sponsors, the publicity-seeking junket met hostility or indifference nearly everywhere, attracting attention only after a crash killed two aviators.) The mission showed that the government, not simply private lobbyists, now seriously sought to promote American air service throughout the hemisphere. The government then announced it would award airmail contracts to an airline serving the Caribbean—contracts that amounted to an indirect subsidy of private aviation.

Pan American Airways, chartered in March 1927, became the beneficiary of the government's new determination. The Post Office awarded Pan Am a contract to carry airmail from Key West to Havana, and the President personally urged the airline to expand as quickly as possible into the Canal area. Pan Am was soon dominated by a twenty-eight-year-old Yale graduate and ex-navy pilot, Juan Terry Trippe. Trippe, whom *Fortune* magazine described as having "an almost psychic grasp of the future," combined the business acumen and personal connections that made his company the perfect chosen instrument. In 1928, Trippe married into the prominent Stettinius family; his new father-in-law was a Morgan House banker and his brother-in-law, Edward Stettinius, would later become Secretary of State.

Trippe also forged a useful friendship with the hero of aviation, Charles Lindbergh. Lindbergh had followed up his famous trans-

Atlantic flight of 1927 by an even more daring, though less heralded, nonstop journey from Washington, D.C., to Mexico City.
Lucky Lindy—who subsequently married Anne Morrow, the
daughter of the well-liked American Ambassador to Mexico
Dwight Morrow (also a Morgan House banker)—received a tu-
multuous welcome in Mexico City. Then, capitalizing on Lindbergh's fame and popularity in Latin America, Trippe and Lindbergh and their wives flew a publicity mission to most nations
bordering the Caribbean in the fall of 1929. This flying quartet,
symbol of youth, talent, adventure, and romance, tapped the kind
of enthusiastic responses that had eluded the earlier, government-
sponsored missions. Trippe's tour gave American aviation—and
Pan American Airways—a perfect image among Latin America's
modernizers.

Trippe quickly developed a successful strategy for rapid expansion. First, he continued to rely upon exclusive government airmail
contracts, a subsidy that made it nearly impossible for any other
airline to compete successfully with Pan Am's service. In fact,
government policymakers purposely used contracts to perpetuate
Pan Am's monopoly. Ignoring the principles of free competition
that they upheld on other issues, officials argued that only a protected monopoly would have the strength to expand its service
quickly. In order to obtain landing rights in various Latin-American countries, Trippe also linked his operations to those of previously established and powerful American interests, especially
United Fruit, RCA, and W. R. Grace. The airline serving Peru, for
example, was Panagra, the joint creation of Pan Am and Grace.
Using such strategies, Trippe drove out or swallowed up fledgling
competitors and extended Pan Am's empire to Mexico, Central
America, the West Indies, and most of South America. Then he
went to work planning trans-Pacific service—Pan Am's agenda for
the 1930s. Pan American Airways continued to be the prototype
of a chosen instrument, a governmentally favored private company, informally designated to carry out national security functions.

In little more than a decade after World War I, the United States
constructed the foundations of an extensive communications empire. Before 1914, Americans owned few means of international

communications. By 1930, American movies were dominant nearly everywhere; American radio, newspaper wire services, and commercial airlines were preeminent in the Western Hemisphere and pushing into the Pacific; and an American cable company had broken the British monopoly in the Western Hemisphere. The 1920s were a truly revolutionary decade in America's international communications.

Enterprising pioneers such as John Merrill, Owen Young, Kent Cooper, and Juan Terry Trippe pushed American communications into the world, but they did so with substantial government assistance. Some Americans supported direct governmental ownership of international cables, radio, and airlines. They feared that private enterprise would not be sufficiently independent of European cartels or would not develop their networks fast enough to beat out European competitors. But government ownership always seemed too dangerous a precedent in a liberal state, and none of the Administrations from Wilson to Hoover supported nationalized communications. But all of these Presidents placed a high priority on an expansion of American communication and placed the promotional state strongly behind certain American companies, making them quasi-official agents of the national interest. All-America Cables, RCA, and Pan American Airways were adopted as chosen instruments, and government assisted their monopolies abroad. American wire services and the motion-picture industry also relied on strong government action in support of free-flow doctrines. Maintaining a climate in which American communications could expand became a basic goal of the promotional state.

Six

★═★═★

FORGING A GLOBAL FELLOWSHIP: THE INTERNATIONALIST IMPULSE OF THE 1920s

WHILE the remarkable growth of American-owned communications was spreading culture, other organizations also attempted to spread American values in a more personal fashion. Before World War I, such direct efforts at Americanization were closely identified with missionary groups offering Christianity and Americanization as a package. Although missionaries continued their efforts in the 1920s, a greater awareness of obstacles, a growing sensitivity to cultural diversity, and rising resentment within host countries changed the direction of missionary work. With several decades of cross-cultural experiences behind them, the missionaries of the 1920s were too sophisticated to promise the evangelization of the world in one generation.

Businessmen and members of the rising new professional groups, however, inherited much of the missionaries' zeal. They formed voluntary associations and foundations endowed by some of the large fortunes made in the late nineteenth century, and forged alliances with foreign business and professional people. Spreading their own gospel of Americanism, most sought to convert the world to American business-oriented values and to American prescriptions for change.

INTERNATIONALIST ASSOCIATIONS

When the French visitor Alexis de Tocqueville toured the United States in the 1830s, he noted that Americans' most distinguishing characteristic was their widespread use of voluntary associations. Long organized for purposes of self-help, reform, or social control at home, many associations naturally broadened their geographical focus as the nation itself became involved abroad. And the 1920s, a decade when most prominent citizens exalted private solutions to public problems, proved a fertile time for the internationalist spirit of a variety of private voluntary groups.

The YMCA, still led by John R. Mott, evolved from a Bible-carrying group emphasizing individual salvation into a scientific and professionalized cadre stressing regeneration through social engineering—the application of the new social sciences to social problems by trained professionals. The emphasis on social science had begun before World War I, as YMCA missionaries recognized the failure of purely religious appeals and the need for a more comprehensive approach to reform. World War I, however, turned the Y decisively in a more secular, service-oriented direction. During the war, thirteen thousand members of the Y handled almost all welfare and recreational work for American armed forces overseas. In organizing for war work, Y leaders reconceptualized the role of their organization, moving away from the moral uplift of Christian boys toward ministering to a broad array of social needs. Both at home and abroad, the Y continued in the decade after the war to deemphasize evangelical Protestantism and devote itself to helping anyone—even non-Christians—reform degrading conditions. G. Sherwood Eddy, a man whose name would become virtually synonymous with Y work, wrote in the foreword of a social-science survey of Peking in 1921 that the new missionary might seek "not merely to rescue a few individuals, but . . . that the whole Gospel may be applied to the whole of life and all its relationships —political, social and industrial, as well as religious." Helped by its new progressive image, the Y flourished in the twenties. Its budget for foreign work soared, reaching a peak in 1928, and the number of branches worldwide increased rapidly.

The Y's new role drew heavily from the progressive, bureaucratic mentality with its penchant for statistics-gathering and fact-finding. A "social survey" of Peking, conducted under Y auspices during the 1920s, for example, illustrated the new direction. Beginning with the proposition that in China "there are no facts" and that facts were necessary for uplift, the Y study became the first in the Far East to use the "survey method" of fact-finding, an approach employed by progressive reformers in American cities prior to World War I. The Y extended the new emphasis on social engineering in 1925, when its Far Eastern representatives established the Institute of Pacific Relations (IPR). Designated as a scientific and educational body without any specific religious attachment, the IPR received support from the Carnegie Endowment for International Peace and became a major forum for American internationalist views during the late 1920s and 1930s. If the turn-of-the-century YMCA had hoped to convert foreigners, the Y and its offshoots of the 1920s hoped to reform them by scientific social analysis.

The Y saw itself becoming a truly international organization, espousing universal goals free from narrow nationalism or sectarianism. John Mott, for example, became one of the most prominent leaders in the ecumenical movement. His experience with the Y led directly into his efforts to begin the World Council of Churches, an association composed of major Protestant denominations. The Y also adopted a policy of "devolution," by which Americans would gradually prepare native followers to continue the process of reform and then turn authority over to them so that social progress could come from indigenous development rather than externally imposed pressures. In 1922, for example, the Y established a special college in Latin America, the Instituto Técnico, to train for association work, and the many new Y branches in postwar Eastern Europe were entirely nationalist controlled, offering what they termed "a typical Y.M.C.A. program adapted to a Catholic environment." In China, native-born YMCA leaders sponsored a "mass education movement," promoting grass-roots literacy and public-health programs.

As Y reformers cut through old ways and indigenous leaders worked to change their own societies, Y-supported activities sometimes shook the status quo, and the line between acceptable and radical reform became hard to draw. When some foreign Y leaders turned to socialism, the Y quickly tried to distance itself from any position that imperiled fund raising at home. Some Y-trained men, especially in the Far East, became such fervent nationalistic reformers that they turned violently against anything identified with foreign missionaries and, ultimately, against the Y itself. A hard question emerged: was the Y's primary mission to engineer social reform or was it to provide the type of recreational programs that could divert attention from social ills? Eventually, as it did at home, the Y increasingly stressed recreational activities and steered away from reform. The contradiction between advocating structural reform and trying to remain true to a liberal-capitalist world order (the order, after all, of Y donors) bedeviled many Y chapters in less-developed countries, and after 1929 the Y's foreign programs withered. The Y's retreat also was made more rapid by worldwide depression.

The Y experience of the 1920s epitomized the dilemmas of cultural interchange. An American-based international organization, dependent on American funds, could not really become transnational. As long as the Y spread American ways, it thrived because of donor contributions. When it diversified its membership and goals, it became more attractive to foreigners but withered because of the suspicion of domestic contributors.

Rotary International, a businessmen's association begun in Chicago in 1905, also rapidly expanded worldwide during the 1920s. In 1920, Rotary International included 758 clubs; nine years later, the figure had grown to 3,178, of which 725 were outside the United States and Canada. Reflecting its increasingly international character, the Rotary convention in Edinburgh in 1921 formally added a "Sixth Object" to Rotary's traditional five purposes: "To encourage and foster the advancement of understanding, good will, and international peace through a world fellowship of business and professional men, united in the ideal of service." One convention speaker in 1928 reflected the seriousness with which Rotarians viewed their international mission: "Let me confess the time has passed when the world trusted the politician, the statesman. One is accused of duplicity and treachery. The other with evasion and desertion. To someone somewhere civilization must turn with confidence and with hope. To whom shall it turn if it be not such as you."

Unlike the Y, some of whose members did pursue structural reforms and grass-roots programs, Rotary aimed at creating a fellowship that would uphold Americans' "propertarian" values (to borrow the historian Marcus Cunliffe's term) and an individualistic approach to social problems. With the mottoes "Service above self" and "He profits most who serves the best," Rotary exhorted its members to mix fairness and social service into their business and professional decisions. Although Rotary stressed its devotion to ethical capitalism, a 1935 study indicated that a large majority of Rotarians admitted they did not know what constituted ethics in business. At the same time, Rotary promoted a conservative philosophy of limited government and consensus politics. "Any man who excites class hatred," proclaimed Rotary president Everett W. Hill before the international convention in 1925, "is a traitor to mankind, a traitor to his country and a traitor to his God."

Although the number of Rotarians abroad may have been rather small, they were nonetheless influential. Rotarian Richard Momsen, for example, once a consul to Brazil devoted to strengthening America's economic position there, reported toward the end of the decade that Rotary in Brazil had attracted such influential members that "today many of our meetings are attended by members of the Federal Cabinet, mayors of cities, educational, health and other officials who come to us to lay before us their problems and welcome our support and cooperation." In an international trip in 1925, Rotary president Everett Wentworth Hill, according to his biographer, associated "on the free, easy basis of Rotarian intimacy" with Mussolini in Italy and King Albert of Belgium and "won the hearts of royalty and bourgeois alike."

Rotarians of the 1920s, of course, truly believed they were internationalists. "The principle of Rotary applied the world over would make enmities impossible," declared Hill. But, in this faith, perhaps no group better displayed the confusion between Americanization and internationalism that characterized the 1920s.

PEACE AND INTERNATIONALISM

The internationalist spirit of the 1920s reached its apogee in the loosely organized "peace movement." The most active groups included the World Peace Foundation, the Foreign Policy Association, the Woodrow Wilson Foundation, the Council on Foreign Relations, the League of Nations Non-Partisan Association, the Carnegie Endowment for International Peace, the Social Science Research Council, and the Institute of Pacific Relations. These groups never attracted a large popular following. They drew most of their supporters from the Northeast and from old-stock, Protestant business and professional people. But the prominence of their members and their organizational skills compensated for their narrow base.

The most prominent of the peace societies preached the old Wilsonian ideals of liberal-internationalism, especially to educated elites. Free discussion and the process of collective arbitration, members urged, would harmonize interests and bring international cooperation and peace. Because they believed the world was evolving into an organized community of nations, leaving behind the war-ridden past of narrow nationalism, many hoped for America's eventual cooperation with the League of Nations, for worldwide disarmament, and for participation in the World Court. Connected in various ways to the overseas economic expansion of their time, these liberal-internationalists shared a cosmopolitan attitude. They believed that national interests were intimately connected to the preservation of a liberal world order based on a commitment to the open door and to the free flow of information. Collective security was central to the maintenance of world peace; but most favored containing aggression through economic sanctions rather than military force.

The Kellogg–Briand Pact of 1928 loomed as a central victory for groups associated with the peace movement. Eventually signed by most nations of the world, the pact outlawed war, but provided no punishment for transgression. James T. Shotwell, a prominent internationalist connected with Columbia University and the Carnegie Endowment, was a major architect of the pact. He and other liberal-internationalists hoped that outlawing war would be a step toward American acceptance of the concept of collective security and the League of Nations.

In supporting the pact, however, Shotwell and his followers joined forces with a very different group, the "outlawry of war" movement led by Salmon O. Levinson, a Chicago lawyer. Levinson's group stoutly opposed collective security arrangements as too entangling and enjoyed the backing of notable Americans such as John Dewey, perhaps the nation's most prominent intellectual, and Senator William E. Borah of Idaho, head of the Senate Foreign Relations Committee. The outlawry group saw the Kellogg–Briand Pact as an alternative to membership in the League, rather than a first step toward it. The United States could remain aloof from most of the world's troubles, Levinson argued, if only war could be eliminated. "We can outlaw this war system just as we outlawed slavery and the saloon," one of Levinson's supporters proclaimed.

Even more unstable than the coalition between advocates of collective security and of outlawry was their temporary alliance with a third group that favored the Kellogg–Briand Pact—organizations emphasizing pacifism, rather than collective security, and favoring socialism. The Women's International League for Peace and Freedom (led by pacifist Jane Addams) and the Fellowship for Christian Social Order, organized largely by leaders in the international YMCA, strongly supported the Kellogg–Briand agreement. But unlike liberal-internationalists, members of these groups doubted that the competitive nature of a liberal-capitalist order could ever lead to real peace. Most favored some kind of Christian socialism and collectivism, though their faith in America's international leadership toward this future seldom wavered. Support for the Kellogg–Briand Pact reflected the diversity of the American peace movement.

Most peace groups claimed to be internationally minded, but this claim raised important questions of definition. Did internationalism mean joining in a collective security arrangement to preserve the status quo dominated by Euro-American capitalist interests? Did it mean strict nonentanglement in world affairs and a commitment to avoid war? Or did it involve working with worldwide movements on behalf of popular reform along a socialist or Christian collectivist model on the assumption that greater social justice would enhance the possibility of peace? Among these possibilities, it would be the old Wilsonian position that would increasingly become identified with the word "internationalist," and the other positions were frequently given the pejorative labels "isolationist" or "radical." Thus, the definition of "internationalism," like the definition of "national interest" earlier, became closely associated with liberal expansionism; "internationalists" became the term for those who held the view that peace and international harmony depended on the globalization of the American liberal tenets of private enterprise, the open door, and free flow and on the development of international policies to ensure the triumph of these conditions.

Despite their narrow base during the 1920s, the liberal-internationalist groups played an important role in the conceptualization and conduct of foreign relations. Many of these groups, particularly the Carnegie Endowment, viewed their primary function as the financing of scholarship from a Wilsonian liberal-internationalist perspective; writings undertaken by the endowment would eventually come to dominate—some would say suffocate—both historical interpretation and political debate after World War II. But, aside from helping a future generation of policymakers learn the historical "lessons" about America's global responsibilities and special mission, some of the leaders of these groups maintained informal ties with people in other countries. Prominent liberal-internationalists constituted a private diplomatic presence during the 1920s and 1930s.

During the 1920s, the American government held to a policy that the historian Joan Hoff Wilson has appropriately termed "independent internationalism"—that is, a concern for international issues but an opposition to direct governmental commitments, especially to international organizations such as the League of Nations or the World Court. Responding to the popular distrust of government and dislike of foreign political entanglements, the Republican Administrations of the 1920s displayed aloofness toward other nations. In this environment, private groups could have a significant impact or even be extremely useful to government. The Carnegie Endowment, for example, stocked foreign libraries with its internationalist publications and sponsored the interchange of foreign and American scholars; it became the chosen instrument for extending cultural influence, a task that government did not assume until World War II. Moreover, some of the representatives of these private groups came very close to carrying on diplomatic conversations with foreign governments. (Technically, private contacts of the kind carried on during the 1920s violated the Logan Act, a statute which bars private citizens from engaging in diplomatic activity.) The Carnegie Endowment's James T. Shotwell, for example, regularly visited the Foreign Ministry of France and offered his advice on diplomatic issues. And members of the Institute of Pacific Relations met, on occasion, with the Chinese government about quasi-official matters. Private efforts did trouble the State Department, especially when conducted by people they deemed radical (some were even placed under surveillance during foreign travels). Nonetheless, such private diplomacy seemed to expand as governments of the 1920s sought to project a limited international role, for most policymakers recognized the usefulness of unofficial initiatives and cultural exchanges. Private citizens could spread American views or maintain important contacts (including with the League of Nations) without government involvement. If private diplomacy could be a nuisance, it could, as a chosen instrument, make America's "independent-internationalist" position more viable.

Some of the liberal-internationalist peace organizations even acted as private research arms of the State Department (that is, as chosen instruments for gaining specific information). In late 1925, when the Council of the League of Nations invited the United States to participate in a preliminary conference on disarmament, the president of the Carnegie Endowment, Columbia University President Nicholas Murray Butler, offered his group's research services to the government. The State Department official Allen Dulles subsequently requested the endowment to send all of the reports prepared by Shotwell's Committee on Security and Disarmament. The Carnegie Endowment, its former president Elihu Root wrote, "has been almost a division of the State Department, working in harmony constantly." The IPR, the Council on Foreign Relations, and the Brookings Institution also provided private research or public-relations work for policymakers, though not all the members of these organizations—especially the Wilsonian Democrats—liked the determined noninvolvement of the Coolidge–Kellogg years.

Although a basically Wilsonian version of internationalism was not the only one espoused by peace groups during the 1920s, it did become the most important in prestige and ultimate impact on policymakers' attitudes. The peace groups themselves declined after the mid-1930s, torn by rifts between those favoring greater involvement to stop Japanese, German, and Italian expansion and those hoping to advance peace through strictly nonmilitary means, but their general outlook became dominant after World War II. The global fellowship defined by liberal-internationalists foresaw a world dominated by American values and held together by American-based institutions.

INTERNATIONAL RELIEF

Closely related to the peace organizations were the American associations devoted to overseas philanthropy; the government built on wartime precedents and continued to employ the chosen-instrument strategy in dealing with international relief. Some private groups, especially Herbert Hoover's and the Red Cross, received special governmental blessing in return for fulfilling foreign-policy objectives.

In the winter of 1919–20, Herbert Hoover reorganized the American Relief Administration to form the European Relief Council (ERC). The ERC became an umbrella organization for the previous ARA, the American Friends Service Committee, the Red Cross, the Federal Council of Churches and other groups. By conducting a public appeal for funds, the ERC hoped to obtain the resources to relieve hunger in Europe and to undercut the appeal of radical movements.

In 1921, Hoover, now Secretary of Commerce in the new Harding Administration, followed up this European campaign by creating a similar umbrella organization, the American Federated Russian Famine Relief Committee, to relieve the massive famine developing in the Soviet Union. Like the ERC, this committee worked closely with the government, even though its sponsorship was technically private. Here again, the motives were both political and humanitarian. Hoping to stop declining farm prices at home, Congress gave the committee $20 million from the funds of the United States Grain Corporation (a wartime agency) and stipulated that the appropriation be used to purchase America's surplus corn. Philanthropy doubled as a farm subsidy.

Hoover also viewed Russian relief as an anti-Bolshevik measure;

he believed that starvation in Russia would serve to strengthen the new Bolshevik regime and that American relief might help to turn the Russian people away from Communism. Hoover forced Lenin to allow the committee to distribute aid directly to the Russian people. In addition, his umbrella agency attempted to monopolize Russian relief, co-opting or discrediting American efforts friendly toward the Bolshevik regime. Socialist and left-leaning nonsocialist relief groups that sought to send aid independently of Hoover's agency charged that the Secretary of Commerce blocked their attempts and clearly showed the political nature of his efforts. Despite Hoover's anti-Bolshevik objectives, however, Soviet officials gratefully accepted aid; in fact, by removing the immediate threat of malnutrition, Hoover probably eased the Bolsheviks' task of legitimizing their power. (Ironically during the late 1930s, the fervently anti-Communist Dies Committee of the House of Representatives would characterize Hoover's assistance as part of a "Communist drive.") In any event, Hoover's dual role as cabinet official and private-aid coordinator graphically reflected how the new wartime connection between government and philanthropy continued into the 1920s.

The Red Cross, which had gained chosen-instrument status during the Cuban crusade of the late 1890s, also continued its special role. During the disastrous Japanese earthquakes of 1923–24, President Coolidge ordered the Pacific fleet to speed food and medical supplies to Japan and asked Americans to channel all relief donations through the Red Cross, thus discouraging the proliferation of unregulated charities. Response was rapid. Large sums of money and supplies poured in from Bethlehem Steel, Guggenheim Brothers, J. P. Morgan, Standard Oil, General Motors, Bell Telephone, and U.S. Steel. American businessmen believed that if they were generous with their money, the Japanese would purchase American materials, hire American firms for reconstruction, and generally solidify the economic relationship between the two countries. "Japan's Disaster to Boom American Industries," read a 1923 headline in *Nation's Business*.

The efforts to assist Europe, Russia, and Japan in the early 1920s showed that Americans were beginning to understand how foreign aid could stimulate business ties as well as build diplomatic friendships. This principle would find expression in the Marshall Plan after World War II. But in contrast to aid programs of the cold-war era, Republican governments of the 1920s channeled foreign assistance through private donations and chosen instruments.

The government also supported the private efforts of Elizabeth Washburn Wright, who mounted an international crusade against opium cultivation. Taking the progressive movement's "purity crusade" worldwide, Wright attempted to attack the narcotics problem by limiting production at the source. She traveled around the world, seeking support from the League of Nations and from the governments of Turkey, Persia, and Yugoslavia, the major opium producers. In Persia, she worked with an American financial mission that was advising the Persian government. Its head, Arthur Millspaugh, endorsed the principle of reducing opium production, but he also realized that rapid reduction of Persia's principal cash crop would greatly decrease governmental revenue and undercut his goal of saving Persia from economic ruin. Wright and the American financial advisers finally worked out an official position committing Persia to a gradual reduction of opium exports while it developed crop substitutes. (The program stalled after 1927, when the American advisers were asked to leave.) In the end, Wright's efforts scarcely affected the narcotics traffic, but her informal working relationship with government officials was typical of the 1920s private approach to international issues.

The upsurge of international philanthropy in the 1920s was closely associated with the growth of American foundations. In many ways, private foundations were the most direct heirs to the nineteenth-century missionary tradition. The Rockefeller Foundation, formed in 1914, for example, immediately launched its first overseas philanthropic program in China. The China Medical Board formally depicted its work as an extension of Protestant missionary work, and it attracted as employees the same kind of people who might have taught the gospel earlier. After accepting a position with the China Medical Board, Roger Sherman Greene received the following congratulatory message from his brother: "The Foundation offers a real opportunity for a continuation of the missionary tradition to the fourth generation of our family." But Greene, like many other professionals of the 1920s, believed that missionaries "justify education, medical work, etc. merely as baits to catch the people so they can be preached to." He and others in the new "helping professions" sought social improvement for its secular, rather than spiritual, rewards. Like his missionary predecessors, however, he too usually defined improvement in terms of American models. The China Medical Board consistently chose to promote high-quality, high-cost medicine, rather than less-sophisticated, cheaper health-care programs that might have brought minimal improvements to large numbers of people.

During the 1920s, American foundations underwrote a variety of international philanthropies. In addition to the China Medical Board, the Rockefeller Foundation helped to establish women's colleges in China, India, and Japan. Its International Health Board promoted public-health measures in various parts of the world and made notable progress in eliminating epidemic disease. Other foundations were also prominent. The Carnegie Endowment established libraries throughout the world. The China Foundation, established in 1924 with the second portion of an indemnity paid by China to the United States government for damages inflicted during the Boxer Rebellion, promised "the development of scientific research" in China. It hired experts to conduct soil surveys and engage in regional planning aimed at fighting famines.

Countless individuals, as well as foundations, plunged into the effort to bring American-style expertise to the world. John Dewey once defined an American as "a type of mind that is developing, from like causes, all over the world." That mind was heir to the progressive tradition; it stressed the application of scientific procedures—in an efficient, rational manner—to economic, political, and social problems. Dewey, like others of his time, saw expertise and technology as instruments of reform that were culturally and ideologically neutral. Dewey involved himself in the task of revamping China's educational system. Charles Beard, a historian firmly identified with the progressive tradition, accepted an invitation from the mayor of Tokyo to launch a new research bureau for promoting urban reform. Later, after Tokyo's destruction in the earthquake of 1923, Beard returned to help plan the city's reconstruction. The intense worldwide involvement of American reformers after World War I is a comparatively unexamined analogue to the prewar domestic progressive movement.

Following familiar precedents, then, much of America's international philanthropy remained in private hands, but was closely tied to governmental objectives: to decrease agricultural surplus, to check Bolshevism, to cement economic and political ties, and to encourage international reform on an American model. The nature of foreign assistance was transformed by the new foundations and by a zealous desire to bring America's progressive movement to the world in the form of modern health care, rational land use, urban planning and professionalized social services.

Cultural expansion during the 1920s took many forms. Mass communications became vital to spreading American influence; international associations boosted liberal-capitalist, Protestant values; philanthropic groups exported a secularized version of America's mission. For the most part, the internationalism of the 1920s implicitly assumed the superiority and inevitable spread of American techniques and values. Expansionism, national interest, and international betterment were fused.

Although the government limited its formal international commitments during the 1920s (even seeming isolationist to some historians), it was partly because internationalist and expansionist impulses were so strongly and successfully manifested in the private sector. After the political and diplomatic disappointments following World War I, many Americans hoped that privately led efforts, rather than governmental crusades, would succeed in bringing about a peaceful and liberal international order. Harding's Secretary of State, Charles Evans Hughes, explained his opposition to American participation in the League of Nations by stressing that informal, private dealings among people provided a firmer bulwark of peace than formal, governmental ties. "Helpful cooperation in the future will . . . depend upon the fostering of firm friendships springing from an appreciation of community of ideals, interests and purposes, and such friendships are more likely to be promoted by freedom of conference than by the effort to create hard and fast engagements." The government was involved in expansion during the 1920s, but it preferred to operate behind the scenes, encouraging, guiding, or even delegating to chosen instruments those functions that policymakers deemed crucial.

Seven

★═★═★

ECONOMIC EXPANSION: THE 1920s

THE exporting of communications and culture coincided with the unparalleled global expansion of the American economy. After World War I international conditions were overwhelmingly favorable to Americans. The war weakened competitors yet stimulated America's own industrial plant and enlarged its supply of investment capital. The United States flooded the world with products, branch plants, and investment capital in the 1920s, making that decade one of the most economically expansive periods in the nation's history. The search for raw materials took on growing importance as the United States became more dependent on global supplies, and many countries with large stores of resources became the hosts of American global enterprises.

FOREIGN TRADE AND BRANCH BUSINESSES

Throughout the 1920s, the United States enjoyed a very favorable balance of trade; Americans exported much more than they imported. The exceedingly high protective tariffs of the Republican-dominated decade contributed to the country's position. The postwar disarray in Europe also helped; it not only weakened Europe's strength as a competitor but created a market for products needed in reconstruction. Essentially, though, America's favorable trade balance derived from the strength and dynamism of its export sector. American producers continued to display their scientific leadership, mass-marketing skills, and innovative technology. During the 1920s, America's manufacturers showed an astonishing and greater increase in productivity than at any other time before or since.

America did not so much surpass as bypass its principal competitor, Great Britain. England had based its preeminence as an exporter on textiles, coal, and railroad parts. All these items had nicely fit world needs during the nineteenth century. After World War I, however, these commodities suffered a relative decline in demand. The war had stimulated native textile production in Latin America and Asia, areas that had previously imported from Britain. New energy technology—the spread of the internal-combustion engine that had proved so successful during the war and the switch from steam power to electric power—encouraged greater worldwide demand for oil. Oil, rather than coal, was the energy source of the future. Automobiles and trucks came off the assembly lines, and railroad systems stagnated. In short, American oil, autos, mechanized farm implements, electrical and telephonic equipment, and advanced machinery supplied the wants and needs of the twentieth-century world market. The demand for America's products soared, while the demand for Britain's exports grew at a significantly slower pace. Just as Americans challenged the British dominance in cable communications by building up strength in the newer technology of radio, so in their trade rivalry Americans did an end run around the British, rather than confront them head-on.

Trade figures reveal a great increase in American exports in the 1920s, but even they fail to reflect the worldwide demand for American products. Building on late-nineteenth-century trends, many American manufacturers met the growing international demand by moving complete operations or assembly plants overseas. Through such direct investment, businessmen could avoid foreign tariffs, take advantage of cheaper labor costs, and be closer to markets and materials. American direct investment in the 1920s increased from an estimated book value of $3.8 billion in 1919 to $7.5 billion in 1929.

Operating branch plants abroad was not without hazard. World War I and revolutionary conditions in Mexico and Russia provided some cautionary lessons to international businessmen. The experience of the Singer company, America's pioneer in foreign fields, well illustrated how international turmoil might disrupt business operations. During the war, Great Britain nationalized Singer's enormous plant in Scotland and retooled it to make munitions; and even though Singer's German division proclaimed its local patriotism and donated 300,000 sewing machines to the German and Austro-Hungarian army, Germany also sequestered Singer's plant. A few years later, Singer suffered the largest loss of any American business that operated in the Soviet Union when its operations were confiscated by Bolshevik authorities. The turmoil of the Mexican revolution after 1910 also brought large losses to many investors, as mines and other enterprises suspended operations or closed their doors altogether. Frightened by a decade of revolution, Americans hardly increased the overall value of their direct investment in Mexico during the 1920s.

Despite setbacks, American entrepreneurs realized that foreign investments could be profitable. In fact, while some investors lost from war and revolution, others prospered greatly. American corporations derived enormous profits from Mexican oil, so badly needed for the Allied war effort, in spite of the Mexican revolution. Many other international companies benefited by providing the food and strategic goods needed during the war. American businessmen, then, constantly talked about foreign risks and emphasized the hazards of doing business overseas to justify the large profits they gained from foreign investment. But most of the largest enterprises emerged from the war with a solid financial base and an even greater commitment to overseas expansion and geographic diversification.

Market-oriented investment tended, as before, to expand mainly into Europe, an area with well-developed consumer demand. Almost all manufacturing firms that had launched international ventures at the turn of the century greatly increased their branch operations. General Electric's policy during the 1920s was to buy into every important electrical company in the world in order to stabilize markets, diversify holdings to protect against occasional losses, and increase the export of parts from United States plants. Under the skilled management of Gerard Swope, who took charge of all of G.E.'s foreign holdings in 1919 and became president of the company in 1922, G.E. gradually acquired interests in the dominant companies of Canada, England, Germany, and elsewhere. By 1930, the giant G.E. cartel controlled or influenced most of the major electrical manufacturers in the world. American car makers also came to dominate the world market, even opening assembly plants in such unlikely places as Japan, Turkey, and the Soviet Union. During the 1920s, Ford gradually transferred its tractor plants to Great Britain, until the entire output of Ford Tractors was manufactured in the U.K. Monsanto Chemical bought into a British firm and became one of the largest chemical companies in the world. American retailers—including Woolsworth, Montgomery Ward, A & P, and Safeway—also opened stores around the world. They revolutionized retailing practices by their American-tested sales techniques: mail order, attractive packaging, glass display cases, money-back guarantees, high-pressure tactics. International Telephone and Telegraph, a small, Puerto Rican-based company before World War I, also expanded extravagantly during the 1920s. By the end of the decade, ITT had more employees abroad than any other American company; it owned or supplied most of the world's telephonic equipment. (ITT did not try to challenge American Telephone and Telegraph's position in the domestic market and ATT did not rival ITT abroad.)

RAW MATERIALS

While market-oriented investment expanded, particularly in Europe, the more important economic trend of the 1920s was America's new emphasis on supply-oriented investment—that is, development of raw materials. Generally, these resources were located in non-European areas.

The United States had based its rise to industrial power on the wealth of its own landed domain, and American businesses dealing overseas in raw materials before World War I primarily exported and distributed resources from its vast domestic stores. But the war demonstrated the growing importance of foreign resources, both as a cause of international tensions and as a factor in America's security. During the 1920s, Americans, for the first time, began seriously to face the choice of whether they should try to meet their raw-material needs from their own sources—a policy of self-sufficiency—or develop ways of gathering resources from many other lands—a global strategy.

Some people argued that the national policy should be to gain supplies abroad through direct ownership by American companies, coupled with liberalization of the mechanisms of international trade. This view had a fervent champion—Charles K. Leith, a professor of geology at the University of Wisconsin. Wisconsin had long been progressive in its social policies, and Leith carried domestic progressivism's zeal for the efficient use of resources into the conduct of foreign policy. Leith believed that the future of the world depended on the rational use of global resources and that the United States was best equipped to avoid waste in mineral exploitation. Although he recognized that growing United States control over the world's mineral resources would likely interfere with the sovereignty of other nations, he argued that the economic benefits to the general welfare would be worth the political price. Just as progressives supported government efforts to rationalize the economic environment at home, so Leith and others did not fear an active government abroad. The result of governmental action, after all, would be to bring greater efficiency to the production of resources.

As Leith understood it, efficiency involved not only a search for the best productive techniques but a commitment to the liberal doctrine of comparative advantage. It was simply inefficient for the United States to produce minerals from low-grade, high-cost domestic deposits rather than to import from high-grade locations overseas. And even if foreign supplies were not of the highest quality, it could be more efficient to use them if they were located in undeveloped countries in which labor rates were low. In addition, American-based companies could cajole local governments into granting terms that would make overseas operations more profitable than domestic ones. To Leith, America's resource strategy would mean cheaper resources for everyone. His economic equation, though, did not include any calculation of the political or military costs of protecting these "cheap" foreign supplies.

Leith's devotion to an open, liberal order led him to espouse a position even more internationalist than Woodrow Wilson's. Leith, who accompanied Wilson to Versailles in 1919, believed that Wilson had failed to realize that a League of Nations would be inconsequential without an international economic body that would insure a postwar liberal order for trade and help guarantee unfettered investment in raw materials. But Leith's plan for an international economic order, regulated by the kind of expert commission popular with domestic progressives, was much too ambitious to be accepted at Versailles. Besides, it was clear to the leaders of other nations that the United States had by far the most to gain from Leith's scheme. Still, throughout the 1920s, Leith continued to urge the coordination of an efficient, global raw-materials strategy. His ideas and vision eventually influenced America's economic policies after World War II.

In contrast to Leith, other Americans emphasized the military advantages of maximizing domestic production of minerals rather than relying on foreign sources. Whereas the advocates of the use of foreign resources found strong support from American multinational companies, advocates of self-sufficiency derived their principal strength from Western mining states. Spokesmen for domestic mining interests pointed out that, at governmental urging, many marginal mines had opened production during World War I. Government now had an obligation, they argued, to insure the continued profitability of these mines; otherwise, their owners would be penalized for their patriotism. They wanted the government to encourage use of low-grade domestic deposits and to fund research programs to find domestic substitutes for imported raw materials.' Responding to this pressure, Congress did raise tariff duties to enable some marginal domestic enterprises to continue. For the most part, though, Congress placated the mining bloc by passing the War Minerals Relief Act. The law provided compensation payments to mine owners who would cut back their expanded wartime operations and helped defuse any strong movement on behalf of self-sufficiency. The government and American international companies could embark on a global, "cheap" resource strategy without significant opposition.

During the 1920s, policymakers never developed the comprehensive planning urged by Leith, but they did adopt a relatively consistent approach to raw materials. Recognizing the importance of ownership of global resources, the government's promotional apparatus assisted American enterprises to gain access to supplies; and when American businessmen seemed insufficiently aggressive, policymakers sought corporations that could become chosen instruments. Government-industry cooperation emerged especially in the case of oil and rubber, the two raw materials most critical for America's expanding automobile production.

Oil companies made the biggest plunge into overseas supplies during the 1920s. A book by a Frenchman, Pierre de la Tramerye, *The World Struggle for Oil,* published in 1924, proclaimed the faith, and fear, of many: "The nation which controls this precious fuel will see the wealth of the rest of the world flowing towards it." Although Americans had dominated the worldwide production and distribution of oil before the war, this dominance was based on domestic supplies and Mexican fields that, together, comprised over 80 percent of the world's total. After the war, demand for oil rose sharply, yet the international dominance by United States oil distributors seemed threatened by the revolutionary Mexican constitution of 1917, which permitted nationalization of the subsoil, and by declining reserves at home. Government geological surveys mistakenly predicted imminent exhaustion of domestic oil.

In light of the projected shortage, the government committed itself, for strategic and economic reasons, to developing oil supplies in other parts of the world. Official interest in foreign sources began immediately after World War I. In 1919, for the first time, the State Department asked its foreign-based diplomats to report on opportunities that American oilmen might investigate. Noting "the vital importance of securing adequate supplies of mineral oil for both present and future needs of the United States," the State Department also asked the diplomatic corps "to lend all legitimate aid to reliable and responsible citizens who are seeking mineral oil concessions." By the early 1920s, alarmed by further reports of near depletion at home, Congress launched several investigations to identify overseas oil sources and to force the elimination of foreign restrictions against American investors. In 1926 a Federal Oil Conservation Board, consisting of four Cabinet heads, including Herbert Hoover, told the President:

> That American companies should vigorously acquire and explore such [foreign] fields is of first importance, not only as a source of future supply, but supply under control of our citizens. Our experience with the exploitation of our consumers by foreign-controlled sources of rubber, nitrate, potash, and other raw materials should

be sufficient warning as to what we may expect if we should become dependent upon foreign nations for our oil supplies.

To maintain United States dominance in oil, government officials challenged what was perceived as Britain's bid for paramountcy in oil and encouraged an aggressive search for new supplies in Latin America.

The exclusion of American oil interests from the Middle East created a major diplomatic controversy between the United States and Great Britain in the early 1920s. After World War I, British oil companies, with some French participation, secured an oil monopoly in Mesopotamia (Iraq), a League of Nations mandate assigned to Great Britain. Standard Oil of New York, however, had conducted extensive marketing operations in the area before the war and had planned to expand into production, until Britain's exclusionary action stopped them. Washington strongly supported the American oil companies' claims that League mandates should be subject to the open door—the principle of equal opportunity for all. But Britain responded that America's failure to join the League gave the State Department little justification for lecturing Britain on its treatment of mandates. Moreover, Britain charged, the United States did not itself uphold the open door. In 1920, Congress had restricted foreign production of oil in America's public lands, and in Latin America the United States government actively hampered British oil interests and worked to expand its own monopolistic control.

In 1928, after eight years of negotiations, the rivalry was finally resolved. British companies allowed Americans (four of the Standard Oil group plus Gulf) to purchase a 25 percent share in their Mesopotamian concession. The State Department supported creation of this new cartel, the Iraq Petroleum Company, even though such an action could hardly be seen as consistent with the open-door policy it had so long advocated.

A similar Anglo-American partnership emerged in Persia (Iran). Standard Oil of New Jersey gained a concession from the Persian government in the early 1920s, when the country was under the economic tutelage of Arthur Millspaugh, a former State Department official and a vigorous advocate of America's petroleum expansionism. Anglo-Persian Oil claimed that the Standard Oil concession conflicted with rights previously granted to them. As in the case of Iraq, the oil dispute was eventually resolved by a cartel arrangement between Standard Oil and Anglo-Persian. In the late 1920s, then, American oil interests in the Middle East remained small, but producers had forced an opening wedge that, after World War II, would be pried wider.

The cartel agreements of 1928 came largely as a result of economic pressures. The newly available oil supplies in the Middle East and Latin America had caused a glut on the market and threatened an imminent collapse of prices unless major companies ceased cutthroat competition. In the so-called Red Line agreements of 1928, the major oil companies of the world, most of which were British and American, promised to curtail competition by operating within the oil-rich Red Line district (roughly the old Ottoman Empire) only through their multinational cartel. This understanding, together with price-setting agreements, prevented extreme oversupply from driving down the price of oil; the international oil industry thus abandoned the liberal marketplace for the protection of a managed system.

As American companies broke into the Middle East and rationalized world pricing and distribution, they also sought new supplies, especially along the northern coast of Latin America. Colombia, in the early 1920s, seemed to be the most promising territory, but its government opposed any oil concessions to American companies unless the United States ratified a treaty expressing regrets for the Roosevelt Administration's role in the Panamanian secessionist movement of 1903. Republican supporters of Teddy Roosevelt in the Senate had long blocked such a treaty. But T.R.'s death in 1919, together with pressure from oil companies and congressional fears of domestic depletion, finally brought ratification of the treaty in 1921. American oil companies then beat out their rivals, obtaining a virtual monopoly over Colombian oil resources.

In 1924, a strongly nationalist government in Colombia tried to cut back the Americans' dominant position by nullifying Gulf Oil's title to rich fields in the "Barco concession." The United States government, working with the oil company's attorney, Allen Dulles, the future director of the CIA, and with Jordan Stabler, a former top-ranking State Department official who then worked for Gulf, issued stiff warnings about protection of United States interests. Later, the Department of Commerce cautioned American investors about the wisdom of granting further loans to Colombia. Under this political and financial pressure, Colombians finally reached an agreement satisfactory to Gulf—and then received a loan from National City Bank.

In Venezuela, American petroleum interests, encouraged by the United States government, also elbowed their way past British oilmen and rushed to develop newly discovered fields. Venezuelan strongman Juan Vicente Gómez allowed oil companies, working with the United States minister, to write much of his country's petroleum laws; not surprisingly, these laws established tax rates and royalty provisions that granted lavish profits to the oil companies. By 1928, American companies had made Venezuela the world's greatest oil exporter. And although the State Department remained publicly committed to an open-door oil policy, it strongly supported the American petroleum monopoly in Venezuela, just as it had done in Colombia.

In part, American interests pushed vigorously into Venezuela because of their troubles in Mexico; but they also continued to seek a solution that would safeguard their Mexican properties. Article 27 of the Mexican constitution of 1917, asserting Mexico's ownership of mineral rights, threatened American oil investments. The United States government therefore tried to force Mexico to grant explicit legal guarantees of American property by organizing a banking consortium that promised loans in return for such safeguards. In 1921, after consultation with the State Department, the banker Thomas Lamont went to Mexico to negotiate. After more than a year of complicated discussions, the United States and Mexico finally reached a series of agreements that ultimately became known as the Bucareli accords of 1923. The Mexicans recognized American citizens' claims against Mexico and promised to respect recent Mexican supreme-court decisions declaring article 27 of the Mexican constitution inapplicable to oil properties acquired before 1917. In return, the United States recognized (and supported with arms sales) the Mexican government of Álvaro Obregón. This combination of private and public diplomacy did not permanently settle the oil controversy (it flared again in 1926–

27, and Mexico finally nationalized oil in 1938), but it did safe-guard American holdings for the time being and demonstrated the close connection between diplomacy and oil.

During the 1920s, then, American companies continued to ex-port large quantities of oil from the United States, but they no longer relied quite so heavily upon domestic supplies to fill their worldwide distribution network. Jersey Standard emerged as the biggest producer of the Big Three global companies (Royal Dutch–Shell and Anglo-Persian were the others). During the 1920s, Jersey Standard alone distributed nearly a quarter of all petroleum con-sumed outside the United States, and at the end of the decade it dominated the international cartel that controlled the world oil market. In undertaking their great expansion, American oil inter-ests enjoyed wholehearted governmental support. When American interests did not control a foreign source of oil and wished to gain access, as in the Middle East, Washington favored the open door. Where American oil interests were firmly entrenched, as in Latin America, officials talked about the sanctity of contracts and the importance of the Monroe Doctrine. By the end of the decade, the government rather quietly acquiesced to the creation of an Ameri-can-dominated international oil cartel that scrapped liberal princi-ples almost completely. In short, the government adopted what-ever policy advanced American control over the world's petroleum.

American rubber companies also received strong governmental encouragement for expansion. British interests had long produced most of the rubber in the world, and in the spring of 1925, rubber prices began to skyrocket. American manufacturers blamed high prices on the British government's new scheme (the Stevenson plan) to regulate rubber production in its colonies. (The lower the world price, the more restricted the quota on rubber exports.) American tire manufacturers charged that British limitations on rubber exports were too drastic. The British, of course, maintained their right to regulate commodity supplies and blamed the rapid rise in prices on the development of balloon tires and the unexpect-edly large growth of demand for rubber by the American auto industry.

As American manufacturers railed against the British govern-ment's international price management, the United States Con-

gress decided to investigate. Congress held hearings on restriction-
ist policies and urged Americans to be more aggressive in developing overseas sources of strategic raw materials. The House even
appropriated money for a technical study of the world's rubber-
production potential. The geological survey of the Amazon in
Brazil in 1923, probably America's first exploration for foreign raw
materials at government expense, represented an extension of the
promotional state.

Secretary of Commerce Herbert Hoover turned the rubber controversy into a major diplomatic issue. He protested the British
restrictions, arguing that interference with the free international
marketplace was a basic cause of international antagonism and a
dangerous reversion to practices of a less-enlightened age. He also
warned Britain that the precedent of government-manipulated
prices on raw materials, if followed by other primary producing
states, could prove extremely dangerous to the industrialized
world. And while Hoover chastised Britain, he also encouraged
American companies to invest in the Dutch East Indies, Brazil,
and Liberia. The Liberian venture proved by far the most successful.

In the early 1920s, Harvey Firestone offered to arrange a badly
needed loan to the Liberian government in return for a concession
to develop a rubber-growing empire. But in light of Liberia's unstable politics, Firestone was reluctant to invest the enormous sums
required for facilities unless the United States government assured
Firestone that it would support the security of his investment. In
the final agreement, a classic example of the chosen-instrument
approach, Liberia received its loan, Firestone got his extensive land
rights, and an American commission, under the thumb of Firestone but with an adviser appointed by the President of the United
States, took charge of Liberia's finances. But Firestone's new land
rights covered territory the Liberians had previously promised to
Marcus Garvey's Universal Negro Improvement Association. A
black nationalist group with an estimated half million Afro-Ameri-
can followers, the UNIP preached a back-to-Africa philosophy.
("We say to the white man who now dominates Africa that it is
to his interest to clear out of Africa now, because we are coming
. . . 400,000 strong," Garvey proudly proclaimed.)

The Liberian government had once promised Garvey that he

would "receive every facility legally possible" to launch his colonization project, and one Liberian mayor had even accepted a post
as secretary of state in Garvey's provisional government. In the
summer of 1924, however, under pressure from United States diplomats, the Liberian government abruptly withdrew its support,
denounced the "incendiary policy" of Garvey's organization, and
repudiated its promises of land. From the mid-twenties until the
mid-fifties, Firestone Rubber, for all practical purposes, ran Liberia's economy. Liberia was a private protectorate with just enough
involvement on the part of the United States government to make
Firestone feel secure.

Hoover's denunciation of Britain for interfering with the "natural" price of rubber constituted only one example of a larger battle
against foreign producers' monopolies. With strong congressional
support, Hoover fought to undermine Brazil's coffee monopoly and
Germany's potash syndicate. He opposed Mexico's sisal monopoly
by encouraging American-owned production in Cuba. (American
farmers used binder twine made from sisal.) Hoover stated:

> . . . it is not until recent years that we have seen government revive
> a long-forgotten relic of medievalism and of war-time expediency by
> deliberately erecting official controls of trade in raw materials of
> which their nationals produce a major portion of the world's supply,
> and through these controls arbitrarily fixing prices to all of the
> hundreds of millions of other people in the world. It is this intrusion
> of governments into trading operations on a vast scale that raises
> a host of new dangers—the inevitable aftermath of any such efforts
> by political agencies to interfere with the normal processes of supply
> and demand.

Significantly, Hoover objected only to government-imposed controls, not to interference with the free market by private enterprises. To Hoover, American business abroad was individualism at
work; it was the essence of a liberal order. Monopoly itself was not
the problem, only monopoly directed by foreign governments.
United States copper firms, for example, used the Webb–Pomerene
Act of 1918 to form an export association that flourished in the
1920s. Eventually, these firms brought in foreign companies, until
the association controlled 95 percent of the world's refined copper

and could easily control the world price. Like its counterpart in oil, the copper cartel, even in the face of substantial overproduction, raised prices dramatically. Although the association fell apart during the Depression of the 1930s—when it could no longer paper over the huge copper surpluses generated by the price-fixing policies—during the 1920s it successfully removed copper from "the normal processes of supply and demand." Yet the American government tolerated the copper combination (as it did similar American cartels in the electrical and petroleum industries), because United States companies, which opened tremendous new deposits in Chile and Peru in the 1920s, controlled 75 percent of world production. As many foreigners correctly charged, Americans' love for free international markets was highly selective.

Oil, rubber, and copper were not the only strategic raw materials that interested Americans. W. Averell Harriman's large contract to develop manganese was one of the largest foreign investments in the Soviet Union during the 1920s, although it was never profitable and was dissolved at a loss in 1928. Harriman and the Anaconda Company in 1926 bought the second-largest zinc deposits in the world, located in both the German and Polish portions of Silesia. In Africa, Union Carbide gained large manganese and chrome properties. Other American entrepreneurs gained access to various minerals in South Africa and Rhodesia, but, because of colonial restrictions, they had to cloak themselves as British or Canadian businesses. In the Western Hemisphere, the Guggenheims established control over Chile's nitrate industry, and United States-based International Nickel turned to Canada and became the largest mining company there.

The 1920s was also a halcyon period for American expansion into nonstrategic foreign commodities, although the government involved itself much less in this process. United States investments in Cuban sugar soared after the depression of 1920–21, which drove many marginal Cuban mills out of business. (National City Bank alone foreclosed on sixty mills.) During the 1920s, Hershey, Coca-Cola, Charles Hires, and other processing companies integrated backward, investing in Cuban sugar-growing lands and sugar refineries. In Central America, United Fruit continued to expand and became even more influential in Costa Rica, Guatemala, and Honduras, nations in which United Fruit's political leverage insured rigidly controlled stability. Investments in processing also rose. W. R. Grace enlarged its textile production in Peru and Chile; American timber barons purchased huge tracts of Canadian woodlands and dominated the Canadian pulp and paper industry; by the mid-1920s, American meatpackers—especially Armour and Swift —slaughtered two-thirds of all Argentine cattle.

The tremendous American foreign investments and the resulting rising level of world trade during the 1920s contributed to important shifts in the world economy. One change was the growing divergence between the industrialized and nonindustrialized world. Underutilized land and untapped resources came into production in the 1920s and provided less-developed countries with new exports to finance a growing volume of purchases, particularly manufactured goods from the United States. The result was an increase in international trade that integrated more and more people into the world economy and substantially raised the national incomes of most regions. But the gains were lopsided, weighted in favor of the industrialized leaders.

The reasons were clear. First, the profits from increasing trade largely went to the industrial nations, whose corporations controlled the international networks of wholesaling, banking, transportation, and communication. Second, the profits from the new production of raw materials accrued largely to the foreign investors, whose companies could often dominate political processes in a poor country and create a climate in which they could extract huge revenues. The liberal-developmentalist rhetoric of limited government and maximum freedom for private enterprise worked to enhance the power of large American overseas investors. During the 1920s, profit levels were extraordinary. Third, entrenched political power in underdeveloped areas largely prevented those economic gains that were made during the 1920s from trickling down to the bulk of the population or from going to promote economic diversification or domestic manufacturing. Until World War II, local landholding interests, allied with foreign traders and investors, largely prevented most primary exporting nations from undertaking economic programs that would have kept profits in the country and generated balanced development. (Mexico was a notable exception.)

Another emerging trend was the increasing predominance of international cartels, generally Anglo-American. Alfred Eckes, a historian of America's mineral use, concludes that by 1929 mostly Anglo-American commercial monopolies "dominated production" of nickel, vanadium, aluminum, potash, asbestos, mercury, diamonds, bismuth, sulphur, natural nitrates, copper, iron, lead, petroleum, tin, and manganese. These "monopolies and cartels, often operating independently of national political power," he writes, "established the prices and terms of trade for key industries vital to the prosperity and defense of independent states, raising serious problems about the coexistence of private and public power." The oil empire, after the 1928 agreements, advanced the furthest along this path of transnational integration, but the same trend held true for electrical companies, cable companies, copper, and others. Cartels could beat off upstart competitors, maximize profits, and extend their empires; they rendered free marketplaces obsolete. Despite this, it was still foreign-government restrictions and monopolies, not privately operated cartels, that American policymakers assailed as the principal threat to a liberal international order.

Large American-based international enterprises also developed a strikingly different set of interests from domestic businesses. The business community had never been monolithic; exporters and importers had often differed over foreign economic issues, especially the tariff. But a generation of global expansion created an unprecedented gulf. As the historian Joan Hoff Wilson points out, "internationalist" businesses, especially those that had large direct investments abroad, promoted policies that would integrate the world economy, while smaller, "nationalist" businesses usually sought to insulate themselves from foreign competition. The split between the groups, which grew ever wider in the 1920s, resulted in a struggle over government policy and contributed to an inconsistent approach to international economic problems.

Eight

★═══★═══★

THE COOPERATIVE STATE OF THE 1920s

DURING the 1920s, the Republican Administrations of Harding, Coolidge, and Hoover based their foreign policies on a presumed mutuality of interests of the public and private spheres. Like their predecessors under Taft and Wilson, Republican policymakers of the 1920s believed that government should clearly show businessmen and private groups how they might assist the public good, but then government should allow this presumably progressive and enlightened private sector to carry out the suggestions voluntarily. Suffusing the Republican philosophy was the belief that business, if informed and encouraged, would act in the public interest; that government need only advise private groups what actions would contribute to national or international well-being. "Reactionaries and radicals," Hoover wrote in *American Individualism* (1922), "would assume that all reform and human advance must come through government. They have forgotten that progress must come from the steady lift of the individual and that the measure of national idealism and progress is the quality of idealism in the individual." Government, in short, would encourage responsible private initiatives, but not replace them.

During the 1920s, government officials maintained a low political and military profile overseas; in a variety of ways, they attempted to disengage themselves from global conflict. They avoided any identification with the League of Nations and backed disarmament. In the Washington Naval Treaties of 1921–22, the United

States joined other major naval powers in agreeing to limit construction of capital ships; and the United States, of course, signed the Kellogg–Briand Pact of 1928, renouncing war. Even in Central America, the traditional zone of gunboat diplomacy and interventionism, Secretaries of State Charles Evans Hughes and Frank Kellogg tried, though not always successfully, to minimize direct political or military involvement. They began phasing out the protectorate system. In 1928, Undersecretary of State J. Reuben Clark prepared a 238-page memorandum that traced the history of the Monroe Doctrine and concluded that it did not justify United States intervention in Latin America. Clark's narrow interpretation of a doctrine that had expanded to imperial proportions from the 1890s through World War I received mixed reviews within the Hoover Administration, but it pointed to a new direction that would culminate in Franklin D. Roosevelt's good-neighbor policy of the 1930s.

Yet, as most recent historians have stressed, such policies of disengagement did not reflect an isolationist attitude. Herbert Feis, an influential historian of United States policy, who began his long government career by joining the State Department in 1931, called the cooperative ethic of the 1920s the "diplomacy of the dollar"— diplomacy that encouraged the outflow of private capital. As Feis argued, policymakers believed that economic expansion would, to some extent, replace traditional political and military involvements; economic connections with other states would provide the substance of national security. Feis wrote in *Diplomacy of the Dollar, 1919–1932* (1950):

> the American people had a hazy, lazy faith that their loans and investments would spread American ideals, foster good will and trust between ourselves and foreign countries, encourage disarmament, and bring reconciliation and peace. The soldiers and sailors had done their part, the dollar was counted on to carry on their work. It was regarded as a kind of universal balm, good for all people and all ailments. The American Executive shared this attitude.

In short, foreign entanglements could remain minimal as long as businessmen were expansionist and public-spirited; disarmament and economic expansion seemed compatible, indeed mutually supporting.

In promoting economic expansion, the Republican Administrations of the twenties displayed continuity with Wilson's Presidency. Democrats and Republicans agreed that expansion was in the national and international interests; both sought to shape a liberal international order granting open access to trade and information. Republicans shared with Democrats the "progressive" mentality of the new professionals and had also participated in building the bureaucratic structure that rose with the promotional state. Herbert Hoover, director of Wilson's wartime Food Administration, Secretary of Commerce under Harding and Coolidge, and ultimately President, epitomized the faith in professional expertise and the continuities between the Wilsonian and Republican years. Hoover, whom President Harding called the "damnedest smartest man I have ever met," expanded the apparatus of the promotional state during the 1920s and employed a variety of practices designed to wed private initiatives to public goals. The 1920s were the most economically expansionist decade in American history (until the 1960s), and Republicans like Hoover encouraged this private internationalist impulse.

ASSISTING COMMERCE

Herbert Hoover, Secretary of Commerce from 1921 to 1929, dominated foreign economic policy. Building on the progressive model of the governmental agencies in World War I, Hoover emphasized efficiency and expertise. But his Commerce Department, according to Hoover's biographer, David Burner, "had little desire for supervisory control; it wanted to be a center for communication among manufacturing and distributing bodies." Hoover used new public-relations techniques to exhort the private sector to act on behalf of the public interest.

Under Hoover, the small Bureau of Foreign and Domestic Commerce became one of the Commerce Department's major divisions, quintupling its staff to 2,500. Although the State Department complained bitterly, the expansion of the BFDC marked the ascendancy of the Commerce Department in most matters of foreign economic affairs. (The State Department retained primary authority only over the economic issues of loans, oil, and reparations; and Hoover influenced these issues as well.) The BFDC hired more special commercial agents and staffed some fifty offices throughout the world. It organized commodity divisions, each specializing in a single item of foreign trade, to advise appropriate American companies. It created a Division of Foreign Tariffs to keep track of foreign budgets, exchange conditions, and credit risks. Hoping that industrial cooperation would replace wasteful competition, the BFDC also actively encouraged the formation of private trade associations. Agents from the Commerce Department assisted private enterprise in the 1920s as never before. "If we are to maintain the total volume of our exports and consequently our buying power for imports," Hoover argued, "it must be by steady pushing of our manufactured goods . . ." He called his commercial cadre "hounds for possible American sales."

In addition to promoting trade, Hoover helped to shape a trade policy, the general outlines of which the government would uphold for the next quarter century and beyond: support for global adoption of the most-favored-nation principle. (A most-favored-nation provision meant that a nation would be granted the same tariff schedule as that applied to the nation receiving the most advantageous treatment; global acceptance of the principle would mean equal treatment on trade duties and equal access to markets.) Since the 1890s, the American government had championed the concept of equal access to China, a proposition that was officially accepted by major nations, including Japan, in the Nine-Power Treaty of the Washington Conference of 1922. But at the same time the United States government employed bargaining tariffs to force special privileges for American traders in Latin America. In the early 1920s, the Tariff Commission, insulated from protectionist pressures exerted on Congress, recommended against such inconsistency and urged the President to advocate applying the most-favored-nation, or open door, everywhere. Tariff bargaining, the commission hoped, might compel Britain and France to drop the discriminatory trading practices that they had established after World War I and gain America wider access to their special spheres of influence.

In adopting these proposals, the Tariff Commission reflected the philosophy of the business internationalists, who favored liberalized integration of the world economy. Naturally, the enthusiasm of international businessmen stemmed from their confidence that America's competitive position was so strong that they needed only equal, not advantageous, terms in order to prosper. It also reflected a recognition that the health of American-based transnationals depended on an expanding world market. But smaller, nationally based businesses that did not need world markets were understandably suspicious of the commission's recommendations, and they urged Congress to retain a protectionist tariff policy that would protect them from foreign competition. To force others to grant open-door treatment to Americans, they feared, the United States would have to promise greater access to its own domestic market.

The Fordney–McCumber Tariff Act of 1922 was an attempt to satisfy both the business internationalists and the nationalists. It endorsed the most-favored-nation principle and authorized the President to raise tariff rates on goods from any country that did not give the United States most-favored-nation treatment. Yet the rate structure was highly protectionist and therefore palatable to the business nationalists. Hoover and other Republicans claimed that the protectionism of the tariff did not violate the concept of a liberal international order: Americans stood for equal opportunity and access, not freer trade. "We are not seeking special privileges anywhere at the expense of others," Charles Evans Hughes explained. "We wish to maintain equality of opportunity; as we call it, the *open door.*" Hoover also justified a high tariff by arguing that it simply compensated for the cheaper wages and production costs of foreign goods and thus equalized competition, rather than interfered with it.

Although Hoover and other officials tried to make protectionism and the open door sound compatible, progress in gaining acceptance of the most-favored-nation principle went slowly. In 1923, the United States and Germany concluded a commercial treaty incorporating a most-favored-nation clause that the United States hoped would become a prototype. But most major trading nations balked at even considering similar agreements; France became positively indignant that the United States wanted equal access to all markets of the world while it shut foreign traders out of its huge domestic market. By 1929, the United States had signed eight treaties and a dozen executive agreements binding nations to the most-favored-nation principle, but most were with minor trading partners.

Although Hoover, among others, consistently maintained that the United States could have both protectionism for the nationalists and the open door for internationalist enterprise, it was clear that there would be only limited foreign acceptance of the open door as long as America maintained a high tariff. And with support from the Republican Presidents, the advocates of protectionism gained, rather than lost, strength during the decade, ultimately even capturing the Tariff Commission. Protectionists had their greatest triumph with the passage of the Smoot–Hawley Tariff of 1930, the highest in American history. Business internationalists would not succeed in their campaign for both the most-favored-nation formula and lower tariffs until after World War II. During the 1920s, equal access, rather than free trade, was the goal of foreign-trade policy.

GUIDING INVESTMENT

Even if the open door had been accepted by other nations, it could not have increased American exports unless foreign buyers had money to spend and international finance and exchange mechanisms were operating smoothly. World War I had left European nations—America's best prewar customers—starved for capital and greatly in debt to the United States; Latin America and Asia, needing greater stability and economic growth, were still only potential markets. The United States, which emerged from World War I with a great surplus of capital and owned the majority of the world's gold, could hardly expect to sell exports without first transferring some of its wealth to foreign buyers.

There were several ways to recycle America's wealth to foreign customers. Many people in the international business community favored large government programs for foreign lending, but both the Wilson and Harding Administrations rejected that on ideological and political grounds. Another partial solution was to cancel the Allies' war debts to the United States so that the Allies would reduce the heavy reparations they levied on Germany. Lessening debt in Europe would leave more money there to buy American products and would also hasten the Continent's recovery. Although a few Americans—such as the governor of the Federal Reserve System, Paul Warburg—initially favored this proposal, during the postwar recession of 1919–20 it became obvious that the American public demanded repayment of war debts and that Congress would take a tough stand on the issue. A third way to get money to foreign buyers was to purchase more goods from them. Business internationalists argued that if America eased its protective tariff, foreign reconstruction and development would be encouraged and America's exports would flourish. Business nationalists and agricultural exporters, however, not only blocked any attempt to lower tariffs but got them raised higher and higher. The Republican Administrations' policies of vigorously promoting exports while demanding repayment of war debts and endorsing a high tariff infuriated foreigners, who believed such a narrow, self-serving approach undermined any hope for long-range global stability and prosperity. The British ambassador to the United States, for example, wrote home bitterly in 1921 that Americans' "central ambition" was "to win for America the position of leading nation in the world and also of leader among the English-speaking nations." To do this, he reported, they intended "to prevent us from paying our debt by sending goods to America and they look for the opportunity to treat us as a vassal state as long as the debt remains unpaid."

The narrow vision of American policy has long been criticized, especially by those who came into the government after 1929 and tried to mop up the international economic wreckage. Herbert Feis suggested the version of Republican shortsightedness that became conventional wisdom for both Democratic policymakers of the 1930s and liberal-internationalist historians of the post-1945 era. "The course we followed in our foreign economic relations . . . was selfish as well as lax . . . We sought and rejoiced in the expansion of our foreign trade. But we refused to face the fact that it lacked a healthy balance." In his influential study of the causes of the Depression, C. P. Kindleberger echoes the charge that the Republicans possessed a flawed vision of America's responsibilities for interwar financial stability; he describes the Republican Administrations as isolationist in their foreign economic policies and uncertain in their international role.

The myth of Republican shortsightedness may have been pushed too far. Experienced and worldly-wise policymakers such as Hoover did clearly understand that American prosperity was dependent on a stable and prosperous world system. They recognized that the United States, the only major power to emerge from the war with a strong economy, had certain international responsibilities. But instead of instituting government foreign loans, lowering tariffs, or canceling debts—all of which they considered politically impossible—the Republicans encouraged private loans abroad as the primary way of recycling cash for purchase of more American exports. According to Hoover's view, Britain in the latter half of the nineteenth century exported more than it imported, invested the profits abroad, and thus created new markets for itself. In doing so, the British "not only extended the capacity and the absorption of British goods, but they lifted the standard of living of the entire world." The United States, Hoover argued, should play a similar role, sending out private investment capital, further enlarging its export sector, and bringing more and more of the world's productive capacity under its control. In this typical liberal-developmental formulation, Hoover stressed mutual advantage. "The making of loans to foreign countries for productive purposes not only increases our direct exports but builds up the prosperity of foreign countries and is a blessing to both sides of the transaction."

Hoover encouraged investment in industrial or transportation projects that could require the purchase of American machinery and replacement parts. He also urged greater cooperation between American investment bankers and manufacturers. If American lenders would require that their loans had to be used to purchase only American products, as Europeans frequently did, export trade would boom. Hoover actually wanted to require bankers to attach a buy-American provision to loans, arguing that they had "certain internal responsibilities to our commerce." The banking community successfully fought any formal requirement about where loans had to be spent, but investment bankers between 1924 and 1931, with government encouragement, absorbed over $9 billion of foreign bond issues and turned New York into the undisputed center of the world's capital markets.

Hoover stated clearly why he thought private international loans were preferable to governmental lending agencies (which Americans would adopt after World War II):

> The resort to direct loans by our Government to foreign governments to promote commerce can only lead to a dozen vicious ends . . . Our Government cannot haggle in the market to exact the securities and returns appropriate to the varied risk that merchants and banks can and will extract. Finally, the collection of a debt to our Treasury from a foreign government sets afoot propaganda against our officials, against our Government. There is no court to which a government can appeal for collection of debt except a battleship. The whole process is involved in inflation, waste, and intrigue.

By encouraging lending through private banking channels, Hoover hoped America could exercise economic leadership yet maintain a limited government and minimize diplomatic conflict. It was the Republicans' cooperative philosophy, with its liberal faith in the private sector, not their international vision and notions of American responsibility, that proved limited in the 1920s.

One of the most controversial actions of the cooperative state was the General Loan Policy, which called on private lenders to act according to official guidelines. In 1922, the State Department requested that bankers notify them before extending foreign loans, so that the department would, "in view of the possible national interests involved," be able to indicate "that there is or is not an objection to any particular issue." The department set forth several categories of investments that would not meet approval: loans to meet budget deficits created by insufficient taxation; loans for armaments; loans that would assist foreign monopolies maintain high prices on goods needed by Americans; loans to unrecognized governments (the Soviet Union); loans that might finance Japanese expansion into Manchuria; loans to countries that were in default to the United States government (that is, those who had suspended payment of World War I debts). Hoover wanted to expand this supervisory function to include oversight of the economic viability of the loan; unwise, unproductive loans, he argued, could lead to default and ultimately to demands that the government should intervene to bail out American lenders. But Secretaries of State

Hughes and Kellogg insisted that judging a loan's economic character would be more, not less, likely to involve government in private financial disputes. The General Loan Policy, they argued, only dealt with political, not economic, appropriateness.

The loan policy did achieve some successes. After several years of bitter diplomatic haggling, and under pressure from the informal American embargo on capital, France resumed payments on its World War I debt. Some Americans refused to lend to Japanese enterprises seeking privileges in Manchuria. Sales of armaments were discouraged. The U.S.S.R. received no long-term credit from the United States. Some of the strongest words and actions were reserved for countries that sought to control the price of basic commodities by monopolizing supply. Hoover especially fought against Brazilian valorization of coffee. Under the valorization plan, the government of São Paulo would buy the country's coffee crop, and since Brazil produced most of the world's coffee, the government agency in charge of valorization would then set the world price. Assailing valorization as monopolistic, Hoover refused to endorse a loan to São Paulo to finance the plan in 1925. A loan, he argued, would help "bolster up the extravagant prices to the American consumers." On the same grounds, Hoover also quashed a loan to the German potash syndicate. The pressure to deny loans to government-managed producers' monopolies was an important part of Hoover's broader campaign—also waged against price-manipulation of rubber by foreign governments.

The General Loan Policy also showed the limits of the cooperative ethic. The House of Morgan issued loans to Japan even though the money ultimately bolstered Japan's position in Manchuria. (Lamont argued that the capital helped support liberals in Japan against the militarists.) American loans to Germany freed up German capital that was then lent to the Soviet Union. When public policy became too great an obstacle to private profits, bankers could find detours around the guidelines.

Some Americans criticized the informal control of the General Loan Policy. Senators such as Carter Glass, who opposed the policy, reflected the banking community's displeasure at even informal government restrictions and maintained that the State Department had no more right to review and, in effect, embargo foreign loans than other nations did to restrict exports through producers' monopolies. Owen D. Young remarked that "our position would be much stronger in criticizing their artificial restraints if we did not indulge in them ourselves." *The Nation* charged that the high Republican tariff obstructed a liberal-internationalist trading system more than foreign monopolies and that Hoover's antimonopoly campaign was a case of "the pot calling the kettle black —in which Mr. Hoover is obviously the pot."

But Hoover held that embargoing loan capital served to police rather than to subvert the liberal-international order. World progress, in his view, depended on maintaining open, responsible states, and the General Loan Policy was an attempt to punish any transgression through the "voluntary" actions of private enterprise. The General Loan Policy, combining private investment decisions and public policy, was a perfect expression of the cooperative state.

Hoover's justifications showed how policies to America's advantage could always be supported on some higher plane of liberal principle. Denouncing what he called an "autocracy of economic power" controlled by foreign governments, he nonetheless justified America's wielding of economic power, because it came from the private sector, was "voluntary," or was compensatory (as in the case of American tariffs, which he said only equalized differing wage scales). Such distinctions gave American liberalism a quality that smacked more of expediency than of principle.

In addition to devising general policy guidelines for lenders, the government used a wide variety of chosen instruments to stabilize the international economic order. Through the J. P. Morgan banking interests, the Federal Reserve Bank of New York, and private financial commissions-for-hire, policymakers hoped to stabilize weak sectors of the international economy (Europe, especially Germany) and to rehabilitate and integrate new areas (such as China, Mexico, or Persia). Chosen instruments for financial rehabilitation deserve to be recognized as parts of a comprehensive and thoughtful, if not ultimately successful, policy.

The Harding Administration continued Woodrow Wilson's use of international banking syndicates to bring stability to Mexico and China. Thomas Lamont became one of the most important diplomats of the 1920s: he held no governmental post but orchestrated the House of Morgan's role as a financial chosen instrument. In Mexico and China, the State Department discouraged other

Americans from offering competing loans, in order to enhance Lamont's position as the sole source of available foreign capital; Lamont, in turn, tried to use this economic leverage to accomplish other diplomatic objectives in consultation with the State Department.

In Mexico, Lamont's efforts led to a *modus vivendi* over the issues of oil and American claims against property damage arising from the revolution. Lamont's negotiations helped moderate the Mexican revolution and secure, for a time at least, Americans' oil and mining properties. The historian N. Stephen Kane concluded that policymakers considered economic pressure applied through private bankers more effective than military force. Diplomats and bankers working together, he wrote, "demonstrated faith in the efficacy of financial power to secure political as well as economic goals."

In the Far East, Lamont also worked closely with the government. Japan was reluctant to join the new international banking consortium for China, which Wilson had helped create in 1918, because joining the group would mean abandoning the old sphere-of-interest approach to China in favor of a cooperative (American-dominated endeavor). Japan was tempted to participate in an international attempt to stabilize China (and to exclude Japan's traditional rival in the area—Russia), but it did not want to relinquish its special privileges in Manchuria, where it had built a strong economic presence. Lamont conducted prolonged negotiations with Japan and finally in 1920 reached an agreement suitable to Japan, the bankers, and the State Department. Japan joined the consortium, thus implicitly agreeing to cooperate on China policy rather than try to carve out a sphere of special privilege, but a number of Japanese holdings in Manchuria, mainly the South Manchurian Railway, were preserved as "outside the scope of the joint activities of the consortium." In these Lamont–Kajiwara agreements, which officially recognized Japan's special predominance in certain enterprises in Manchuria, Japan also accepted the open door and territorial integrity of the rest of China. These arrangements were the basis for the Nine-Power Treaty at the Washington Conference of 1922.

With Japan's participation in the consortium secured, Lamont continued throughout the 1920s to conduct intermittent negotiations between the consortium and China. The bankers offered a variety of loans to China in return for some supervision over Chinese finances and control over all of China's nationalized railways. Despite the United States government's interest in China loans and stabilization, however, Lamont's enthusiasm about the project lagged and no consortium loans were ever consummated. (In view of the severe conditions the bankers attached to the loan, one wag suggested that the consortium's most valuable contribution to China was to give nothing.)

The Chinese loan negotiations demonstrated the limitations as well as the possibilities of privately conducted economic foreign policy. While Lamont appeared to support the government's policy for a China loan, in fact he formed a close association with the Japanese and seemed much more interested in lending them money. Such a bias was understandable: Japan offered immeasurably greater investment security and opportunity for profit. The House of Morgan actually helped deprive China of capital (because no competing loans could be offered while the consortium's negotiations were proceeding), while—contrary to the General Loan Policy—it helped build Japan's economic strength. Carrying out foreign policy through the private sector raised other uncomfortable dilemmas. The United States government supported the Federal Telegraph Company's attempts to extend American-controlled cables into China, but when Federal Telegraph sought to float a loan to finance this effort, Lamont and the bankers' consortium successfully pressed the State Department to disapprove it. The State Department was forced to choose between two of its chosen instruments. In this case the bankers won, retaining their monopoly over potential loans to China. In China, the contradiction between public intentions and private action and the conflicting interests of American businessmen both reflected the difficulties of the cooperative approach and foreshadowed the breakdown of Hoover's vision after 1929.

The House of Morgan also became the principal actor in one of the most important economic events of the 1920s—the massive loans to Germany associated with the Dawes Plan of 1924. The German economy, disrupted by war wreckage and saddled with impossible reparations, was unable to attract loans. In 1924, Hoover helped establish a commission—headed by Charles G.

Dawes, a Chicago banker, and including Owen D. Young of G.E. and RCA—to work out a plan for German recovery. Dawes's arrangement provided that J. P. Morgan extend a $100 million loan to Germany, and scaled down reparations payments to ease Germany's financial burden. The State Department turned to Morgan partly because he had been so accommodating in organizing a stabilization loan for Austria in 1923. At that time, Morgan announced that his company, unlike other American banks, would "even be willing to incur a temporary financial lockup of reasonable proportions rather than have America fail to do its proper share" for European recovery.

Initially, Morgan was reluctant to finance such an investment in Germany, but Secretary of State Hughes again made the appeal that European recovery depended on American bankers. Hughes wrote Morgan's representative about his concerns:

> I believe that the execution of the Dawes Plan is necessary. . . . In the event of its failure, we should have, in my judgment, not only chaotic conditions abroad but a feeling of deep despair . . . We had hoped that while this Government could not make a loan or give any guarantee, the American financiers would see their way clear to undertake the participation which the world expects and which is believed to be essential to the success of the loan.

After strong pressure from the government, Morgan finally consented; afterwards, Germany became the most popular country for other American investors. Between 1924 and the crash of 1929, Americans contributed 80 percent of the capital borrowed by German credit institutions, 75 percent loaned to local governments, and 50 percent loaned to large corporations.

The American stake in Germany became so large that Hoover and others in the government began informally to advise against further investment there. They particularly feared that claims by private American bondholders might ultimately clash with Allied governments' claims for reparations. American industrialists, alarmed at the enormous stimulus given to German competitors by American investment capital, also urged a slowdown in United States loans. But State Department warnings scarcely dampened investors' enthusiasm; it became increasingly evident that private investment decisions did not always work in the public interest, nor could they always be controlled by cooperative techniques. Hoover's version of "jawboning" proved a poor way of ensuring the government's control over economic foreign policy; the contradictions of the cooperative, voluntaristic approach became more and more apparent.

Republican Administrations of the 1920s also encouraged the Federal Reserve Bank of New York (FRBNY) to undertake programs of international economic stabilization. Benjamin Strong, the governor of the FRBNY, became a close personal friend of the head of England's central bank during the 1920s. Together with the heads of other central banks, they tried to function like an international bank—granting loans to countries that followed their stabilization procedures, selling and buying foreign exchange to influence gold movements and exchange rates, and trying to coordinate the domestic monetary strategies of other countries. Strong initiated these activities after a meeting in 1921 with President Harding, Secretary of Treasury Andrew Mellon, and Hoover. The meeting was concerned with Eastern Europe, an area Hoover had special interest in because of his relief work there. After the meeting, Hoover wrote Strong:

> The economic rehabilitation of these 100,000,000 people is vital to our commerce, not only directly with them but also with the other states whose prosperity so much depends upon them . . . I believe that most men of economic and commercial thought are agreed that if these states are to recover it must be by forces entirely divorced from political origin or action, that is through the healing power of assistance of private finance and commerce.
>
> Therefore it is the hope of the President and my colleagues in this Administration that you can pursue the conversations which have been suggested, that is to determine whether the great public banks in the interested countries as well as the United States could not formulate a plan for financial cooperation with these states of purely private character . . . as would give promise of economic stability.

Cooperation among central banks, with the FRBNY representing the United States, worked fairly well to stabilize Europe. The bankers' programs for each country it assisted generally included a promise to balance the national budget and return to the gold standard, in return for a loan that reduced and consolidated the national debt and an understanding that other private bankers would lend additional money once the central bankers' loan had strengthened the currency. Between 1925 and 1928, almost all the nations of Europe were moved onto a gold standard (most had abandoned it during World War I). In each case, Strong consulted with Secretary Mellon, a prominent banker himself, and usually with Hoover. Mellon supported Strong's efforts because, he said, "the return to a common international standard will tend to stabilize industry in foreign countries and increase their purchasing power . . . This means a greater demand for our surplus products." Moreover, he argued, the gold standard would facilitate international exchange, thus contribute to more trade, and improve foreign credit ratings so that more American investment might be attracted. Mellon saw America's domestic economic health closely connected to the efforts of the international bankers.

There were advantages to having the international economic system organized by the private central banks of the major nations. As Hoover pointed out, the government did not shoulder the burden of enforcing certain economic requirements on foreign states; ostensibly, the system removed the "science" of economics from the "unscientific" realm of politics. Hoover and Strong both consistently viewed the central bankers as apolitical and held that they never wielded financial power to extract political concessions, as they believed government agencies might do. Such a view implied an exceedingly narrow definition of politics. The bankers were concerned with integrating countries into a Euro-American capitalism, and by exerting vast influence on a nation's fiscal policies, they clearly imposed political priorities. Yet, as long as the bankers were not technically the arm of any government, the myth of apolitical economic forces was perpetuated.

The disadvantages of this chosen-instrument approach to international economics would become increasingly obvious after 1928. Each loan granted required a separate negotiation, and by 1928 the haggling over terms among the central bankers became so great that there no longer existed a common basis for monetary cooperation. Despite the veneer of cooperation throughout the 1920s, both British and American bankers struggled to make their respective currencies the preeminent unit of international exchange, and the inclusion of French central bankers later on further complicated national economic rivalries. The process of international stabilization fell apart when it was most needed—after the onset of the Depression in 1929. The private approach simply could not operate in bad times as well as good.

In addition to using the House of Morgan and the FRBNY, the governments of the 1920s also encouraged the use of American financial commissions or advisers. These private financial experts also sought to rehabilitate and put other areas on the gold standard. Before World War I, Charles A. Conant had guided United States colonies and protectorates onto the gold standard and helped them to develop strong national banks and strict budget and accounting procedures. Such measures encouraged private loans from United States investors and integrated foreign economies into America's needs. With Conant's death in 1915, the mantle of master currency-organizer fell primarily on Edwin Kemmerer, a professor at Princeton, who had supervised the Philippine currency system before the war, and some of his former students, especially Arthur N. Young and William Wilson Cumberland. Kemmerer later recalled that he had acted "as financial adviser to two silver-standard countries and eleven managed paper-money standard countries in the transformation of their currencies to a gold-standard basis." The countries included China, Colombia, Chile, Poland, Germany, South Africa, Ecuador, Bolivia, Turkey.

Although the financial missions were technically private, there was a large degree of official involvement behind the scenes. The State Department often suggested or urged a foreign government to hire an American adviser, informing them that such action would improve their chances for obtaining loans or receiving greater consideration from the United States government on other issues. The State Department usually suggested a suitable expert, such as Kemmerer, who might be retained. Foreign governments always understood that the missions kept in close touch with the State Department, as well as with the higher circles of American finance. Poland illustrated the close connection between private and public spheres. Kemmerer, the FRBNY, and Assistant Secretary of the Treasury Charles S. Dewey drew up a financial plan for Poland, and the tough new Polish dictator, who overthrew Poland's weak parliamentary government in 1926, then hired Dewey as a financial adviser to implement it. Dewey left his government post and became Poland's principal economic planner for the next three years. In Poland as elsewhere, writes the historian Frank Costigliola, "Americans sought involvement that was economic rather than political, unofficial rather than official, private rather than governmental."

Some American financial missions attracted loans and, in the short run at least, stabilized economies. But often they displayed a parochial vision that assumed reform simply meant copying American techniques. One group of financial experts, led by Charles Dawes, was dispatched to the Dominican Republic in the late 1920s to recommend solutions to the egregious financial problems that previous American advisers had only managed to exacerbate. The group wrote a 200-page report of financial recommendations, all modeled on United States practices, while on a ship sailing *to* the Dominican Republic.

But worse were the erroneous assumptions of the developmentalist credo. Financial reorganization and economic stabilization gave greater borrowing capacity, yet too often failed to stimulate growth. The influx of new money might strengthen and enrich a self-serving oligarchy, leaving the nation with greater long-term indebtedness and dependence. In 1921, for example, the Peruvian government requested an American to administer its customs services, in the hope that United States loans would follow. The adviser, William Cumberland, did help Peru to get a loan. But, unable to meet the payments, the country then sank into an even deeper financial morass. When Cumberland finally left Peru a few years later, he felt his financial mission had probably done more harm than good; he had only deepened Peru's indebtedness by temporarily strengthening its credit rating. A decade after Cumberland's "reforms," the Peruvian government was in even worse shape and was again asking to be "rehabilitated" by American advisers.

The case of Persia (Iran) provides another example. In the early 1920s, Persia asked for an adviser, and the State Department suggested Arthur C. Millspaugh, a State Department financial expert. Millspaugh then resigned from government and took charge of a commission to run Persia's economy. From 1922 until 1927, the Millspaugh mission attempted to manage Persian finances, but because Millspaugh wanted to raise revenue by levying some taxes on the wealthy, he encountered growing opposition both within the Majlis (Parliament) and from Reza Khan, Minister of War. After Reza Khan declared himself Shah in 1927, disagreements became even sharper, and Millspaugh left. He evaluated his mission this way. "Success," he wrote, "was partly illusory and almost entirely transitory. Our financial reforms helped Reza to consolidate his dictatorship. Our main accomplishment was to finance the forces of reaction and degeneration; and we could not help ourselves."

The problem of the financial commissions of the 1920s, as the cases of the Dominican Republic, Peru, and Persia suggest, stemmed from the fact that progressive "expertise" was seldom transferable. Technical missions were stymied by deeply rooted social structures that impeded Americanization, even when it came under the guise of scientific process. Insolvency in undeveloped nations was less the result of financial mismanagement than of grossly inequitable social structures and dependent economies. Again and again, financial missions trying to create "developmental" conditions merely enriched the existing oligarchy and reinforced dependency. Financial reforms in an oligarchy could only make the maldistribution more efficient. (Arthur Young felt his lengthy mission in China, beginning in the late 1920s, made great progress, but unlike similar efforts, his mission worked without foreign loans and, according to Young, thus increased China's self-sufficiency rather than its indebtedness.)

Still, Millspaugh and most other Americans did not lose faith in their expertise or in the theoretical possibility of financial regeneration and American-guided development. They failed, they supposed, because they held insufficient power over the country. In 1946, Millspaugh suggested that success might have come from a division of responsibilities. He wrote in his memoirs:

> It seems clear that if Reza could have restricted himself to the function of keeping order, and if a continuing American mission had guarded the treasury and guided the country's development, Persia might gradually have achieved the requisites of self-government and permanent stability.

In the post-World War II period, Americans learning from these "lessons" would devise various ways of achieving greater control over societies to be "developed." In addition, they would have the force of their government squarely behind them; the chosen-instrument approach was scrapped. Mark Twain's *Connecticut Yankee,* with Hank Morgan as a government-approved expert, continued to be an appropriate parable for twentieth-century policy.

LIMITS OF COOPERATION

The close connection between private loans and public policies, illustrated by the General Loan Policy, the banking consortiums, the role of the FRBNY, and the private financial missions, drew increasing domestic criticism throughout the 1920s. Some business interests resented government's guidance and assailed Hoover as a meddling opponent of the free marketplace. Anti-imperialist groups warned that encouragement and supervision of economic expansion could ultimately force the United States government to become a global bill collector. They argued that a policy designed to substitute private economic ties for political-military involvement could easily reverse: the dollar might become the cause, not the solution, of diplomatic problems. Their fears grew when Coolidge, in a speech before the United Press Association in 1927, presented an exceedingly broad view of America's police power:

> We live under a system that guarantees the sanctity of life and liberty through public order and protects the rights of private property under the principle of due process of law . . . We have adopted these ideals because we believe that they are of universal application and square with the eternal principles of right . . . It would seem to be perfectly obvious that if it is wrong to murder and pillage within the confines of the United States, it is equally wrong outside our borders. The fundamental laws of justice are universal in their application. These rights go with the citizen. Wherever he goes, these duties of our government must follow him.

Coolidge's attitude reflected how the global expansion of American property holding would lead the government to broaden its protective shield. If the American government's primary overseas duties were to uphold the property rights of its citizens and enforce due process, then revolution, disorder, or nationalization was everywhere the enemy, the antithesis of progress, the obstacle to development. Under Coolidge, more gunboats appeared in the Caribbean, more patrols in the Yangtze River. United States aerial attacks showed Sandinista rebels in Nicaragua (and other revolutionaries in the Western Hemisphere) the new hazards of activity against American-dominated governments, while 1,500 marines stationed in Shanghai protected the nearly 4,000 Americans who lived there. But because they were protecting American rights, policymakers refused to consider their troops as the tools of interventionism. Charles Evans Hughes had explained: "In promoting stability we do not threaten independence but seek to conserve it. We are not aiming at control but endeavoring to establish self-control." But many foreigners found it difficult to understand such high-mindedness, domestic critics also scoffed at such obfuscations, and, by the end of the decade, even some people in the State Department began to rethink the implications of a decade of unbridled economic expansionism. According to Herbert Feis, who entered the department in 1931, policymakers of the late 1920s had begun backing off from promoting economic expansion and suggesting voluntary guidelines, as they realized such activities implied a protective shield that the government's political and military policies could not support.

Coolidge's formulation of policy showed how the expansionism of the 1920s—though private in nature—could work to transform foreign policy, as Americans came to have ever-greater stakes in expanding and enforcing their concepts of the rule of law abroad. In the end, encouraging private investment did not replace the game of power politics (as Hoover had hoped); it merely upped the stakes. The political and military involvements that policymakers wanted to avoid would follow close behind an expanding, privately controlled economic role.

The fear of excessive government involvement in global affairs —a fear shared by both right and left for entirely different reasons —kept Hoover and others within the bounds of a cooperative ethic. As in domestic matters, it would take the Depression and another war to convince the American public and its leaders to set aside their fear of a larger role for government. Beginning with Franklin Roosevelt, policymakers would gradually create official structures and a military establishment to advance the open and integrated world order in which American influence could spread. Still, if the private approach did not last long, many of the devices to promote international financial stability in the 1920s became cornerstones of economic foreign policy in the next postwar period: standardization of international exchange rates, appropriately placed loans to stimulate purchase of exports and accomplish other goals, and expert financial commissions that worked to integrate other nations into the world economy.

In the 1920s, United States private enterprise greatly expanded the nation's export trade and foreign investment, and the government, building on prewar trends, worked through private interests to guide United States participation in the international economy. But contradictions undermined cooperative notions. Conducting an economic policy through the private sector assumed an identity of interests between private enterprise and the national state. Often the interests did coincide, and then, as Hoover clearly understood, it greatly simplified government's tasks to have private citizens, rather than policymakers, involved in international economic details and negotiations. Not only did this private approach remove highly technical discussions from the political arena and put them into the hands of "experts"—bankers, businessmen, or economists —but it accorded with the liberal bias against large government. Often, however, the private sector could not or would not execute public policy. Private bankers were ultimately bound by their own standards of liquidity and their stockholders' expectations, not by government's prescriptions for international interest. Capital, particularly toward the end of the decade, did not always flow as officials desired. In addition, private chosen instruments acted in the name of American interests, but had no public accountability, or even much visibility, in the political process. The American public believed that the Republican Administrations were following a policy of disengagement from international affairs, yet the private sector was involving the United States in the intricate world system at government's behest and making enormous profits by this economic entanglement. The private approach to economic diplomacy ultimately made the public less able to understand their country's relationship with the rest of the world.

The liberalism of the cooperative state contained even more profound dilemmas. Republican Administrations of the 1920s made equal access, not free trade, their basic goal in commercial policy; Americans sought equality of opportunity abroad, yet enjoyed protectionism at home. Moreover, policymakers fought attempts by foreign governments to manipulate world prices, while they instituted "voluntary" restrictions on investment capital and acquiesced in price-setting cartels dominated by American companies in the oil, copper, and electrical industries. Hoover suggested that because American economic controls sprang voluntarily from the private sector, they were somehow more benign and acceptable. By such policies, American liberalism of the 1920s actually distorted liberal, free-marketplace doctrines. A liberalism that would not recognize that high tariffs and private cartels constituted restrictions within the world marketplace bore little similarity to the ideas of Adam Smith, who had warned against concentrations of private power, as well as against government interference.

Nine
★ ═ ★ ═ ★
DEPRESSION AND WAR: 1932–1945

THE central assumption behind the foreign policy of the pre-Depression era was that the United States could simultaneously enjoy great international economic power and limited government. But the cooperative state proved unable to halt the spiral of declining trade and rising default on debts that set in after 1929. During the 1920s, America's high-tariff policy had strengthened its position as a creditor; foreigners used American loans in part to meet previous debts and to purchase American exports. When American lenders slowed their extension of credit in late 1928 and then stopped foreign lending altogether after the stock-market crash of 1929, foreign trade declined, export inventories mounted, and debts went unpaid. America's combined imports and exports fell from $9.5 billion in 1929 to less than $3 billion in 1932; in September 1931, Great Britain left the gold standard, and forty other countries followed during the next six months; after 1931, there was large-scale international default on governmental war debts and on private securities. (By 1935, for example, Germany's default rate was 99.6 percent, Brazil's was 93 percent, China's was 100 percent.) The international system of trade, finance, and exchange was in collapse. It needed a massive infusion of capital to make up for the retreating investment and to reverse the downward trend, but there was no adequate governmental or international mechanism to provide it.

The private banks, experiencing their own liquidity crises, could not be expected to resume massive international lending. The Young Plan of 1929 tried to scale down war debts and reparations and to schedule German payments on private American loans; in 1931, Hoover declared a one-year moratorium on war debts. But neither measure arrested the crisis. The Young Plan, reflecting the views of the internationalist business community, proposed a Bank of International Settlements (BIS) that could coordinate international monetary policy through the central banks of the leading nations. But it was too late to construct institutions to stop the depressionary spiral; nationalist pressures were strong and the American public viewed with suspicion any proposal advanced by international business interests. Without strong American support, the BIS was useless. Hoover's inability to fashion any significant response to the crisis highlighted the inadequacy of a structure based on private capital.

If the private sector could not resuscitate the international economy, neither could the government save the private sector. Governmental institutions possessed few means of protecting the private businesses and chosen instruments that had ventured abroad during the 1920s at government's urging. Despite the cries of Americans that foreigners should be forced to repay their debts and despite business's appeal for greater governmental support of their foreign claims, the government was helpless to prevent massive defaults.

The cooperative ethic thus collapsed along with the international economy. The private sector was unable to work in the interests of international stability; the public sector was unable to protect the foreign stakes of its citizens. Franklin Delano Roosevelt, who became President in 1933, gradually moved toward more governmental regulation and greater executive-branch power over foreign economic policy. The largest globally oriented corporations also hoped for a stronger governmental role in assuring a stable international system, but they did not wait for that. Most sought to secure their own international positions through greater geographical diversification or stronger monopolistic arrangements. Both government and private capital, then, moved to bring order out of international chaos; and both moved further and further away from a liberal marketplace model.

RATIONALIZATION IN THE PRIVATE SECTOR

Depression gave birth to neomercantilist restrictions and political uncertainties. In 1930, Congress enacted the extraordinarily high Smoot–Hawley tariff. Nationalist business interests backed this tariff to preserve the dwindling domestic market for themselves. Despite the objections of a thousand American economists, pressure from internationalist business circles, and protests from more than thirty foreign countries, Hoover signed the bill, hoping that if domestic prosperity was restored, international health would also return. Yet, while Hoover futilely struggled to prove that nationalistic measures and international health were not at odds, in fact, the tariff was seen, as Dana F. Fleming has written, as a "declaration of economic war by the strongest economic power against the whole of the civilized world." Other nations responded with similar economic nationalism. By 1932, American traders and investors began to discover a radically changed international environment: higher tariffs; special trading agreements; import quotas; regulations on prices, exchange rates, and profit remittances; and, in some places, pressure to cooperate with national, government-sponsored cartels.

As they looked beyond America's borders in the early 1930s, most traders and investors felt alarm and pessimism. The rules of the international economic game were changing. In 1932, American financial journals advised against investments in firms with significant foreign holdings. From 1933 to 1940, statistics on direct investment revealed a net *inflow* for the first time since records had begun to be kept in 1900.

Extractive and agricultural investments suffered most. The great investments in raw materials that the American government had encouraged after World War I produced a surplus in most commodities during the 1920s. During the 1930s, these surpluses glutted the marketplace, and prices declined sharply. The Guggenheim's huge nitrate holdings in Chile went broke: the value of United Fruit's investment in Central America dropped sharply under the combined impact of depression and a new banana disease. As copper prices plummeted, the American-dominated copper cartel collapsed. American companies with foreign investments in copper, nitrates, tin, bananas, rubber, and sugar generally showed losses after 1930.

Price stabilization became the object of the private diplomacy carried on by the many international companies that had large stakes in raw materials. During the 1930s, some American companies joined in privately arranged cartels—the tactic of a producers' monopoly that, when practiced by foreign governments, had been anathema to Hoover. American investors signed price-setting agreements with other tin producers to boost their profits. Goodyear and U.S. Rubber Company, operating in Dutch and British colonies, participated in an international rubber agreement, even though the United States government had loudly denounced the British government's rubber controls in the 1920s. A similar private accord over the price of sugar, backed by significant American interests in Cuba, was also tried, though it failed because too many growers remained independent. All in all, international stabilization of prices, a principle that ran directly counter to liberal pricing by supply and demand, became one method of survival. By mid-decade, Franklin Roosevelt, reflecting the government's growing acceptance of a regulated international market, even came out in favor of government-enforced commodity agreements, at least those that would raise the price of America's major agricultural exports, wheat and cotton.

For some companies, diversification and further international expansion also became strategies for survival. United Fruit posted financial losses during the 1930s, but its overall position grew stronger and stronger. Its local competitors, less able to withstand the pressures of banana disease and depression, failed; impoverished Central American governments borrowed money from United Fruit in order to keep their national budgets afloat. And, while Central Americans became more dependent upon United Fruit for their prosperity, United Fruit became less reliant on them after it launched a major diversification program in Africa.

American oil companies, adopting strategies of both price-management and diversification, turned the Depression decade into an era of unprecedented foreign gains. In 1929, the American Petroleum Institute approved a plan to limit exports by holding back production in the United States, and although domestic oil operations still produced a surplus, America's high tariffs left foreigners too short of United States currency to purchase much American oil. Therefore, oil companies increasingly supplied their international markets from foreign wells. And with nations striving to curtail imports and achieve energy self-sufficiency in the 1930s, oil companies could find countries willing to grant incentives if they would agree to produce and refine in new places. Several European and Latin-American governments established state oil companies that operated in partnership with the international giants.

Geographical diversification also reduced the impact of political instability in any one country. During the 1930s and 1940s, American oil interests greatly expanded their production in the Western Hemisphere; Mexico nationalized oil in 1938, but oil companies enlarged their investments in Venezuela and moved into South American countries in which they had not previously operated. Companies also made their first really significant investments in production outside the Western Hemisphere. They entered the Dutch East Indies and began developing Middle Eastern fields in Saudi Arabia, Bahrain, and Kuwait. In 1929, Standard Oil of New Jersey refined and produced more oil at home than abroad, but by 1939 it refined 15 percent more abroad than at home and produced more than twice as much. And Jersey Standard, which had been the only American company with significant international holdings in the 1920s, was not alone. By 1939, four more United States companies had become integrated, multinational enterprises: Socony–Vacuum, Gulf, Standard of California, and Texaco. These five American companies, plus Shell and British Petroleum, became known as the "seven sisters." In a series of meetings in the early 1930s, the international oil barons reaffirmed the price-setting, profit-splitting, and market-dividing provisions of the Red Line agreements of 1928. Although the new cartel did not achieve total dominance everywhere, oil companies did rationalize prices and production well enough to flourish despite the world Depression.

On the whole, the Depression hit American manufacturers and processors operating overseas less severely than most supply-oriented investors. Some manufacturers and processors expanded cartel arrangements to shield themselves from the uncertain economic environment. In 1931, General Electric and Westinghouse, the two major American electrical companies, formed an export association (the Webb–Pomerene Act of 1918 had legalized monopolistic associations in the export trade) and then joined major foreign electrical enterprises in an international agreement to regulate

prices and divide markets. This cartel virtually eliminated international competition in electrical parts. More importantly, the tariff
barriers and quota systems that contributed to a decline of trade
gave enormous stimulus to market-oriented investment. Taking
advantage of incentives offered by Latin-American governments
wishing to boost domestic textile production and save foreign exchange, a Texas-based multinational, Anderson, Clayton, and
Company, expanded its cotton-producing and processing industries and became one of the largest business empires in Latin
America. American drug companies also extended their operations
into Latin America during the late 1930s. Thus, at the same time
that Latin Americans tried to legislate restrictions on the American (and other foreign) firms that controlled their basic raw materials, their policies designed to encourage new domestic manufacturing provided opportunities for other American investors. Latin
America's dependence on foreign investment was not broken, only
transformed, by the nationalistic legislation of the 1930s.

A similar process took place in Canada. In the Ottawa agreements of 1932, Britain launched a full-fledged imperial preference
system: a system of tariff preferences for nations within the empire
that effectively ruptured most trading links with nations outside it.
As trade with Canada and other parts of the British empire became
difficult, incentives to produce within the empire became greater.
American investment in Canadian industry boomed as investors
sought to penetrate imperial markets.

American manufacturers also expanded in Germany. International Harvester, GM, Ford, IBM, for instance, greatly increased
the size of their operations; all gained from orders generated by
Hitler's decision to rearm Germany. Although remission of profits
to the United States was illegal under German law, American
businessmen were content to reinvest in Germany, profits were
high, and labor's demands were tightly controlled by the Nazis.
Many American industrialists entered into joint ventures with the
German industrial giants I. G. Farben and Krupp. If the politics
of Hitler's Nazi state bothered some businessmen personally, others admitted that Fascism had more benefits than drawbacks for
their businesses. *Fortune* reported that George M. Moffett, president of Corn Products Refining, preferred "the tangible, explicit
Nazi interference to the half-defined meddling of democracy."

Japan was one of the few places that experienced a significant decline in American direct investment in manufacturing. Under the strongly nationalistic policies of the 1930s, Japanese businessmen were under heavy government pressure to gain control of joint Japanese-American ventures or abandon them. Japan sought not only greater self-sufficiency in trade but greater native ownership of its industrial sector during the 1930s.

Although overall foreign investments showed losses, many of America's major international companies survived and even flourished during the 1930s. By the end of the decade, many had expanded and diversified their operations, aided by cartel or price-setting agreements, by foreign protective tariffs, by cooperation with state-sponsored foreign enterprises, or simply by taking advantage of the bankruptcy of smaller firms. To a large extent, business leaders still talked in marketplace terms: they continued to exalt the hallowed virtues of "free" enterprise, to decry state interference, and to uphold the principle of equal access for trade and investment. But as American direct investors searched for ways to lower risks, foreign investment veered sharply away from the marketplace model of free competition and toward what one scholar has called a "negotiated environment," characterized by national regulations, international cartels, and in some cases close association with state-owned enterprises. Successful international companies had to develop their own diplomatic capabilities to negotiate with countries over terms of doing business.

As America's multinationals developed their own strategies for growth, their relations with the United States government became much more complex. Policies of government and the objectives of private businesses had in the past so often run parallel. But the more nationalistic countries became in the 1930s, the more internationally minded the largest American corporations grew—and the more their outlook could differ from Washington's. Businesses still lobbied to influence government policy, and government still pulled strings to affect business decisions, but their interests were less interdependent.

Many American companies argued that government had a responsibility to protect their foreign interests; they correctly pointed out that government had urged them to invest overseas in the first place. In 1933, for example, Liberia defaulted on its debt to Firestone, and Firestone asked the government to send gunboats in view of their past chosen-instrument relationship. F.D.R. refused, and the new arrangements finally devised between Liberia and Firestone did not have the type of governmental involvement that had prevailed in the 1920s. Officials of the 1930s had to take a broader view of the nation's economic interest; they feared that strong action on behalf of corporate interests might push countries into alliances against the United States. They were particularly cautious with nations—like Mexico, Venezuela, and Japan—that had vital supplies of strategic raw materials or were America's important trading partners.

Oil diplomacy of the 1930s showed the significant gaps between the objectives of the international oil companies and those of the United States government. Negotiations between the two frequently became as complex as their dealings with third parties. Many Latin-American countries created state-owned oil monopolies or passed restrictions on foreign oil companies during the 1930s, but the United States government, interested primarily in strengthening good relations within the hemisphere (and thus insuring strategic supplies in the event of war), would give only modest support to oil companies' demands for more favorable treatment. In cases of outright nationalization—in Bolivia in 1937 and Mexico in 1938—the Roosevelt Administration urged the oil interests to act with moderation and flexibility. Mediating between nationalist demands and oil companies' rigidity in both cases, the government pressured all sides into compromise settlements that recognized nationalization but provided enough compensation to satisfy the oilmen. During the war, the State Department also urged the oil companies to compromise on Venezuelan demands that oilmen felt were both unreasonable and illegal. Under government pressure, Jersey Standard's officials came to terms with Venezuela in 1943 rather than risk letting antagonism build into expropriation that would have damaged the war effort and further destroyed the oil companies' Latin-American empire. The companies agreed in principle to what they considered a revolutionary fifty-fifty profit split.

Oil-company desires met governmental coolness in other areas of the world as well. When the Japanese Petroleum Control Bill of 1934 and Japanese refinery construction in Manchuria threatened

Standard–Vacuum's position in the Far East, the State Department failed to support the company's request for a crude-oil embargo against Japan. (It did, however, register no objection to a privately arranged embargo that Stanvac tried unsuccessfully to organize.) In 1935, the State Department also advised Stanvac to drop a concession that the Ethiopian government had granted just before Italy invaded the small African nation. Secretary of State Cordell Hull feared that a dispute over the concession's validity would exacerbate tensions with Italy. In 1941, American oil companies with interests in Saudi Arabia tried to get F.D.R. to grant loans through an executive agency, the Reconstruction Finance Corporation, to King ibn-Saud in order to help maintain America's postwar position there, but the request was refused. Protecting private financial empires at the jeopardy of other traders or investors—or to the detriment of broader strategic interests—was not possible.

THE CROSSROADS OF LIBERAL INTERNATIONALISM

As the Depression undermined the ethos of the cooperative state, government policymakers increasingly sought to fulfill national goals through direct involvement in the international economy. The United States government moved toward becoming an international regulatory state. Such a state, as this term must be understood, did not provide a set of controls over American business practices (though it did include a few); rather, it created a variety of government-operated mechanisms to promote economic recovery and to safeguard against the kind of breakdown experienced after 1929. It created significant new powers for the executive branch and allowed for direct governmental intervention in international economic and cultural realms. The international regulatory state developed slowly, not reaching its peak until the cold-war period, but its origins were in the crises of the 1930s.

Before policymakers really began to fashion a regulatory state, they had to define America's position in the world and to set particular goals. American economic and cultural expansion had long proceeded under the umbrella of liberal-developmental faiths that linked free enterprise, equal access, and free flow to a vision of international development and global progress. As nations threw up economic barriers during the 1930s and began to rearm, Americans debated what policies would be appropriate to the new, more restricted world order.

Many internationalists called on the government to take more vigorous action to restore an integrated, liberalized, and peaceful international system. Many urged the United States to join, or at least to act in concert with, the League of Nations in order to attack economic problems and punish military aggression. To these internationalists, spheres of interest and mercantilistic restrictions were characteristic of a less-enlightened past, and they could only breed international rivalries and, ultimately, wars. In his book *At the Rim,* James T. Shotwell wrote that civilization in the 1930s was at a turning point. "The issue before us is whether we shall have to turn back the march of progress and accept once more the anarchy of the old state system, with all its risks and dangers, its accentuation of conflict, and its acceptance of war as an instrument of policy. It is a contest of the future with the past." This internationalist group, of course, contained many factions. Some wished primarily to restore international stability, to accelerate a Pax Americana in which American economic might could expand without obstruction. Others, who would find a leader in Secretary of Agriculture Henry Wallace, urged Roosevelt to forge an international system that would support social reform and popular control worldwide. Both groups of internationalists favored an open world, but the first cared most that it was open to American business and the other that it was open to the New Deal's concern for social justice. This difference in emphasis, muted at first in the common effort to promote international recovery and to eliminate restrictive nationalism, would grow into a major split within the Roosevelt and Truman Administrations during and after World War II.

Other people, who considered themselves more nationalistic— more American—than the internationalists, embraced the concept of spheres of interest and advocated greater national self-sufficiency. They warned against the globalism inherent in policies of open-door liberalism. Expansionist policies, they believed, could only bring Americans into conflict with others; spheres of interest, they maintained, offered the surest road to peace. Like the internationalists, the advocates of greater American self-sufficiency were a diverse lot, and they did not see eye to eye on all issues. Some

tended to be arch-protectionists, closely allied to domestic interests
that resented the domination of international corporations and the
competition of imported goods. Mining interests from Western
states, for example, advocated developing domestic raw materials,
rather than importing them, and strongly opposed the internationalists who sought further to integrate American and foreign economies. George Peek, a leading spokesman for agricultural interests,
whom F.D.R. appointed administrator of the Agricultural Adjustment Act and special adviser on foreign trade, also argued in favor
of protecting domestic markets and encouraging exports only of
"those products we can best produce, particularly those agricultural products which are the backbone of our prosperity." Peek
warned that increasing economic interconnections with the world
in a liberalized order would continue to sacrifice agricultural interests for the well-being of industrial exporters, something he felt had
happened during the 1920s. And the agricultural depression of the
1920s, he believed, was a major cause of the worldwide Depression
of the 1930s. Peek's book *Why Quit Our Own?* (1936), written with
economic isolationist Samuel Crowther, invoked the historical tradition of George Washington's Farewell Address and Henry Clay's
American System to advocate a new "American program" that
would boost agricultural exports without committing the United
States to a general lowering of tariff barriers or to international
economic cooperation. He also advocated extension of government
credits to finance agricultural exports; he became the first president
of the Export-Import Bank of 1934. Peek, like other business nationalists, wanted to halt (through protectionism)—not to accelerate—the integration of the United States into the world economy.

Charles Beard, one of the era's most prominent historians and
a bitter foe of internationalism, developed a different formulation
of the dangers of globalism and the advantages of self-reliance. In
The Idea of National Interest (1934), Beard rejected the liberal
faiths that had posited economic expansion as a means of achieving
prosperity and world peace. War, not peace, he maintained, was
the inevitable result of global economic aspirations. Like Peek, he
called for a revival of Alexander Hamilton's vision of "national
interest," that is, self-sufficiency in the nation's primary needs—the
"means of subsistence, habitation, clothing, and defense." By invoking the economic philosophy of Hamilton, and even of Thomas

Jefferson (the two political adversaries disagreed on many points, but not on their desire to break the new nation's economic dependence on Europe), Beard tried to elevate self-sufficiency into a strong and still-viable American historical tradition. As Beard explained in *The Open Door at Home* (1934), a companion volume to *The Idea of National Interest,* America should "substitute an intensive cultivation of its own garden for a wasteful, quixotic, and ineffectual extension of interests beyond the reach of competent military and naval defense."

But Beard's invocation of tradition and his unfortunate use of the nostalgic garden metaphor did not reflect a mindless desire to retreat into a simpler past. His vision of America's proper path looked to the future. New technology, Beard believed, made self-sufficiency more practical than ever before; technology could create substitutes for products hitherto supplied only from foreign lands. America could break its dependence on foreign sources of supply by development of synthetics (he provided the example of nitrates) and could, through careful social engineering, convert the economic surplus it currently exported into programs to achieve real social justice at home. Beard, in short, believed that international liberalism was expansionistic and ultimately militaristic; he wanted the term "national interest" once again to be identified with the strength of the national economy, rather than being defined by the business internationalists and other expansionists. The open door to new opportunities and profits could be found at home.

In retrospect, it may seem that Franklin Roosevelt, who took office in 1933, had to make a clear choice between nationalist and internationalist policies, but Roosevelt, without doubt, was a master of inconsistency. Initially at least, he tried to cultivate support from both groups. During the Presidential campaign of 1932, for example, he assailed the Republicans' high tariff but also emphasized the need to preserve domestic markets. (Given two contradictory drafts of a speech on tariff policy—one advocating protectionism and one favoring reciprocal lowering of tariffs—Roosevelt told an adviser to "weave the two together.") It was clear that the President favored both international cooperation toward a liberalized and more integrated world order and maximum national flexibility that might insulate Americans from international troubles. His earliest appointments included both prominent internationalists, such as Secretary of State Cordell Hull, and others, including George Peek, who believed that recovery had to come from purely domestic measures. Although there was much confusion, Roosevelt actually did follow both policies, emphasizing nationalism in the first year and internationalism thereafter.

During 1933, Roosevelt's actions had an ultranationalist tone. That year a World Economic Conference, which outgoing President Hoover strongly endorsed, convened in London. European leaders hoped to bring Americans into a cooperative effort to stabilize exchange rates (as a first step toward raising world price levels and restoring trade) and to counteract the nationalistic restrictions that were contracting world trade. Although Roosevelt's Secretary of State, Cordell Hull, who believed in trade liberalization as a primary means of recovery, received F.D.R.'s preliminary support for such measures, the President decided at the last minute not to go along with the London conference's internationalist approach. The President wanted to maintain maximum flexibility for domestic policy and announced that he was unwilling to stabilize the dollar. Roosevelt thus doomed, or at least delayed, cooperative attempts to restore the international economic order. In the process, he incurred the deep distrust of most European leaders. (A notable exception was John Maynard Keynes, a prominent British economist and treasury official who advocated the same sort of nationally contained capitalism envisioned by Beard.)

Most American internationalists lashed out against F.D.R.'s actions and warned that the President's narrow nationalism would only incur retaliation. Internationalists were even more horrified when Roosevelt announced his decision to begin massive gold purchases, a scheme that would inflate the dollar by manipulating the price of gold and thereby raise prices for American commodities. It was just such competitive inflation of national currencies that the Europeans (and Hoover) had hoped to prevent through international agreements. Internationalist critics also attacked the New Deal's Agricultural Adjustment Act (administered by George Peek), which temporarily banned all agricultural imports in order to reduce domestic farm surpluses. They charged that the AAA presented one more obstacle to the restoration of world trade and represented the kind of governmental restrictions that Americans had traditionally opposed.

A few months after the London conference, at a Pan-American gathering in Montevideo, Uruguay, the President once again showed his reluctance to liberalize trade. Cordell Hull, though feeling the sting that Roosevelt had handed him in London, continued to proselytize for free trade. He introduced a resolution calling for hemispheric efforts to reduce tariffs and to embrace most-favored-nation policies. But again Roosevelt undercut his Secretary of State. He summoned reporters to the White House to inform them that Hull's proposals were an independent action to which his Administration attached little importance. To underscore his reservations, Roosevelt used the occasion of Hull's absence in Uruguay to appoint protectionist George Peek as an adviser on foreign trade.

In Congress, where nationalist interests had always been strong, the suspicion of international economic ties brought new protective legislation supported by Roosevelt. In 1933 and 1934, lawmakers mandated formal regulation of the sale of foreign securities. The new laws required foreigners (as well as Americans) to file detailed prospectuses and information with the newly created Securities and Exchange Commission. When foreign governments were the sellers, their information had to describe existing indebtedness, itemize governmental receipts and expenditures, and list any defaults within the previous twenty years.

Congress also toughened its policy on war debts. Throughout the 1920s, the United States had taken a hard line, insisting on repayment while refusing to recognize that Europeans' ability to repay had any relationship to America's high tariffs or to Germany's payment of reparations. In response to the general economic collapse, Hoover in July 1931 accepted a year-long moratorium on debts; but, despite European pleas that cancellation of both reparations and war debts would serve the interests of recovery, the President rejected outright cancellation. After the moratorium expired in the summer of 1932, most countries defaulted, and Roosevelt's failure to try a cooperative approach to international economic difficulties at the London conference precluded any comprehensive solution to the war-debts problem. Angered by foreign defaults, Congress then took the initiative. In the Johnson Act of January 1934, Congress forbade private loans to any country that had defaulted on debts owed to the United States government. Realizing the Johnson Act's popular appeal, Roosevelt quietly supported the measure, though he also recognized how unpopular it was with foreign governments and with Americans who had favored international cooperation. He did manage to slip in an exception for *governmental* loans made to foreign nations so that the act would not hamstring operations of the new Export-Import Bank. The Johnson Act and Roosevelt's halting endorsement of its nationalistic approach reinforced the notions that countries too poor to pay their debts should be punished, rather than assisted in recovery, and that American lenders should go slow in their international dealings.

American policy in the first year of the New Deal, then, shaped by Roosevelt's nationalist advisers, by the President's desire to give himself maximum flexibility in international matters, and by Congress's response to nationally based special interests, was cautious toward foreign economic involvement and primarily addressed the problem of domestic recovery. Charles Beard and other advocates of nationalism or self-sufficiency applauded Roosevelt in early 1934 for his reluctance to embrace internationalist solutions. It looked as though Roosevelt might repudiate expansion and global economic integration. But nationalists mistakenly interpreted the President's actions as a reflection of his commitment to their position. In fact, however, as the historian Robert Dalleck has stressed, Roosevelt saw his early policy only as a response to short-term emergency conditions. He maintained a philosophical commitment to cooperative internationalism.

During 1934, Roosevelt began to emphasize how national security was dependent on a liberal world order that could be open to American goods, capital, and culture. More important, he began to develop new governmental mechanisms for making internationalism work. Because of the great domestic opposition to foreign entanglements, these efforts were sometimes halting; but their ultimate purpose was nonetheless clear. Under pressure from the unrelenting economic depression and the growth of Fascism's military challenge, F.D.R. devised new governmental powers to reinstate a liberal order that would supposedly benefit all nations, without some needing to pursue policies of aggressive territorial expansionism.

THE EARLY REGULATORY STATE

The international turmoil of the 1930s arose, partly at least, out of the Anglo-American economic dominance of the 1920s. During that expansionary decade, Americans rolled up favorable trade balances and, together with Britain, came to monopolize three-fourths of the world's mineral resources. At the same time, America's balance of trade and position as a World War I creditor gave United States lenders predominant control over international purse strings.

Internationalists justified Anglo-American control over minerals and investments as efficient and advantageous to all, but other, less-favored industrial countries came to believe they were entrapped as second-rate powers. During the 1930s, writers and politicians in Germany, Italy, and Japan pointed out that their countries had insufficient raw materials to maintain their industrialized economies and complained that they could not depend on purchasing raw materials from others, because the breakdown of international lending and closure of foreign markets left them short of funds. Increasingly, political groups in Germany, Italy, and Japan turned away from international liberalism toward national self-sufficiency. To shield themselves from dependence on an unstable economic order dominated by others, they sought to acquire territory that would bring them both mineral wealth and a captive market. Japan's move into Manchuria in 1931, Italy's invasion of Ethiopia in 1935, and Germany's reoccupation of the Rhineland in 1936 were all designed to achieve a more viable and self-sufficient economic base.

Anglo-American dominance gave them the economic power to choke off the strategic raw materials needed for war and thus check these early signs of aggression. But after Japan absorbed Manchuria, the League of Nations placed no economic sanctions on Japan (despite the fact that Japan's move clearly violated the Washington Treaty and the Kellogg–Briand Pact), and the League's economic restrictions against Italy omitted the most important commodity of all—petroleum. In part, the League acted weakly because economic sanctions served little purpose without

United States cooperation. And the Roosevelt Administration seemed ill-disposed to cooperate, because popular sentiment ran so strongly against involvement in foreign quarrels.

Congress balked at any Presidential effort to favor one side in a conflict. The revisionist historians of World War I and the Nye Committee's Senate hearings in 1934 had hardened beliefs that involvement in World War I had been the unfortunate result of pressures from international bankers and traders whose profits became tied to an Allied victory. In 1935, Roosevelt asked Congress to give him discretionary power to embargo war supplies to belligerents; he wanted to be able to deny arms to an aggressor while supplying them to a victim. But Congress refused. F.D.R.'s congressional critics charged that the grant of such authority would allow the President, at his own discretion, to act in harmony with members of the League of Nations and to become allied with one side in a foreign war. Roosevelt accepted, instead, Congress's Neutrality Act of 1935. Rather than giving the Executive discretionary power over commerce, the Neutrality Act specifically mandated an absolute embargo on the sale of munitions to all belligerents in a war. A few months later, Congress went further and forbade the purchase of securities issued by belligerent nations and created a new National Munitions Control Board to license all peacetime trade in "arms, ammunition, or implements of war." This neutrality legislation, passed during the Italian invasion of Ethiopia, seemed primarily concerned with barring practices that, in the name of neutral rights, had led America into a war to support the Allies in 1917.

After World War II, internationalists faulted Roosevelt for not fighting harder for economic sanctions to choke off aggression in its early stages. Yet the reluctance to jump conspicuously into economic warfare in the mid-1930s did not mean that Roosevelt employed no economic diplomacy in an effort to ameliorate international problems. Roosevelt, in fact, was increasingly listening to internationalist advisers such as Cordell Hull, who believed that if the machinery of world trade was lubricated, Germany, Italy, and Japan could once again make up their deficiencies through purchase rather than conquest. Roosevelt came to believe that measures to restore international prosperity would alleviate pressures for aggressive acts more effectively than isolating the aggressors economically. Economic weakness was, after all, the problem; the wisdom of further aggravating the deprivation was not at all clear, even from an internationalist point of view.

Roosevelt tackled the problem of international disorder by using economic measures that, unlike an embargo, did not attract the public spotlight. With surprisingly little public notice, he widened the Executive's authority over international economic policy and gradually accumulated substantial power to parcel out economic rewards and punishments. From 1934 on, the economic foreign policy of the New Deal—trying to reestablish an open, liberalized order without controversial entanglements—embraced two goals: trade liberalization through tariff policy, and an increase of discretionary power over loans and trade that could be exercised by the Executive largely outside the control of Congress.

In 1934, the President clearly endorsed Secretary Hull's beliefs and began to work seriously on Hull's dream of trade reform, producing what became the Trade Agreements Act of 1934. In stating his new internationalist approach to peace and prosperity, Roosevelt announced that his goal was to create a more equitable world order by seeking to restore "commerce in ways which will preclude the building up of large favorable trade balances by any one nation at the expense of trade debits on the part of other nations." Hull's assistant in the State Department was Francis Sayre, a law professor from Harvard and Woodrow Wilson's son-in-law. In elaborating the philosophy behind the Trade Agreements Act, Sayre offered this archinternationalist analysis of the Depression:

> One of the important underlying causes of the existing financial difficulties which are so grievously delaying the return of prosperity is the failure of international trade, due to its diminished proportions, to offer a sufficiently broad base to support the volume of international debts and credits and thus to stabilize the financial situation of the various countries. Without an increased international trade it is difficult to see how to meet the problems of international finance which press in on every side.

The Trade Agreements Act of 1934 gave the President authority to raise or lower existing tariff rates by as much as 50 percent. Tariffs would be lowered against the products of nations that granted American goods reciprocal concessions, and because of America's adherence to most-favored-nation treatment, the reductions given to one government would then extend to all except those that continued to discriminate against American commerce. Countries that did not grant most-favored-nation status to Americans could still, under the 1922 tariff law, be penalized by an increase of 50 percent. The act had two purposes: to contribute to a general lowering of tariff and to effect the spread of the most-favored-nation doctrine of equal access. It represented a victory for the internationalists, who had long favored both equal access and freer trade, and a major setback for the business nationalists, who had always tried to merge equal access with protectionism. Reflecting the nationalists' anger, George Peek excoriated Roosevelt for becoming a tool of the Carnegie Endowment, the World Peace Foundation, and other pro-League, internationalist groups and soon resigned from the Administration. He charged F.D.R. and Hull with adopting trade policies that, in Peek's words, were "un-American" and "Internationalism Gone Wild."

Cuba became the first country to benefit from a reciprocal trade agreement under the new law. But, since tariff agreements with Cuba had been specifically exempted from most-favored-nation generalization, this was a special case. Lower duties on Cuban sugar would apply exclusively to Cuba, without automatically being accorded to others under the most-favored-nation policy. Such exemption obviously preserved markets in the United States for Cuban growers, most of whom were American investors. The special situation of Cuba meant that reciprocal lowering of duties with Cuba was more easily agreed upon, because reductions did not raise complications over their extension to others.

There were also pressing political reasons for rapidly lowering duties on Cuban sugar. In 1933, Cuban reformers had unseated the long-time dictator Gerardo Machado and established a government that American landowners in Cuba feared might embark on a program of agrarian reform. Roosevelt refused to send American marines to ward off the threat, but he made it clear that a trade agreement placing lower duties on sugar would not be negotiated with the existing government. He also promised Cuban army leaders, notably Fulgencio Batista, that the United States would support a coup against the reformist government and reward its leaders with a trade agreement that would bolster Cuba's depressed economy. After the coup, Roosevelt not only signed the trade agreement with Batista but also formally abrogated the Platt Amendment of 1902, the hated clause that had turned Cuba into a U.S. protectorate after the Spanish-American War. These actions made Batista appear to be an ardent nationalist, the hero who ended Cuba's demeaning status as a protectorate and alleviated its economic depression. The case of Cuba illustrated the great power that control of tariff duties could bring to the American Executive.

Elsewhere, however, Executive authority under the Trade Agreements Act of 1934 never became the formidable force in diplomacy or recovery that Hull and other champions had sought. Since each reduction had to apply to every other country, except those specifically under penalty for discrimination against American goods, the writing of reciprocal trade agreements became an intricate task. Instead of cutting through the tangle of trade and tariff policies to make trade less complicated, the Trade Agreements Act itself got lost in the morass. Although the Roosevelt Administration eventually signed agreements with eighteen governments, it found these of little help in boosting the overall volume of international trade.

The significance of the Trade Agreements Act of 1934 was less its impact on economic recovery than the fact that it made tariff negotiations a more direct tool of Executive diplomacy and that it made the U.S., for the first time, an advocate of both equal access and freer trade. In an article in *Foreign Affairs,* Henry F. Grady lauded the 1934 act: "This new policy is of an importance that can hardly be exaggerated. We are to a greater degree than ever before meshing our domestic economy into the world economy." The economic internationalists were in the ascendancy.

Roosevelt embraced Hull's internationalism, but he still threw some crumbs to the nationalists, who favored protection from the world market. He instituted a system of import quotas for certain products (wine and sugar, for example) to protect domestic suppliers against foreign dumping. Resorting to quotas involved certain ironies. United States policymakers had for years opposed import quotas as unnatural barriers to trade; they had, for instance, issued strong diplomatic protests over motion-picture quotas in the late 1920s. In addition, domestic critics charged that Roosevelt's policies worked at cross-purposes: he tried to stimulate trade through the Trade Agreements Act while he simultaneously restricted it through quotas. As usual, Roosevelt was trying to play on both sides of the fence. Like the Trade Act, however, quotas again increased the power of the executive branch to punish or reward.

As the Roosevelt Administration sought to lower tariff barriers, it also attacked another obstacle to restoring international trade—lack of money for purchasing. In peacetime, Americans had always relied completely on the private banking community to finance export trade. Except during World War I and for a year afterward, when the War Finance Corporation (WFC) lent funds to war-related industries to finance their exports, government itself had no lending authority. The Depression, however, showed the inadequacy of this arrangement. Private capital withdrew at precisely the time when trade most needed to be encouraged. Borrowing from the pattern of the WFC, President Hoover had created the Reconstruction Finance Corporation (RFC) just before he left office in 1932. The RFC's primary function was to provide investment capital to spur industrial recovery at home, but Congress also stipulated that it could make loans to finance the sale of surplus agricultural crops abroad. The RFC subsequently financed small agricultural sales to China and to the Soviet Union.

The RFC, however, proved inadequate. In 1933, the Russian commissar for foreign affairs announced that Russia, which was not suffering a depression, might place $1 billion worth of orders in the West. A few months later, the Roosevelt Administration granted diplomatic recognition to the Soviet regime, hoping that trade would increase and that the Soviet Union, after years of going it alone, would gradually become integrated into the Western economic structure. Excited by the new prospects for trade, American businesses deluged the RFC with applications for financing exports to the Soviet Union. In response, Roosevelt decided to create a new agency—the first Export-Import Bank—to handle all the requests.

From the beginning, officials of the Export-Import Bank realized that loans could accomplish diplomatic, as well as economic, purposes. They made it clear to the Soviets that loans to finance Soviet purchases of American products were tied to settlement of other grievances. To obtain American credits, the Soviets would have to pay their outstanding World War I debts (something no other European nation had done), pay American claims against damage inflicted during the Bolshevik takeover, and agree to respect American property rights in the future. Disliking the coercive nature of the loan proposal, the Soviet government refused to consummate the deal. Trade with the Soviet Union remained at an exceedingly low level.

A second Export-Import Bank was then established to lend to Cuba and other countries. It subsequently became a permanent institution. Again, the political overtones of lending became apparent; in numerous instances, loans were tied to a variety of diplomatic objectives. The United States government withheld credits to Cuba (just as it had delayed lowering sugar duties in 1934), as long as a government that threatened American landholdings remained in power. Only after the friendly Batista government seized control of Cuba did the bank extend loans to stabilize the island's economy. Loans to Italy for cotton purchases were refused in 1935, during the Italian invasion of Ethiopia. In several Latin-American countries, especially ex-protectorates, retention of an American financial adviser became a precondition for a loan. Thus, although formal financial supervision of protectorates in the Caribbean was phased out during the 1930s as part of the good-neighbor policy, American financial advisers were often reappointed as part of a financial negotiation. Loans to Latin-American countries were also occasionally refused until the governments reached an agreement with America's Foreign Bondholders Protective Council (FBPC), a private group formed with State Department encouragement to represent Americans demanding repayment of defaulted foreign debts. In the late 1930s, the Export-Import Bank made it clear to Bolivia and Mexico that no credits would become available until the controversies over the nationalization of American oil companies were settled. Credits were similarly denied to a popular-front government in Chile in 1939 because of its left-nationalistic stance toward foreign enterprise; after this government's demise, the flow of American credit resumed.

The Export-Import Bank's role in the growing international crisis became especially clear in the case of China. After Japan had consolidated its hold over Manchuria, it turned toward China. China, for its part, attempted to secure a loan from the Export-

Import Bank, but Roosevelt blocked the transaction. The President still hoped that a general world economic recovery would relax expansionist pressures in Japan, and he wished to avoid the impression that he was taking extraordinary measures to capture the China trade, for fear that such an act might inflame the militants in the Japanese government and anger British banking interests. Not until late 1938, after Japan had carried on full-scale warfare with China for over a year and had declared its "new order" in Asia—essentially a restricted sphere of Japanese influence—did the Roosevelt Administration finally extend credits to China. Although more loans followed, much of the money being used to purchase war supplies (contrary to formal contract stipulations), the Chinese could not mount an effective resistance against the Japanese. Still, the decision to extend loans to China in 1938 carried a political message: the United States was switching its policy from economic conciliation of Japan and toward imposition of economic punishments.

The Export-Import Bank, then, institutionalized government-sponsored foreign lending. Initially, the bank represented such a small step away from the normal functions of a promotional state that few people found it objectionable. Like its predecessors, the WFC and the RFC, it seemed simply to provide a needed service to exporters, especially to agricultural interests. George Peek, the ardent anti-internationalist, was Ex-Im's first president. Quickly, however, the bank became involved in the broader game of diplomacy. Through the bank, the Roosevelt Administration could deal out punishments and rewards, depending on political judgments. After 1938, the bank broadened the scope of its lending activities far beyond financing exports. It granted credits to friendly governments to support their foreign-exchange and development programs, and it financed more rapid expansion of the communications networks owned by ITT and RCA.

What Congress had approved as a nationalistic trade-promotion measure thus turned into an executive-branch weapon for economic warfare that Congress, through its neutrality legislation, had tried to avoid. Noting the bank's changing nature, Republicans and isolationists increasingly criticized its operations and tried to limit its funding. But in 1940, after the fall of France to German troops, with the growing fear of Nazi influence in Latin America and with the Japanese in control of large portions of China, Roosevelt beat back the bank's opponents and got Congress to triple its lending authority. The Export-Import Bank proved so useful in the conduct of diplomacy that policymakers overcame earlier qualms and, after World War II, would create many additional government lending agencies.

During the 1930s, the Treasury Department also acquired important new powers for conducting economic diplomacy. Under the Gold Reserve Act of 1934, Congress created a Stabilization Fund under the control of the Secretary of Treasury. Its purpose was to deal in foreign exchange and gold in such a way as to counteract adverse fluctuations in world currency markets. At its inception, the Stabilization Fund reflected the early nationalistic approach of the New Deal; it carried out an extensive gold-buying program designed to inflate the value of the dollar and thus undervalue American exports in world markets. By 1936, however, the nationalistic, emergency phase of the New Deal had ended, and Secretary of Treasury Henry Morgenthau made a Tripartite Agreement with Britain and France (later expanded to include many other nations) to coordinate policies to regularize the entire system of international exchange and avoid further competitive depreciation of currency. The Stabilization Fund thus became a vehicle by which the executive branch, at its discretion, could coordinate monetary policy with other nations and try to regulate the international economy, a function performed in the 1920s by private bankers, particularly Benjamin Strong of the FRBNY.

Moreover (like the FRBNY in the 1920s and anticipating the philosophy of the later International Monetary Fund), the fund also had the power to grant loans to foreign governments wishing to stabilize their currencies. Morgenthau worked on several such agreements, but this expansion of Treasury Department interest in foreign affairs met strong opposition in the State Department. Secretary of State Hull considered trade agreements, not new lending powers, the key to recovery and fought Morgenthau's efforts to enlarge government lending. In late 1939, Assistant Secretary of Treasury Harry Dexter White, for example, called for creation of an inter-American bank to stabilize Latin-American economies and secure them against Axis influence. The proposal, like other similar Treasury plans, was stopped by opposition in the State

Department, whose personnel continued to fear the diplomatic implications of such direct, large-scale financial entanglement. Default on private loans was causing enough diplomatic difficulty; if the government were directly involved as the creditor, collection of debts could become an even greater problem for diplomats. Despite Hull's displeasure, however, Morgenthau did extend stabilization loans to many individual countries, although some were postponed until the State Department was satisfied at least that an agreement had first been reached between the foreign government and the FBPC over repayment of private debts.

The Secretary of the Treasury acquired even broader powers over economic foreign policy by reviving an old World War I statute, the Trading with the Enemy Act of 1917. A clause in this act that gave the President power to regulate foreign exchange, it was discovered, had not been specifically restricted to wartime; nor had it been repealed after the war. On the authority of this old statute, Roosevelt declared his famous banking holiday of 1933, and Congress subsequently passed a Banking Act of 1933 that specifically authorized the Executive to use these Trading-with-the-Enemy-Act powers "during time of war or during *any other period of national emergency* declared by the President" (italics mine). Through this broad grant of power, Roosevelt issued controls over foreign-exchange transactions in 1933, controls that remained in effect for about a year. In April 1940, implementing "measures short of war" against the Axis, he again invoked this authority to freeze any transfers of funds to countries under German control and, later, to European neutrals as well. In July 1941, the freeze on assets was extended to Japan. Given the blanket nature of the 1933 congressional delegation of power, all these Executive actions of economic warfare could be taken without further congressional authorization.

In view of the strong domestic opposition to foreign involvement, then, the Roosevelt Administration avoided military entanglements, binding political alliances, and conspicuous trade embargoes during the 1930s. Instead, it developed new tools of economic diplomacy, many of which either evolved outside the realm of congressional authority (by Executive order) or were based on existing legislation that delegated power to the President. The Trade Agreements Act, the Export-Import Bank, and the new powers assumed by the Treasury Department all represented significant new commitments by government to restoration of a stable international system in which American trade and investment could flourish. The days of the full-fledged regulatory state would not come until wartime and postwar agreements to establish a World Bank, an International Monetary Fund, and a General Agreement on Trade and Tariffs, but the Roosevelt Administration, even before the war, had taken long strides toward replacing the private approach of the 1920s with government-directed regulatory mechanisms.

From late 1939 on, Roosevelt also gradually wrenched from Congress greater control over trade. Trade during the mid-1930s had been the one major field in which Congress had warily circumscribed Presidential authority. Congress's journey away from strict noninvolvement toward increasing support for the Allies closely paralleled the growing gravity of the international crisis. Japan controlled a client government in China and looked toward Southeast Asia, an area rich in raw materials. Germany annexed Austria, then took Czechoslovakia, and in September 1939 invaded Poland, an action that prompted Britain and France to declare war. Only a few months later, Nazi armies swept across Western Europe. After the fall of France in July 1940, Roosevelt, and probably most other Americans, supported a campaign to offer large-scale aid to the Allies and to prepare America for war. In response, throughout 1939 and 1940, Congress gradually strengthened the President's power to exert economic sanctions through trade. In late 1939, Congress modified the neutrality act to permit belligerents to purchase arms on a cash-and-carry basis. The action helped Great Britain against Germany, but unfortunately it worked the opposite way in the Pacific, where Japan—not China—had shipping capabilities. F.D.R. thus supplemented cash-and-carry with a voluntary "moral embargo" on airplane parts and some vital materials to Japan. In July 1939, Congress finally authorized the President to curtail exports of military equipment and raw materials to Japan, although this action was justified primarily as a way to conserve scarce strategic commodities for national use, rather than as an instrument of economic pressure. Materials that were plentiful in the United States—copper, petroleum, nickel, cobalt, and others—were thus not included. Gradually, however, more and more commodities were added to the proscribed list, until finally, in July 1941, the most important one of all—oil—was cut off.

In 1941, the President persuaded Congress to pass the Lend-Lease Act, allowing the United States to sell, lend, or lease any article to any country whose defense the President considered vital to national security. He also instituted total export control, requiring government licenses for all foreign trade, and he banned trade with the Axis powers. A blacklist against German firms operating in Latin America was drawn up by the Office of Inter-American Affairs (OIAA), headed by Nelson Rockefeller. Rockefeller not only asked American firms to halt business dealings with Nazi-tinged enterprises in Latin America but also requested that they fire any employee that sympathized with the Axis. These tight trade controls, as they had in World War I, substantially harmed America's German competitors worldwide and provided the executive branch with substantial new economic leverage for use in a variety of diplomatic controversies, whether war-related or not.

Congress also authorized the Executive to take a direct role in insuring American supplies of strategic raw materials and in denying them to Axis nations. In World War I, the government had given little advance thought to raw-material needs. By contrast, special legislation was passed in June 1940 to allow the RFC to create government-owned corporations to produce or acquire strategic materials. Stockpiling thus began well before Pearl Harbor (though many critics still complained that Roosevelt stockpiled too little, too late). The United States Commercial Company, a government-owned corporation, began buying up commodities, especially in areas close to Nazi Germany—Spain, Portugal, and Turkey. Other public corporations such as the Petroleum Reserve Corporation, the Rubber Reserve Corporation, and the Metal Reserve Corporation all became major purchasers of raw materials. And where production of a commodity was not deemed adequate to meet war needs, RFC corporations actually undertook to explore, mine, and transport the commodity. To safeguard supplies within the Western Hemisphere and to cut off Axis purchases, the RFC in 1941 also entered into agreements with many Latin-American nations, promising to buy their exports at high, stable prices in return for their promise not to sell to nations outside the hemisphere. These accords accumulated needed materials under United

States control, denied them to Germany, and helped stabilize Latin-American economies.

By the time the United States entered the war, then, the President had already acquired a full range of controls over foreign economic affairs. The new executive-branch powers constituted a genuine revolution in economic foreign policy and provided the psychological and, to some extent, the statutory bases for a postwar regulatory state that was markedly different from the cooperative state that had followed World War I.

New powers over economic foreign policy, together with the crisis of war, also transformed the business community, rapidly accelerating its consolidation and contributing to greater international expansion. Shortly before World War II, many Americans had grown suspicious of internationalized businesses, because their far-flung operations made their national loyalties ambiguous. Senate committees of the early 1940s—especially the Kilgore Committee on War Mobilization and James Murray's Committee on Small Business Enterprise—assailed participation by American firms in international cartels. Much of the testimony before these committees charged that internationalized control over strategic materials endangered national security and that American firms had conspired in the rearming of Germany. In antitrust actions of the early 1940s, the Justice Department argued that the international cartel arrangements so common in the 1930s prevented free competition, stifled smaller domestic enterprise, and artificially raised prices.

But as the war united them in patriotic purpose, the tension between the New Dealers and the international business community eased. Businessmen staffed the new wartime agencies, and government bureaucrats, charged with winning the war, found it simpler to deal with large corporations than with numerous small entrepreneurs. Large businesses commanded the financial and the engineering skills to undertake technologically difficult projects; similarly, they possessed the facilities quickly to produce and deliver massive war orders. Government also came to rely on American-based international companies to procure the overseas raw materials needed for the war, and government funds assisted the rapid expansion of many raw-materials companies. Concern for wartime efficiency and a global raw-materials base overrode fears about postwar corporate monopoly. The boost given to industrial concentration during the war was tremendous: in 1940, the nation's top hundred companies produced 30 percent of America's manufacturing output; by 1943, the top hundred were filling 70 percent of all war and civilian contracts.

A few members of Congress—led by Representative Wright Patman of Texas, Senator James Murray of Montana, and Senator Robert Taft of Ohio—tried to formulate a government policy that would favor smaller enterprises. They created a Smaller War Plants Corporation to help smaller businesses attract defense contracts, but the effort largely failed. They also advocated new techniques to produce domestic substitutes for scarce resources obtained overseas. They correctly saw that a global resource strategy, however efficient in terms of the liberal economic law of comparative advantage, would leave the country dependent on multinational cartels after the war and would ultimately discourage the kind of technological innovation that could enable Americans to live on their own domestic resources. Secretary of the Interior Harold Ickes testified sympathetically before Murray's committee. "It may be that if we freed technology from the restrictions of interlocking corporate control and the ideology of monopoly, we would reap a harvest of new, highly efficient and self-contained medium- and small-sized operations." But Ickes's warnings that the interests of international corporations might not always coincide with the good of the nation did not prevail.

Wartime expediency buried the distrust of international businesses. When the Justice Department's Antitrust Division began investigating and revealing antitrust violations by Standard Oil, American Lead, and other companies involved in wartime procurement, Secretary of War Henry L. Stimson and others persuaded Roosevelt to order a grant of immunity for defense-related businesses. "We believe," Roosevelt's subsequent directive read, "that continuing such prosecutions at this time will be contrary to the national interest and security."

Moreover, although the government established and ran a few RFC corporations during the war, Roosevelt refused to embark on any long-term program of national ownership over strategic supplies. Public corporations, it was clear, were simply a wartime expedient to supplement, not supplant, private operations. Secretary of Interior Ickes wanted to extend the regulatory state to include public ownership over certain strategic supplies. In particular, he proposed creation of a United States government-owned oil company to develop petroleum in Saudi Arabia. He again argued that international cartels—even if dominated by Americans —might not always serve the national interest; more important, he felt that a government company could better ensure Americans' access to Saudi supplies. Private American oil companies, however, heatedly opposed the plan, and under their pressure the idea was finally dropped. The government did not continue in the postwar period its wartime practice of using government corporations to develop foreign strategic supplies. In fact, it sold to the private sector at extremely low prices most of the holdings that RFC corporations had developed during the war at public expense. After the war, policymakers energetically supported the continued internationalization of American "free" private enterprise. "In fact," the historian John Morton Blum has written, the term "free private enterprise was translated while the war went on to mean immunity for business from federal efforts to free the market from the controls that business had conspired to impose upon it."

THE POSTWAR REGULATORY APPARATUS

Roosevelt's assumptions about the postwar world differed strikingly from those of Woodrow Wilson. Wilson believed that the progressive force of history, embodied in a League of Nations, would usher in a world order safe for the spread of American influence. He greatly extended the structure of the promotional state but never allowed it to take over functions he saw as being proper to the private sector. Tightly bound by the canons of nineteenth-century liberalism, he declined to press for direct, large-scale governmental involvement in the postwar international economy. The policymakers of the Second World War, in contrast, planned to maximize rather than minimize the role of government in the postwar world. They, too, favored an international political structure based on collective security, like the League of Nations; but, more important, they sought to create international economic and cultural institutions that were directly subject to government, especially to the executive branch.

Of course, there was no single "American view," even within the executive branch, on international economic issues. Disciples of Hull such as Francis Sayre and Henry Grady continued to stress free, nondiscriminatory trading practices as the key to a healthy international order. Those in the Treasury Department emphasized loans and monetary arrangements. Henry Wallace, who had become Vice-President, advocated a global version of the early New Deal, with vast public-works projects modeled on the Tennessee Valley Authority and concerted programs to build international highways and airways. These differences in emphasis accompanied bureaucratic power plays and created considerable confusion about America's postwar direction. But although the approaches differed, all saw vigorous United States economic expansionism—this time regulated by government rather than solely by private chosen instruments—as the ultimate goal. And all, to some extent at least, drew similar historical lessons from the experiences of the 1930s.

Greatly simplified, these lessons may be summarized: a purely private structure of foreign lending is unable to correct cyclical international depressions; excessive protectionism and other trade barriers are detriments to international prosperity; the lack of a consistent international standard of exchange and unregulated fluctuation of exchange rates impede international prosperity; international economic instability contributes to political extremism and disorder; aggression must be punished in its early stages through the collective action of an international body or through adequate, ever-ready military forces. All these lessons pointed to the creation of a more integrated, liberalized, and regulated world system, one which could presumably offer prosperity to those who cooperated and punishment to any who remained outside and who tried to create a restricted sphere of influence.

These lessons were not the only ones that might have been learned from the interwar years. Charles Beard and the economic nationalists believed that the instabilities of the 1930s stemmed not from the deficiencies of America's global involvement during the 1920s but from an excessive expansionism that had monopolized resources and capital and created an inequitable—and thus an unstable—international order. The internationalists argued that the United States should increase its economic regulatory power and military shield in order to protect a national interest that was clearly global in scope. The nationalists, or "isolationists," believed that the United States should retract its far-flung economic interests and repudiate globalism, expansionism, and militarism.

The nationalist critique of globalism, which had garnered considerable support in the 1930s, faded during the war and was almost completely discredited in the postwar period. Some of its adherents, especially Charles Beard, lost credibility because of their opposition to World War II. Others linked their nationalism so closely to a special interest or region that theirs really became just single-issue lobbying efforts. Other opponents of internationalism suffered from blatant xenophobia; their nationalism was a form of racism, more than a thoughtful repudiation of expansion. Finally, the crusading anti-Communism of the cold war helped discredit those who opposed internationalist policies. Architects of the regulatory state presented government's new, expansionist role not as a violation of American liberalism but as the only way to preserve America's traditions from a growing Communist threat. The regulatory apparatus within what Daniel Yergin has appropriately termed the postwar "national security state" both sprang from and intensified the cold war. A Soviet sphere of influence, after all, directly menaced the integrated world system propounded by the United States. The ideas of nationalism and self-sufficiency ultimately became the property of ultraconservative, fringe politicians. The postwar opponents of internationalism in Congress increasingly tended to oppose an international economic role for the United States government (foreign aid, loans, and participation in international economic institutions) while they supported both expansion in the private sector and an enlarged military shield; thus even those deemed "isolationists" after the war were often expansionists rather than nationalists in the older Beardian tradition.

As those who opposed expansion and remained suspicious of new executive-branch powers lost influence, the architects of the postwar world order gained considerable latitude to shape their new regulatory state according to their own "lessons" of the past. Through this new structure, developed in the five years after 1944, the United States government planned to stabilize the international environment by interventionary powers; government would operate in the international economy in much the same way that the New Deal government sought to regulate domestic prosperity. The executive branch continued to use its substantial discretionary authority over commerce (for example, to license trade with Communist nations). The United States participated in the International Monetary Fund (IMF), established on American initiative in 1944, to regulate exchange rates, bring nations back onto a common currency standard, and oversee rehabilitation of weak economies. The American government likewise pushed acceptance of a General Agreement on Trade and Tariffs (1947) to moderate trade barriers and insure equal access (most-favored-nation treatment). Congress refused to ratify establishment of an International Trade Organization (ITO), the institution that was to administer the GATT, but the State Department provided funds for it anyway, hiding the request in its departmental budget for international conferences. Although the government still encouraged private investment abroad—particularly in raw materials—to recycle America's postwar wealth to potential customers of American exports, private capital was slow to go abroad after the defaults of the 1930s. Therefore, the government itself directed large-scale foreign loans. The Export-Import Bank was further enlarged and new institutions were created, such as the State Department's Agency for International Development (AID) and more specific programs such as the Truman Doctrine (to Greece and Turkey), the Marshall Plan (to Europe), and Point Four (to less developed nations). The government also helped establish an international lending institution, the International Bank for Reconstruction and Development (later called the World Bank). Although the new bank was theoretically a multinational institution, the greatest amount of its capital and its director came from the United States. The government also created a variety of agencies to send technical, economic, agricultural, or military missions into foreign lands.

Besides these new agencies, the United States helped found the United Nations and its associated bodies; institutionalized scientific research within the federal government (a new extension of the promotional state); created a permanent, peacetime intelligence agency to protect its new global interests; and entrenched a large, peacetime military establishment, one with a strong commitment to contingency planning and military readiness.

All of these new powers contrasted with the policies of the 1920s, but the government's new role in the international economy raised the greatest doubts. In a hearing before the Senate Committee on

Banking and Currency in 1945, Senator William Fulbright questioned whether the Bretton Woods agreements of 1944, which created the International Monetary Fund and the International Bank for Reconstruction and Development, could really remain separate from political entanglements, as the President claimed they would. Secretary of Treasury Morgenthau replied: "These are to be financial institutions run by financial people, financial experts, and the needs in a financial way of a country are to be taken care of wholly independent of political connection . . . " Of course, as Richard Gardner, the preeminent historian of the postwar international economic accords, wrote, "The impracticality of this idea . . . should have been apparent to anyone experienced in the conduct of international affairs." Yet the executive branch continued to sell an international economic role as a purely technical necessity, one without political implications.

Despite disclaimers that economics had no political content, the United States tried to use its strong postwar economic position, manifested in these new powers and agencies, to force countries to accept the policies of liberal-developmentalism: equal and open access for trade and investment and an emphasis on private, rather than public, ownership. A memo of the International Trade Policy Division of the State Department in October 1945 stated: "If we tickle the palms of the foreigners with a few billions," they would conduct "their international economic affairs according to the pattern we advocate." Wartime assistance and postwar loans helped open the Middle East, a traditionally British zone of influence, to a rapidly growing American economic presence. In relations with the Soviet Union, the Administration of Harry S Truman tried unsuccessfully to tie offers of economic assistance to Soviet acceptance of economic liberalization, particularly in the Eastern European areas its armies dominated. As the price of continued lend-lease aid, the United States extracted promises from Britain to abandon the preferential trading practices it had developed in the 1930s and to accept greater American economic access to the British empire. Then in 1946, by using the promise of an American loan, the United States forced Britain to stabilize the value of its currency and return to the gold standard. Despite reservations about such policies, British leaders went along. "We weren't in a position to bargain," said Prime Minister Clement Attlee. "We had to have the loan." The British economy went into a severe tailspin until this requirement was relaxed.

Latin Americans were also pressured into following liberal economic policies. In the midst of the war, the United States had wooed Latin Americans with promises of the two economic commitments most vital to their prosperity: large-scale loans to enable them to diversify their development and become more self-sufficient, and commodity agreements to stabilize prices on the primary products they exported. After the war, however, the United States delayed convening a hemispheric conference at which they feared Latin Americans would form a united front to press these demands. Instead, the United States urged Latin-American governments individually to accept different economic priorities, especially free-market trade practices (instead of commodity agreements) and encouragement of private foreign enterprise and investment (instead of significant governmental loans that Latin Americans could have used to stimulate native-owned businesses and national economic planning).

By formulating Latin America's developmental needs in this way, the United States pitted itself against an alternative pattern that was becoming increasingly attractive to nonindustrialized countries. This pattern, which the United States viewed with hostility, involved foreign aid and technical cooperation, but with local (not American) control; stabilized prices for primary exports, so that economic planning could be more reliable and prices would not deteriorate in relation to the costs of the industrial goods that had to be imported; mixed economies with state-directed enterprises; and the possibility of compensated nationalization of key resources. The United States—guided by policymakers such as William L. Clayton, Assistant Secretary of State for Economic Affairs but formerly of the large Texas-based multinational Anderson–Clayton (one of the largest dealers in Latin America's primary commodities)—not only refused to discuss seriously these proposals but threatened economic retaliation against governments that would not cooperate. Despite its rhetorical endorsement, during the war, of "developing" nonindustrialized nations, then, the American government expected them to welcome foreign private capital with minimal government restriction and to continue to supply raw materials and primary commodities needed by the industrialized world. By following policies promoting free trade and unrestricted foreign private investment, Latin-American economies would continue to be shaped primarily by United States economic needs.

The new powers of the regulatory state and its new capabilities for conducting economic diplomacy were an astonishing departure from the ingrained traditions of limited government and nonentanglement in foreign affairs. Yet government's new role in stabilizing the international economic environment could also be seen as the ultimate extension of the promotional state; it assisted private expansion in every possible way by ensuring that there would be open access for investment, customers for the export trade, and imported raw materials for industry. And none of these powers usurped the normal functions of private corporations; as in the past, those businesses that performed functions deemed especially crucial to national interest were accorded chosen-instrument status. The government's older policy of carrying out economic foreign policy through the private sector continued, especially in the areas of raw materials and international air transportation.

Underlying postwar raw-materials policies was the acute realization that domestic prosperity depended heavily on a stable and open international order. This proposition gained special attention after publication in 1942 of Yale professor Nicholas Spykman's influential geopolitical views. America faced a desperate economic plight, Spykman maintained, if hostile nations succeeded in closing access to significant areas of the world, especially Southeast Asia. America's own continued abundance and wealth, he suggested, was clearly linked to a global predominance that could ensure access to supplies needed by the American economy.

Yet, true to the developmental faiths that Americans had long held, a world open to American access was also supposed to bring prosperity to all. Charles Leith still pressed the argument that a liberal order would be an "efficient" one and that specialization by each part of the world economy would bring rising prosperity for everyone. During World War II, Leith advised both the War Production Board and the State Department. In 1945, he prepared a major memorandum for the State Department, advising, as he had during World War I and throughout the 1920s, against stimulating high-cost domestic production and favoring governmental stockpiling of foreign supplies. America's purchases of raw materials in the postwar world, he recommended, would be one way of recycling capital back into the world system, providing foreigners with the means to pay for American exports and to repay the loans extended for reconstruction or development. Though Congress never passed as extravagant a program of government stockpiling as Leith advocated, it did certainly embrace a "cheap" resource strategy, one to encourage American companies to expand mineral production overseas as part of a global program to ensure America's strategic material base, provide other nations with capital, and restore prosperity worldwide.

Many of government's new powers helped American companies pursue a global strategy. The Export-Import Bank, the International Bank for Reconstruction and Development, and later both the Marshall Plan and Point Four were designed, in part, to open new areas to United States mineral exploration. Marshall Plan legislation stipulated open-door treatment for American firms, and Point Four included surveys by the United States Geological Survey and the Bureau of Mines to identify new mineral deposits overseas. "Washington seized on the idea of encouraging American investment in foreign mining ventures," wrote Alfred Eckes, "not because domestic firms lacked profitable opportunities at home, but because government officials saw an opportunity to achieve an American presence in high-grade foreign deposits which would confer long-range advantage to the United States and provide some repayment for the costs of rehabilitating Europe." In addition, in 1948, the National Security Council approved a plan authorizing the new Central Intelligence Agency (CIA) to help protect American privately owned facilities abroad that dealt with strategic commodities. In the postwar period, the CIA worked to protect copper mines in Chile, oil refineries in Indonesia, the Middle East, and the Caribbean, and cobalt companies in the Congo.

The government especially encouraged the expansion of the oil companies. The promise of postwar governmental loans in the Middle East helped American oil companies obtain rights in Saudi Arabia, and the United States surpassed Great Britain as the predominant owner of oil reserves in the Middle East. By 1945, said one State Department report, Saudi Arabia was "in a fair way to becoming an American frontier." President Truman, just before he left office in 1953, quashed a major antitrust action charging the international oil companies with setting prices and dividing markets. Truman claimed that bad publicity for large capitalists would play into the hands of Communists and that attacking the oil trust would ultimately weaken America's hold on all global resources. The new Eisenhower Administration agreed. The President's Special Assistant wrote Secretary of State John Foster Dulles (whose former law firm was acting as defense counsel for the oil companies) that "the enforcement of the Antitrust laws of the United States against the Western oil companies operating in the Near East may be deemed secondary to the national security interest . . . " As during the 1920s, the American government adopted free-market rhetoric but both tolerated and encouraged American-dominated cartels.

International air transportation was another important sector that continued to have chosen-instrument status. The role of Pan American Airways, however, changed somewhat as the special relationship between Pan Am and the United States government began to break down after 1935. In that year, a Senate investigation of airline subsidies resulted in a revised procedure for competitive bidding among carriers for the overseas-mail subsidies that had underwritten much of Pan Am's international expansion. Pan American's mail contracts were not cancelled but they could no longer be taken for granted, and the new Civil Aeronautics Board, created in 1938, sharply reduced contract rates. (For example, the subsidy for Pan American's Latin-American division was cut by 74 percent.) And as Juan Terry Trippe fought to maintain his company's subsidies (at one point he even suggested that Pan American become a regulated monopoly like the telephone company and offered to sell the government 49 percent of the airline's stock), Roosevelt delivered another blow. He decided to make international air service and landing rights the subject of diplomatic conference on a governmental level, rather than to allow these negotiations to remain wholly in the private sector. The Roosevelt Administration began a long battle to get Trippe to conduct his negotiations with foreign governments through the State Department and in accord with State Department policy.

The government cut Pan American's revenue and tore away some of its exclusive privileges, but the war, beginning in 1939, gave an enormous boost to the airline's profits and power. British, French, and German airways reduced service worldwide and Pan American was left nearly alone in the field. Strategic measures to prepare America for war also assisted Pan American. In 1941 the United States government blacklisted the many German-controlled "national" airlines in Latin America and an RFC-created corporation set aside $8 million to help Latin Americans take over German interests. With the subsequent collapse and conversion of the German-affiliated network, Pan American again had a near-monopoly on air transport in Latin America and business boomed despite diminished subsidy. Pan American also contracted with the War Department to construct or improve airports worldwide. The airline ultimately devoted 60 percent of its greatly expanded facilities to the war; its wartime service helped blur the distinction between commercial and strategic advantage and further convinced Americans that a strong commercial aviation industry served a potentially vital strategic function.

During the war, American aviation became dominant overseas. As part of the lend-lease agreement between the United States and Great Britain, America built almost all of the air transport planes for the Allies and ran the Air Transport Command. America's specialization in aircraft contributed to a remarkable eclipse of Britain's competitive position in international aviation. According to James L. Gormly, who has studied aviation rivalry, in 1938 Britain conducted half of all international aviation traffic and the United States conducted one-ninth; in 1943, even excluding the Air Transport Command carriers, Britain's percentage had fallen to 12 and America's increased to 72. With America's postwar aviation supremacy assured, the Roosevelt Administration no longer needed to rely on one airline (Pan American) as a quasi-national carrier, but began to encourage competition among United States carriers with policies designed to assist the industry as a whole.

To maintain the supremacy of America's aviation industry after the war, Roosevelt began a campaign for unrestricted landing rights, a kind of free-flow doctrine for aviation. The United States forthrightly denounced contracts that gave certain airlines (even if those carriers were American) exclusive landing privileges. This open-door doctrine for aviation, dubbed the Fifth Freedom, became the subject of bitter dispute at the International Civil Aviation Conference in 1945, as American delegates pressed for its acceptance and British representatives, anxious to preserve their dominance in the few remaining places where they could manage to extract exclusive rights, fought it as a tool of American hegemony. Unrestricted access for aviation, of course, did favor United States companies, because they held the strongest competitive position, but, as in the cases of free-trade and free-flow doctrines, Americans presented their case not as one that served their own economic interests but as the incarnation of freedom itself. Anglo-American rivalry over acceptance of the Fifth Freedom lasted long after the Chicago conference; Americans tried to negotiate many international air agreements endorsing the principle, and Englishmen fought them. Though the United States never succeeded in obtaining official international recognition for the Fifth Freedom (only a few Latin-American nations formally endorsed the doctrine), wartime extension of air service and construction of new landing sites, together with cagey postwar maneuvering that traded economic and military assistance for air rights in strategic places (such as Saudi Arabia), did give America's commercial aviation industry undisputed international supremacy. American airline companies, like firms dealing in strategic raw materials, were the special beneficiaries of the government's new powers and new activism on behalf of an "open world."

During the 1930s, both private capital and government moved to rationalize the international environment and bring it under greater control. International businesses sought to minimize competition and to maximize geographical diversification; they adapted themselves to a "negotiated environment" in which they often pursued complex arrangements with like companies, with host governments, with the new international lending institutions, and with the governmental agencies that had taken charge of America's foreign economic policy. Government policymakers from 1933 to 1945 increasingly believed that some direct government regulation of the international economy was necessary to a stable system. The promotional state's bureaucracies continued to assist expansion, and the cooperative approach still largely governed America's attempt to gain control over strategic raw materials, but new attitudes overwhelmed the traditional liberal distrust of government. Administering new loan and assistance programs and new controls over commerce became a major function of government; the State Department lost power as the Treasury and Commerce Departments increasingly became involved in foreign economic policy. Moreover, government developed the political and military tools needed to help ensure a world open to American expansion after the war. A huge military buildup, political institutions like the United Nations, and a strong system of alliances replaced the disarmament and "independent internationalism" of the interwar years. Both government and international business, each in its own ways, abandoned the canons of an older liberalism and accepted greater manipulation of the global system. Although their efforts sometimes pulled in different directions before the war, after 1941 they gradually worked together, drawn by a common effort to win the war and to usher in an integrated and open world system.

In the postwar world, the United States hoped to promote global recovery: United States-sponsored loans would help to reindustrialize Europe; this would be followed by massive European purchases of raw materials (developed by American capital) in the nonindustrialized world; and this would be followed by large purchases from these primary producing countries of goods manufactured in the United States. The integrated system, based on specialization within each sector and careful recycling of capital through American loans and investment, was to bring benefit to all. It depended on others' acceptance of liberal patterns: free trade, open investment, and a limited role for government in the private sector. To American postwar planners, expansion, domestic prosperity, and the world's well-being were complementary goals. To others —especially to nationalists in Asia, Africa, and Latin America— America's crusading commitment to a liberalized international order would perpetuate their second-class position in the world system and ensure unrestrained expansion of America's dominance over trade and investment.

Ten

★═══★═══★

THE CULTURAL OFFENSIVE: 1939–1945

AMERICA'S international cultural influence, like its trade and investment, contracted sharply during the Depression decade. As the world economy fractured into spheres of influence, American internationalists' hopes for an emerging "international [i.e., Americanized] mind" faded.

The private associations designed to create global fellowship in the 1920s fell on hard times. In response to declining contributions, the YMCA's total foreign budget for 1933 was only 22 percent of its average budget from 1925 to 1929; missionary programs were cut back; philanthropic efforts lagged; organizations such as Rotary saw their foreign memberships decline. Internationalist groups met increasing suspicion at home. Revisionist historians denounced United States involvement in World War I as a tragic mistake, while default on war debts and turmoil abroad left many Americans distrustful of foreign connections. A world clearly divided into spheres of influence, advocates of greater national self-sufficiency argued, would produce a healthier and more peaceful international order than one wracked by the clash of globalist ambitions. In 1935, in the spring, 175,000 college students abandoned their classrooms for one hour; they demanded abolition of R.O.T.C. and protested Roosevelt's program of naval rearmament. Meanwhile, most Americans continued to reject suggestions that the United States join the League of Nations. The lines between internationalism and nationalism seemed to be drawn more sharply than ever before—or since. The easy faith in the coincidence of national interest and international betterment, so characteristic of the internationalism of the 1920s, was considerably strained during the 1930s.

Barriers to the expansion of American-based communications also grew stronger, as nations turned sharply away from the liberal policies of the open door—not only in trade but also in information. The 1930s was a neomercantilist age in which nations tried to regulate both their economies and their culture.

To internationalists, the resultant rollback of America's cultural influence in the 1930s, resulting from both domestic financial restraints and foreign restrictions, only confirmed their belief in the indivisibility of a liberal order. American trade and investment seemed to increase or decline along with the expansion and contraction of its communications and culture. If American values were to uplift the world, then, so it seemed, must its capital and its products; and if its goods and capital were to circulate freely, so must American ideas.

Therefore, as American policymakers of the late 1930s devised a more vigorous role for government in restoring a liberalized economic system, they also began to create new ways of ensuring America's cultural expansion. Since private institutions were not always strong enough to undertake the task, they began to revolutionize the government's relationship to cultural expansion. Philip Coombs, who would later become (under President John Kennedy) the first Assistant Secretary of State for Educational and Cultural Affairs, recalled in his memoir:

> After 1938 the United States government, forced to abandon its hands-off position, adopted a policy of supplementing and stimulating private cultural intercourse. The war years that followed planted the seeds of almost every present-day federal program of international education, science, culture, technical assistance, and information.

From the late 1930s on, government itself developed what Coombs termed "the fourth dimension of foreign policy"—the cultivation and active direction of international cultural exchange.

NEW CULTURE AND INFORMATION AGENCIES

Until the mid-1930s, few foreign governments had exercised political censorship of cultural imports. Some moved to eliminate sex or violence from American movies, and some imposed quotas on American films during the 1920s. But neither of these activities, which reflected a growing concern with national cultural integrity, interfered much with the free flow of information and culture. The economic and political instability of the 1930s, however, brought overt political censorship from many different directions. The American film industry, for example, came under new, more severe overseas restrictions. Several countries banned *Mutiny on the Bounty,* an Academy Award-winning film, because it sympathetically portrayed rebellion against authority. The German government barred some American films that were directed or produced by Jews and mounted a growing attack on the entire film industry, because it was allegedly dominated by Jewish talent. After 1939, Germany automatically banned American movies in each newly conquered territory. And after 1937 Japan restricted American movie imports. As the world divided, American news organizations saw their clientele shrink. Friendly relations between the Japanese news agency and the Associated Press, for example, disintegrated, and Japan aggressively sought to push its communications networks into China and to eliminate American outlets there.

Even more threatening were the aggressive propaganda campaigns mounted by the Axis. Joseph Goebbels, Hitler's minister of propaganda, truly revolutionized the use of mass communications, demonstrating their political power. During the late 1930s, Germany launched a mass-media offensive that paralleled its military one: it broadcast highly political programs worldwide, built high-power radio transmitters, produced skillful and effective documentary films, and erected a strong network for distribution of Germany's government-controlled "news."

The Americans were comparatively slow in developing an "information policy" to combat restrictions, censorship, and aggressive propaganda. Liberal traditions nurtured a deep distrust of direct governmental involvement in the dissemination of culture and information; Americans had always insisted that "freedom" meant privately controlled mass media. Although nearly every other major country in the 1930s had a government office that directed foreign-information policies and cultural exchange, the United States did not formally establish similar agencies until after 1938. And, not surprisingly, the first agencies that were finally established were specifically directed toward Latin America, America's own special sphere that seemed to be the target of growing Nazi influence. Only after the United States entered World War II did the government become actively involved in promoting American information and culture outside the Western Hemisphere.

At an inter-American conference held in Buenos Aires in 1936, the United States, as part of Roosevelt's good-neighbor policy, proposed greater efforts to encourage cultural relations between the United States and Latin America. Consequently, in 1938, the State Department established a Division of Cultural Relations to implement the Buenos Aires convention. Because of its small budget, the new agency relied heavily on existing institutions to administer its programs, especially on the Institute of International Education, the American Council on Education, the American Library Association, and the American Council of Learned Societies. The first head of the new division, Ben Cherrington, said he wanted "partnership between government and private initiative, with the government the junior partner." The Division of Cultural Relations used private groups as chosen instruments and channeled much of its appropriation through them; it mounted the first official governmental peacetime effort to encourage overseas student and faculty exchanges, to support American schools abroad, to build libraries, and to facilitate the dissemination of American films and broadcasts.

From the first, the Cultural Division confronted the dilemmas involved in purveying an official culture. Was culture to be an instrument of government policy? Or, in order to maintain its credibility and integrity, was the spread of American culture to be insulated from government purposes and propaganda? Factions lined up on each side of this question, and, in theory at least, the dilemma of how to disseminate an unofficial official culture was never resolved. Cherrington insisted that his division would be free from the State Department's positions on international political issues. In practice, though, cultural programs were seldom shielded from foreign policy. The war made such links inevitable, but it was difficult, even in peacetime, to maintain an independent cultural program.

Moreover, the same liberal tradition that made official culture seem incongruous could, with a slight shift, make it eminently acceptable. Policymakers, after all, could reason that because United States foreign policy sought to encourage the free flow of ideas and international understanding within a liberal order, a cultural policy closely linked to these diplomatic goals was less objectionable than the cultural diplomacy of other nations. In 1942, for example, the Advisory Committee on Cultural Relations used this rationale when it recommended increasing the cultural offensive "as a means of strengthening resistance to attack on intellectual and cultural freedom and of reinforcing moral unity among free peoples." The Nazis' aggressive use of culture made it easy to identify America's own cultural offensive with "freedom" and eased the problem of blending educational and cultural exchange with official policy. The subsidized chosen-instrument approach, in which the State Department relied on preexisting private organizations, also softened the dilemma; it insured government direction but preserved the illusion, especially to foreigners, of independent, privately sponsored exchange.

The Cultural Relations Division in the State Department remained a small-scale operation, and by 1940 many Americans began to believe that the Axis threat required a harder sell. In 1939, Nelson Rockefeller, who had developed a concern for Latin America because of Standard Oil's operations there, traveled around the continent with a group of other businessmen. He returned home alarmed at growing Nazi influence and promptly submitted to Roosevelt a proposal recommending creation of an agency to promote pro-American information. Over the objections of the State Department, which did not want a new propaganda bureau outside its control, the President created the Office of the Coordinator for Inter-American Affairs and appointed Rockefeller as a dollar-a-year-man to serve as its director. The agency later became the Office of Inter-American Affairs—OIAA.

Unlike the Division of Cultural Relations, the OIAA was less concerned with scholarly and artistic exchanges (these accounted for less than 10 percent of its budget) and more with extending

American communications and increasing technical assistance programs. It was staffed primarily by people from the private commercial sector. Its budget soared from an initial $3.5 million, taken from the President's Emergency Fund, to $38 million by 1942, a figure ten times greater than that allotted to the State Department's Cultural Division. Both before and during the war the OIAA mounted a thorough cultural offensive in Latin America, operating motion-picture, press, and radio divisions, while devising numerous technical assistance programs. A skillful bureaucrat operator, Rockefeller succeeded in keeping OIAA's propaganda empire separate from the other information agencies that grew up in wartime Washington.

The OIAA's film section censored movies sent to Latin America. Some it banned outright; it suggested deletions and additions for others. The OIAA, for example, got the producers of *Down Argentine Way* to spend an additional $40,000 to reshoot scenes that Latin-American audiences might have found objectionable. The film section also made Spanish-language newsreels and entertainment-with-a-message films. Rockefeller enlisted the cooperation of America's premier producer of popular culture, Walt Disney Studios, and produced *Saludos Amigos,* a feature-length cartoon with Disney characters dancing in Brazilian fiestas, riding with Argentine gauchos, and crossing the formidable Andes.

Rockefeller initially asked the Associated Press and the United Press to enlarge their Latin-American coverage, but these commercial press services claimed that their worldwide clients did not wish more Latin-American news. OIAA's press section subsequently became its major enterprise, supplying wire services with photos, news, and background of interest to Latin Americans. OIAA's syndicated material stressed themes of continental solidarity and the good neighbor. The section also published a slick magazine, *En Guardia,* patterned after *Life,* and a news digest called the "American Newsletter." Using techniques similar to those employed by Creel's news service during World War I, the OIAA also worked to deny export licenses for newsprint shipments to anti-Allied papers in Latin America and even subsidized shipments to friendly ones. Reflecting Rockefeller's preference for enlisting the resources of America's international investors in the patriotic cause, the OIAA took advantage of a Treasury Department ruling that allowed "approved" advertising costs to be deducted from corporate income taxes. Businesses could promote both their products and continental solidarity—and earn a tax write-off.

Rockefeller's radio division enjoyed close relations with commercial radio, and together they worked to increase the hours of American programming available to Latin Americans. In 1939, Germany beamed seven hours of programming a week to Latin America, while the United States offered about twelve hours. By 1941, the United States broadcast around the clock, including numerous daily newscasts in Spanish and Portuguese. Rockefeller also drew up a blacklist of pro-Axis firms and threatened to include companies that advertised on, or sold equipment to, Axis-influenced stations. These actions isolated pro-Axis and neutral radio stations and drove many off the air. The OIAA helped to saturate Latin America with programs on democracy and the "common aspirations of the peoples of the Americas"; it also helped spread tastes for the American way of life and its popular music.

After America's entry into the war, the government's cultural offensive gradually became global in scope. The Department of State's Cultural Division extended its activities to China in 1942. It financed grants for many Chinese to study in the United States and dispatched technical experts to China. In 1943, the program began to encompass the Middle East as well. In this region, the many colleges founded earlier by American private groups received financial support for conducting technical projects commissioned by the State Department. In all areas of its operations, the Cultural Relations Division established "cultural centers" offering classes in the English language and United States history and literature.

More important than these expanded functions within the State Department, however, was the creation in 1942 of the Office of War Information (OWI), headed by Elmer Davis, and the Office of Strategic Services (OSS), headed by William Donovan. Roughly speaking, the OWI was to purvey information and the OSS, an intelligence agency, was to collect it. The OSS also had charge of undercover operations. The agencies worked fairly closely together, but problems did arise when, as part of a strategic operation, the OSS wanted inaccurate information spread. The OWI naturally felt that cooperation would compromise its reputation. A *modus vivendi* was finally evolved: the OWI dealt in presumably accurate information, but the OSS alone could disseminate disinformation.

The OWI adopted methods similar to those used by the OIAA. (Rockefeller, however, managed to exclude OIAA from OWI control.) Although OWI published *Victory,* in a joint effort with *Collier's,* and produced Voice of America radio broadcasts, its principal energies went into improving the quality and distribution of materials available from the private mass media. To spread these more effectively, the OWI created information libraries in twenty-eight foreign locations; established exhibits; published and distributed magazines and newsletters summarizing articles in private newspapers and magazines; cooperated with private publishers to distribute cheap, paperback "Overseas Editions" of American books; and sponsored visits to the United States by foreign journalists. Perhaps its two most important endeavors involved the formation of an *entente cordiale* with the motion-picture industry and the tremendous expansion of America's radio capabilities.

Immediately after the Japanese bombing of Pearl Harbor, the American motion-picture industry offered to assist the war effort, and Roosevelt appointed a liaison to advise Hollywood on how it could help. Hollywood's offer reflected both patriotism and self-interest. Wartime rationing might have shut down Hollywood's "dream machine" unless it showed that it could fulfill a useful, war-related function. Moreover, unless Hollywood moguls voluntarily agreed to produce the kinds of films that government wanted, a competing government-run studio might have been created. In June 1942, the government's liaison with Hollywood became a staff member of the new OWI.

Prior to the development of television, movies were America's most effective way of reaching foreign audiences; their international importance in shaping popular perceptions of America in the 1920s greatly surpassed that of radio or press. OWI's Bureau of Motion Pictures (BMP) was instructed to shape Hollywood into an effective propaganda tool. It convinced RKO Studios, for example, not to rerelease *Gunga Din,* a glorification of British imperialism, and advised quashing other films it found harmful to the war effort. Censoring films *after* production, however, seemed an irrational way of functioning, and the BMP soon requested that studios submit their scripts (eventually even their initial treatments) for prior approval. The BMP suggested additions and deletions that it felt would clarify wartime issues; in some cases, OWI even suggested direct dialogue that pounded home its messages. The BMP also cooperated with the Office of Censorship to apply an elaborate code to exported films. It denied licenses to films that portrayed labor or class conflict or presented American life as violent, cynical, idle, or lavish.

The major film resulting from OWI–Hollywood cooperation was *Wilson,* the 1945 Darryl Zanuck picture glorifying the previous wartime President's crusade for a League of Nations and pleading for popular acceptance of internationalism. The most expensive motion picture made up to that time, *Wilson* was pushed vigorously at home and abroad, especially in newly liberated areas.

Although relations between the OWI and the Hollywood moguls did not always proceed smoothly, neither were they as difficult as might have been expected. Demands for prior submission of scripts and requests for changes caused some inconvenience, but the OWI also became a kind of central clearinghouse for the movie industry. Aware of what every studio was planning, the MPB could unofficially advise on production schedules and smooth some of the industry's competitive edges. Moreover, the OWI shipped approved films right behind the liberating armies, reestablishing old markets in Europe and reaching new ones. Government-financed goodwill tours by Douglas Fairbanks, Jr., Alice Faye, and others also did no harm to Hollywood's postwar prospects. The government–Hollywood partnership lasted well beyond the defeat of Japan. Having become used to wartime censorship, the industry developed its own means of making politically acceptable films, and the government, with its new concern for preserving free trade and free flow of culture, took a more active role than ever in ensuring favorable conditions for the export of films.

The OWI could rely on private industry to produce films but not to beam radio broadcasts overseas. America's most important chosen instrument for international radio communications, RCA, had increasingly devoted itself to domestic growth during the 1920s and 1930s. RCA did slowly increase its network of point-to-point radio transmissions, but displayed little interest in international voice broadcasts. Similarly, NBC and CBS, the major domestic broadcasters, only dabbled in international transmissions, which they considered unprofitable. In 1941, there were only seven small American licensees, with a total of thirteen transmitters, engaged in international voice broadcasting, and none showed a profit.

After America entered the war, the OWI moved into the radio business. It assumed control of the thirteen private transmitters, encouraged the industry to build five more, financed construction of three itself, and worked out arrangements with many friendly governments around the globe to use their facilities as relay points. Using this network, the OWI and OIAA developed twenty-four-hour-a-day programming in more than forty languages, reaching every part of the world. (This radio capacity was greatly augmented by the Armed Forces Network [AFN], a network run for American servicemen that also attracted large local audiences and spread the popularity of American music.) Because it could be beamed anywhere, the OWI's Voice of America became the cornerstone of America's informational program. During the war, broadcasting proved itself a truly international medium. Not easily jammed by government barriers, radio became the great hope of those advocating free flow of information in the postwar world.

Despite its successes, the Overseas Branch of the OWI came under considerable strain. In 1940, Roosevelt had appointed Henry L. Stimson Secretary of War, a lifelong Republican of conservative, patrician background, who had been Herbert Hoover's Secretary of State. And after 1941 a large number of businessmen flocked to Washington to staff many of Roosevelt's planning agencies. Such changes in personnel put the New Deal on a more conservative course. Yet, as the nature of Roosevelt's Administration changed, the OWI provided a refuge for many early New Dealers. Robert Sherwood, the famous writer and speechwriter for F.D.R., headed the Overseas Division and staffed it with progressive-minded internationalists such as James P. Warburg and Joseph Barnes. These OWI officers hoped the war against Fascism would become a "people's crusade" based on Roosevelt's Four Freedoms: freedom of speech and religion; freedom from want and fear. These New Dealers disapproved of imperialism and hoped that the war would bring permanent gains for the poor, for nonwhites everywhere, and for women. To them, Fascism was the enemy less because Germany challenged America's national security than because it stood for institutionalized racism, a controlled labor movement, and a subordination of individual rights to corporate privilege. Their internationalism represented their hope for worldwide reform and social justice, and OWI messages abroad tended to reflect these convictions.

The ideals of the OWI staffers did not always square with what defense planners perceived as wartime necessity. In time, the OWI came under attack, especially from the military and from others who felt it exhibited an unhealthy independence from national policy. American wartime policy supported the corrupt regime of Chiang Kai-shek in China, was allied with ex-Fascist, German collaborator Jean François Darlan in North Africa, supported an occupation government in Italy that included Fascist elements, and suspended criticism of British colonial rule in India. In preparing press releases, OWI staffers clearly had difficulty fitting such policies into their own vision of America's wartime goals; sometimes they appeared to criticize such policies. Finally, when the tensions became too severe, Sherwood was sent to London on another mission in 1944, and Warburg, Barnes, and others in the Overseas Division resigned. More conservative successors took their places.

The OIAA and the OWI extended the cultural and informational dimension of foreign policy, but the experience of Sherwood and the others also demonstrated the difficulty of acting independently of the government's larger goals. Informational policies, even after the war, would remain the captive of broader objectives.

A POSTWAR COMMUNICATIONS ORDER

Peace threatened the organizations that had directed wartime cultural and informational diplomacy. Prewar suspicions about governmental involvement in the dissemination of information and culture remained strong, and many members of Congress expected to eliminate the agencies just as they had done after World War I. The OWI and OIAA were cut back and consolidated into the State Department's Cultural Division, which in 1946 became the Office of International Information and Cultural Affairs. The agency's new head, William Benton, was an advertising executive, vice-president of the University of Chicago, and publisher of the *Encyclopaedia Britannica*. He and Truman's Secretary of State,

General George C. Marshall, conducted a vigorous campaign from 1945 to 1947 to stave off further budget cuts and to preserve the government's informational functions. But even with such respected and prestigious support, cultural diplomacy remained in limbo for two years immediately following the war.

While Benton tried to wring a larger financial commitment out of a suspicious Congress, much of the wartime cultural apparatus reverted to private hands. Many of the powerful radio relay stations that had served the armed forces and carried OWI messages to every part of the world were returned to former foreign owners or sold at a fraction of their cost to private enterprise. Only the remnants of any coordinated global structure of telecommunications remained. (Voice of America did continue but at a reduced level.) Associated Press and United Press, claiming that the government's wartime news services interfered with their own selling of news abroad, abruptly prohibited the State Department's use of their wire services at the end of the war and lobbied for government to abandon news production completely. The American book industry formed the United States International Book Association to cooperate in trying to maintain an export market that had been well cultivated by the wartime "Overseas Editions," but government involvement ceased.

The State Department's Cultural Division was left to operate a scaled-down program. It continued to maintain American libraries abroad and to sponsor student and technical exchange. On a greatly reduced scale, it also continued shortwave broadcasts, published a Russian-language magazine for distribution in the Soviet Union, and maintained a small flow of visual materials and background news about the United States to its overseas centers. Even though these remnants seemed substantial beside the nonexistent informational capacities of the pre-1938 era, they represented an enormous rollback of wartime efforts.

Returning so much of the "cultural dimension" to private initiatives left troubling questions. Would publishers export their best products or their most sensational? Would the prewar ratio of two hundred copies of *True Confessions* to every copy of *Harper's* sent abroad continue? Would international broadcasters continue to serve the large lucrative foreign markets, while they abandoned the small, marginal ones that might, in some cases, have greater strategic importance? Would Hollywood ever devote resources to high-quality newsreels and documentary films such as the OWI and the army had supervised during the war? (Frank Capra's *Why We Fight* series of documentaries, produced by the army during the war, attracted both widespread critical acclaim and great box-office success overseas; it was frequently touted as an example of the high-quality product that a noncommercial, government agency could produce.)

Would any private press association devote adequate resources to developing multiple-address newscasting, a revolutionary development that OWI had successfully used and that Reuters and other foreign agencies were aggressively pursuing? The multiple-address technique involved sending news items from a single press association on a wide beam, to be picked up simultaneously by perhaps hundreds of contracting newspapers. Because the costs of wide-beam transmission could be shared by all users, the service could potentially be provided at a fraction of the cost of the old services, which were sent in separate point-to-point transmissions by cable or radiotelegraph. If Americans, who had been in the forefront of international radio technology since World War I, did not develop multiple-address systems, foreign news would eventually undersell American news in most parts of the world.

And more pressing than any of these questions relating to specific media was a broader one. When all other major governments were coordinating informational and cultural programs—Britain even consolidated and nationalized its cable and radio service—could the United States adequately assert its interests in the world if it depended primarily on private initiatives? Dominant communications networks and national power historically went hand in hand, and the Democratic policymakers of the postwar era had little faith in the old chosen-instrument approach to a global structure of communications.

As such concerns surfaced in the debate over postwar "cultural diplomacy," other problems also became apparent. The remains of the wartime cultural operation were consolidated in a State Department confronting severe budgetary constraints. With too little money to go around, the newly consolidated agency suffered internal divisions, roughly between those whom the historian Frank

Ninkovich has described as advocates of "cultural diplomacy" and advocates of "informational diplomacy."

Those favoring cultural diplomacy tended to argue for the so-called slow media—art, books, scholar exchange—and advanced a kind of "trickle-down" rationale. Cultural exchanges among the literate elite were not well suited to accomplish immediate propaganda objectives, they believed, but these "slow" media would result, in the long run, in greater mutual respect and understanding and would in time provide a sound basis for successful diplomacy. Anything that helped advance the image of America as a truly cultured civilization would counteract the stereotype of materialistic, cultural barbarians. Cultural diplomacy, thus, aimed primarily at affecting the perceptions of foreign elites, at detaching cultural exchange from foreign policy (thereby insuring its "purity" as culture), and at cementing long-term goodwill, even though no short-run payoffs on particular policies might result.

But another, larger group within the State Department wanted the government to emphasize "informational programs," generally a euphemism for propaganda. Caught up in the technology of the so-called fast media—radio, motion pictures, and news—this group argued for short-range impact and mass appeal. It was particularly concerned that America's tremendous capacity for shortwave radio coverage and news dissemination not be allowed to deteriorate after the war. Only government, they warned, could maintain the systems that were vital to national interest but unprofitable to private businesses. These information officers branded the old cultural diplomacy as elitist. They recognized that American popular culture, whatever its artistic worth, could be one of America's most potent weapons in fighting for the "minds of men." Even if the elites scoffed, the masses of the world gravitated to the simplified messages of popular culture. In fact, the potentialities of shortwave broadcasting and the revolutionary multiple-address system for disseminating news made it possible to appeal directly to the people in a country, even without their government's consent. Unlike cultural diplomacy, the type of informational diplomacy conveyed by the fast media could be unilateral; it was not dependent on formal arrangements between governments. Informational diplomacy, then, aimed primarily at mass appeal and short-term impact. It was almost necessarily (as the OWI had demonstrated) linked more closely to the policy objectives of the American government than cultural diplomacy.

Precisely because informational programs were really just another name for propaganda, they initially generated greater suspicion. As a result, William Benton emphasized cultural diplomacy. In 1946, the State Department's Cultural Division decided to put together a comprehensive exhibit of American art for display abroad. Using miscellaneous, end-of-the-fiscal-year funds, it purchased seventy-nine contemporary paintings and launched a show called "Advancing American Art." In artistic circles at home and abroad the display drew great praise. But in early 1947 the American popular media began running sensationalized stories about the frivolity of spending taxpayers' money on what President Truman described as "ham-and-eggs art." Congressmen attacked the exhibit's modern art, charging that it was part of a Communist conspiracy to undermine young people's natural perceptions, common sense, and economic productivity. The House Un-American Activities Committee investigated the political views of the artists included in the display (finding many who had once had Communist sympathies), and the President himself joined the attack. In a letter to Benton, Truman called such art the "vaporings of half-baked lazy people." Under such a barrage of criticism, it became apparent that any cultural diplomacy based on purveying "elite" art that was not in accord with the tastes of the American Congress and public provided an easy target for critics of the government's expanded role in cultural affairs.

At the same time that cultural diplomacy aimed at elite tastes was under attack, however, the case for improving informational services, that is, the "fast" media, was growing stronger. In 1946, the University of Chicago, operating through a grant from Time, Inc., organized an independent, nongovernmental "commission on freedom of the press." The committee was composed of some of the leading intellectuals of the day, including Robert Maynard Hutchins (its chair), Zechariah Chafee, Jr., Harold Lasswell, Reinhold Niebuhr, and Archibald MacLeish. After surveying the state of American international communications, the Hutchins commission warned that the failure of United States leadership in mass communications would "lead inevitably to a rapid acceleration of the . . . sealing-off of peoples from peoples, the substitution of slanted propaganda for truth within these walled 'zones of influence,' and ultimately the reappearance of those nationalistic neuroses that plunge their victims into war." The commission urged the government to take a direct role in consolidating an American-owned global telecommunications network for handling "commercial, military, diplomatic, press, and voice-broadcasting traffic." It recommended that the Congress, the Department of State, and the United Nations work "to secure the progressive removal of political barriers and the lessening of economic restrictions which impeded the free flow of information across national borders." It advised the media to establish self-policing associations on the model of the International Book Association and to encourage exportation of only high-quality informational products that would present a "truthful" picture of American society. Most important, it urged restoration of all OWI and OIAA functions that were not suitably being carried out by private industry and suggested a cooperative effort by industry and government to "formulate an integrated program" for the promotion of international information. Ironically, though the report was titled *Peoples Speaking to Peoples* and its authors genuflected to the traditional liberal faith that greater communication among people would improve international understanding and bring peace, its hundred pages dealt primarily with how the United States should extend its mass media to reach other peoples; it paid virtually no attention to the many obstacles (geographical, economic, and technological) that prevented a return flow.

Such private pressures to restore a hard-hitting informational component of foreign policy helped Benton ward off congressional budget cuts. Although Congress might object on both aesthetic and economic grounds to the purchase of modern art, the dissemination of pro-American "information" into strategic areas in order to shore up friendly forces could not engender the same controversy. Propaganda, quite simply, gave more bang for the buck than "culture." In 1948, with the sharp deterioration of United States–Soviet relations, Congress passed the Smith–Mundt Act (the United States Informational and Educational Exchange Act), finally authorizing a permanent global "information" program and an expanded Fulbright scholar exchange. As Philip Coombs wrote,

Benton finally "won the battle [to restore the informational offensive], but only with the help of a new war, this one called 'cold.' "

Within a few years, the new program degenerated into a strident and narrow anti-Communist "crusade for freedom," whose strategy was to focus on certain specially targeted areas and flood them with propaganda. Later, President Dwight D. Eisenhower removed "information" from the State Department, placed it in an independent agency (the USIA), and left "cultural exchange" behind in the State Department. After nearly ten years, then, the OWI finally had a genuine successor agency, one imbued with a warlike zeal and operating as a regular feature of American diplomacy.

Information agencies had always had a close connection to intelligence, and the wartime Office of Strategic Services underwent a metamorphosis not unlike that of the OWI–USIA. The OSS was disbanded after the war, and other agencies, especially the Federal Bureau of Investigation, and the military fought to absorb its functions. After a period of limbo, however, during which many of the talented officers who had served during the war left for other jobs, a national Central Intelligence Agency (CIA) was re-created in 1947. Like the information agency, the CIA was given new life by the cold war, and it also shaped up as a narrow anti-Communist instrument.

Vigorous government agencies set up to disseminate and collect information became important components of America's postwar information order, but, where possible, they operated through private groups. Both the CIA and the USIA, in variations of the old chosen-instrument approach, subsidized organizations already doing work that they believed advanced the national interest. Foreign schools, prestigious publishers, the foreign affiliates of the American Federation of Labor, philanthropic groups, student-exchange programs, and countless other private organizations that the government deemed useful in the anti-Communist crusade received CIA or USIA subsidies in the postwar period. In trying to preserve something of the liberal belief in private exchange, however, this subsidized chosen-instrument approach eventually led foreigners to suspect that all American private cultural or charitable groups were paid agents of American policy. By trying to strengthen the private sector and limit its own role, the government ironically may have actually weakened the effectiveness of America's private cultural exchange efforts.

Another major ingredient in the postwar communications order was government's effort to hasten the free flow of information, around the globe. The United States became the major champion of "freedom of information" in postwar international forums and used the new powers of the regulatory state to urge others to embrace an open door for information. William Benton, for example, wrote in 1946 that his central problem was "the artificial barriers largely imposed by governments to prevent free exchange of ideas," and he called for their removal. In hemispheric conferences and in UNESCO meetings within the UN, the United States pressed other nations to eliminate censorship and restrictions, improve distribution of information across national borders, widen journalists' access to sources of news, and support private ownership of news media.

United States policymakers pushed these goals in the name of liberalizing the world's communications order and promoting greater cultural exchange. But the liberal idea of free flow, like that of the economic open door, logically led not to a wide-open market full of varied and competing products but to dominance by the most technologically advanced producers. In their formulation of free-flow doctrines, Benton, the Hutchins commission, and most American policymakers considered none of the obstacles to exchange of information that were created by the domination of a few (mostly American) companies. Government's efforts to advance free flow meant an open door for American communications companies, which, especially after the advent of television and high-cost communications satellites, came to provide much of the programming and media advertising in the non-Communist world. Free flow might result in "peoples [Americans] speaking to peoples [foreigners]," but those who lacked a global communications structure could not talk back. America's postwar drive to enshrine free flow sounded like liberalism but looked more like an attempt to dominate the world's media. As a former president of Finland rhetorically asked, "Could it be that the prophets who preach unhindered communication are not concerned with equality between nations but are on the side of the stronger and wealthier?"

RELIEF, TECHNICAL ASSISTANCE, AND TRAINING

Foreign aid, like cultural relations, was a totally private endeavor before 1938 (except during, and immediately after, World War I), but it also came under increasing governmental control as a result of the crises of the 1930s. The New Deal's domestic price-support policies brought the government huge agricultural surpluses, and in 1938, responding to the suffering caused by the civil war in Spain, Congress authorized the United States Federal Surplus Commodities Corporation to give surplus wheat to the Red Cross for distribution in Spain. Although the impact of this aid in Spain was limited, the precedent was important. Distributing government-owned surpluses as relief to foreign nations had not been done before in peacetime, yet the practice would continue after the war, ultimately becoming institutionalized in the Food-for-Peace program.

In 1939, when Congress revised its neutrality legislation to tighten trade restrictions with Axis nations, it also required the State Department to license private philanthropic groups giving aid to countries at war. The Neutrality Act of November 1939 thus empowered the government to block private assistance to Axis countries. At first, the government permitted and encouraged aid to the victims of Axis expansionism. A Commission for Polish Relief, supported by Herbert Hoover and run by some old hands from Hoover's World War I American Relief Administration, even got food supplies into Nazi-occupied Poland. But after the United States entered the war, Roosevelt ruled against such efforts. Despite Hoover's pleas to continue relief into Axis-controlled Europe, the United States government terminated the Polish campaign and refused to license any group that sought to send aid behind Axis lines, for fear it might help the enemy's cause.

As a war-torn world pleaded for more philanthropy, the number of relief agencies proliferated, and the techniques of fund raising became more elaborate. The United China Relief, for example, got Shirley Temple to make a radio appeal asking children to send nickels and dimes to their favorite movie stars, who would forward them to China; Thomas Lamont, John D. Rockefeller 3d, Thomas Watson of IBM, and other socialites attended an elaborate Chinese costume party, featuring Chinese games and a ride on a junk, to raise money for United China Relief. A *Life* magazine headline in

1941—"U.S. Balls, Brawls, Pageants, and Parades Turn War Relief into Show Business"—exemplified the growing public criticism of private philanthropy. Such extravaganzas had too much overhead and presented too many temptations for con artists.

In the spring of 1941, as part of a general program to rationalize available resources, Roosevelt appointed a Committee on War Relief Agencies, headed by the prominent internationalist Joseph E. Davies. The committee recommended an extension of licensing to include all overseas relief agencies and a tightening of licensing requirements to make agencies prove that they operated efficiently and did not duplicate Red Cross work. Both Davies and Secretary of State Hull urged that the Red Cross, already a quasi-official agency, should be strengthened and made the primary organization for dispensing relief. Shortly thereafter, licensing requirements began to whittle down the number of groups competing with the Red Cross, and Congress appropriated $50 million of public funds for the Red Cross to use in purchasing American supplies to send to victims of war on the Allied side.

After America entered the war, Davies' committee became the Relief Control Board, charged with responsibility for licensing and regulating all private philanthropy. It quickly forced even greater consolidation, slashing the number of licensed relief agencies from three hundred at the end of 1941 to sixty-seven by 1943. Only politically acceptable agencies survived. After the war, although the War Relief Control Board became the Advisory Committee on Voluntary Foreign Aid and lost its power to grant licenses, it continued to wield enormous influence over the private relief community. It became a dispensing agent for the government subsidies that began to be given to private philanthropies for the first time in the postwar period. Moreover, in 1944 the Advisory Committee encouraged formation of a private Council of Voluntary Agencies, with which it worked closely. The council unofficially continued the government's wartime role of policing the honesty and political views of "approved" constituents. Thus, if private philanthropy after the war was no longer totally controlled by government, the postwar structures that developed out of wartime controls still made government approval very desirable.

Government not only asserted control over voluntary relief efforts but began to create new structures for the direct dispensation of foreign aid. In 1942, Roosevelt established an Office of

Foreign Relief and Rehabilitation Operations (OFFRO) to use America's agricultural stocks and medical supplies to relieve areas under Allied control. OFFRO was directed by Herbert Lehman, the former governor of New York. A year later, OFFRO merged into an Allied effort called the United Nations Relief and Rehabilitation Administration (UNRRA). Back in 1919, Herbert Hoover and Woodrow Wilson had refused to allow such Allied control over American relief contributions, because they had wanted to retain tight control of the political leverage that relief supplies provided. Roosevelt, however, assumed that the United States would dominate UNRRA; Lehman even remained the director. And Americans did dominate UNRRA at the higher echelons. But without Americans in control over local distribution, trouble sometimes developed. After public criticism that UNRRA supplies were going to Communists, Truman stopped funding the organization in 1946. He announced that from then on America's foreign aid would be supervised at all levels by Americans, and thus have maximum political impact on the targeted area. After 1947, the government developed and expanded a variety of other unilateral methods of dispensing foreign assistance, including specialized agencies for relief in occupied Germany and Japan, subsidies to voluntary organizations, donation of government war surpluses to the private organization CARE, the Marshall Plan of 1948, and Food for Peace after 1954.

During the war, then, the government assumed greater control over foreign relief and became, itself, the most substantial contributor. In the postwar era, American philanthropic aid and foreign policy were merged as never before. The government's principal interest, however, lay less in giving "handouts" to foreigners than in "helping people help themselves." Government-financed technical assistance programs, almost nonexistent before the war, consequently became another prominent feature of America's foreign policy. Technical aid combined government's cultural offensive with its new role in philanthropy.

Nelson Rockefeller's OIAA inaugurated government-sponsored technical assistance programs and, one observer commented, ran them "like a foundation." Applications for projects were reviewed by a committee representing OIAA, the State Department, and private organizations. Approved applications were then implemented by private agencies or corporations on a contract basis. This contract procedure, a variant on the chosen-instrument approach, remained the pattern for future programs.

In developing OIAA's programs of technical assistance (which became a more important part of OIAA than its cultural and informational exchanges), Rockefeller stressed those relating to commercial matters. The OIAA funded cooperative agricultural research into the development of tropical commodities such as rubber and financed surveys to locate mineral deposits such as manganese, chromium, tungsten, and tin. It sponsored technical exchanges that took the form of the United States lending technicians to Latin America and Latin America sending students to the United States. The OIAA also placed importance on public health and food production. In 1942, Rockefeller got Congress to establish a government corporation, the Institute of Inter-American Affairs (IIAA), that could finance health services, especially near United States military bases and strategic mining areas. In many ways, this public corporation was a descendant of the Rockefeller Foundation; much of IIAA's work actually continued previous foundation projects.

The OIAA also planned to exchange information on labor standards with Latin Americans, but Rockefeller clashed on this issue with Secretary of Labor Frances Perkins. Perkins wanted United States agencies to stress the basic labor rights championed by the New Deal. Rockefeller's business-dominated agency was more concerned with maintaining a "free" labor environment—one in which workers were "free" to labor for any wage under any conditions without the "coercion" of militant unions or protective labor statutes.

If Perkins would not cooperate with the OIAA's labor programs, however, the AF of L would. Gradually, during the war, the OIAA and the AF of L formed an alliance not unlike that which the Wilson Administration had forged with Samuel Gompers during World War I. The OIAA tried to help the AF of L gain leadership over the hemispheric labor movement and undercut the strength of Vicente Toledano, the militant Mexican labor chief who headed the strong Latin American Confederation of Labor (CTAL). But the CTAL was difficult to undermine. Toledano was a towering figure in Latin-American labor circles; his personal popularity and the concept of labor solidarity made it hard for the AF of L to start any alternative movement. In the mid-1930s, when the Congress of Industrial Organization (CIO) split with the AF of L and formed a rival union, its leaders developed close ties with Toledano's federation. And in the late 1930s and early 1940s the United States government itself had supported expansion of the CTAL, because its leadership, many of whom were pro-Communist, strongly advocated anti-German measures and helped popularize the war among Latin Americans.

Toward the end of the war, the OIAA and the AF of L laid plans to create a new American-led international federation to replace the CTAL. They began to cultivate ties with any Latin-American labor leader who opposed Toledano. When the war ended, an OIAA staff member who had been engaged in labor diplomacy in Latin America, Serafino Romualdi, joined the AF of L and became their major organizer. Romualdi's goal was to split the CTAL in Latin America and to build a new organization affiliated with the AF of L. In 1946, Romualdi began traveling around the continent, with the unofficial support of the Department of State. (The State Department clearly favored the AF of L's efforts but at first did not do so publicly for fear of charges that they were favoring the AF of L over the CIO, which had always had support from the Roosevelt Administration and still backed the CTAL.) Over the next few years, as the cold war deepened, the government's support, even subsidy, of the AF of L's efforts gradually became more direct, and in 1948 Romualdi officially announced formation of a new organization, which subsequently became the Inter-American Regional Organization of Workers (ORIT). ORIT then affiliated with another AF of L-sponsored international union, the International Confederation of Free Trade Unions (ICFTU).

The ICFTU and ORIT were both virulently anti-Communist and, according to a State Department memorandum of 1949, "a sort of projection of the foreign-policy interests of the governments of its members, most notably the United States and the United Kingdom." Although the AF of L, and then the CIO, which shortly joined both federations, insisted that their international organizing efforts were independent of government involvement (indeed, they claimed, that was what distinguished their federations from Communist ones), their representatives worked closely with embassy personnel and many received CIA subsidies. Their policies aimed at keeping the workers in foreign countries friendly and receptive to American influence and programs. In Latin America, ORIT encouraged labor support for the Clayton program of low tariffs and massive United States investment, and in Europe the ICFTU strongly backed American assistance programs such as the Marshall Plan. Labor diplomacy in the postwar period became an important adjunct to winning foreign support for America's new postwar order.

The OIAA's concept of technical aid proved so popular that the State Department's Division of Cultural Relations also gradually broadened its functions to emphasize technical assistance. Interestingly, the ascendancy of technical aid and the decline of cultural exchange within the Cultural Relations Division reflected an attempt to democratize cultural connections. In response to Congress's mandate that the program should be carried, in the words of one congressmen, "not to the caviar class, but to the bread and butter eaters," the division drew up new guidelines deemphasizing the fine arts in favor of engineering, agriculture, and training programs. Technical assistance, the new policy stipulated, would help men improve their job skills and agricultural methods and assist women in improving home life and "domestic arts." Such assistance, presumably, would help the masses, while the exchange of elite culture would affect only a few.

The technical assistance programs pioneered by OIAA and the State Department during the war eventually merged into a larger structure of postwar foreign-aid agencies. In 1950, President Truman announced his Point Four program to shore up the less-developed areas of the world against Communism by encouraging self-help. The government's technical assistance programs were then centralized in a new State Department bureau called the Technical Cooperation Administration. A year later, the State Department also began assigning science attachés to its foreign embassies, in order to improve technical-assistance programs.

Technical assistance became an integral part of the government's policies to promote America's economic and cultural influence. Spreading American technique and know-how was designed to build friendships. Developing new agricultural and mineral resources was a means of integrating marginal areas more fully into the world economy. The policy of working through contracted private agencies and corporations was a way of preserving the strengths of private initiative. And having the State Department control the allocation of this assistance provided one more economic tool for bolstering friendly governments.

Although Point Four and other technical-aid allocations seemed small beside huge programs such as the Marshall Plan for Europe, these technical-assistance contracts had substantial impact on the general direction of economic development in poor countries. The contract system of assistance caused some foreign critics to note that a major result of technical aid appeared to be to provide employment for American experts and to subsidize American corporations and organizations, whose overseas programs would produce markets or products needed by the American economy. But American policymakers had always presented self-interest and international betterment as identical, and the fact that technical assistance developed the world in accordance with America's economic needs did not, to them, lessen its philanthropic qualities or diminish expectations of foreign gratitude.

Government's new emphasis on foreign assistance also involved the United States more deeply in training foreign military establishments. The United States had begun to take an interest in military missions during the 1920s. In America's Caribbean protectorates, the armed services trained local constabularies, and in 1920 Congress authorized the President to assign naval officers to Latin-American governments. A military mission of sixteen officers and nineteen petty officers served in Brazil for four years during the mid-1920s (the first extensive training mission of its kind), and after that the United States encouraged similar requests for missions elsewhere in Latin America.

Military missions had two interrelated purposes: they were to serve the strategic needs of the United States by binding the foreign armed forces into America's system of training and supply, and they were to create markets for American goods. Although the General Loan Policy of the 1920s had discouraged the sale of military equipment, many Americans argued that because Europeans were willing to sell armaments American self-denial accomplished nothing and damaged the nation's strategic interest. During the late 1930s, the economic and strategic arguments for military missions and sales gained in appeal. After 1938, the United States gradually developed a concerted strategy for expanding its military-assistance programs and for encouraging purchase of its equipment.

Latin America again became the principal target for military-assistance programs. The State Department urged Latin-American governments to terminate pro-Axis military missions and replace them with Americans. In 1938, the United States had assigned twenty-four military officers to Latin America; by 1941, the total reached one hundred and every nation in Latin America, except Uruguay, had received some kind of United States military adviser. In 1940, Congress also promised to help arm the Latin-American military, and this military-assistance program was subsequently expanded through Lend-Lease. Vigorous support for Latin-American military establishments greatly enlarged their power over the internal affairs of their own countries and had lasting consequences. As a result, the Peruvian populist Haya de la Torre denounced the Roosevelt Administration as "the good neighbor of tyrants."

Building strong, friendly military forces seemed to have obvious strategic and economic advantages, despite its potential for encouraging military dictatorship. Under Lend-Lease, which continued after the war, the United States supplied military equipment to any nation deemed vital to America's interests, and the program extended America's influence well beyond the Western Hemisphere, to places not previously associated with American military power. Oil-rich Middle Eastern countries, particularly Saudi Arabia and Iran, became militarily dependent on the United States through Lend-Lease and subsequent military-assistance programs. The Truman Doctrine appropriation of 1947 funded military assistance to Greece and Turkey, formerly in the British sphere of influence. Huge military aid went into the futile attempt to bolster Chiang Kai-shek in China.

Foreign relief, technical assistance, and military aid programs, then, all became associated with official foreign policy during and after the war. They were considered to be humanitarian efforts that would develop and protect others at the same time that they served America's own global economic and strategic interests. Extremely limited before 1938, foreign aid of various kinds became major components of the postwar regulatory apparatus. They aimed at keeping the world friendly, stable, open to American influence, and integrated into an American-dominated world system.

In these years, the American government devised new ways of expanding American information and expertise. Growing Axis influence in Latin America in the late 1930s and, ultimately, the war itself provided the initial stimulus, but the new agencies an ` techniques were continued or revived in the postwar period. The cold war both stimulated and was itself aggravated by the new initiatives of this "cultural dimension" of foreign policy. Direct governmental supervision in peacetime of foreign informational programs, of technical missions, and of large-scale foreign aid marked a significant departure from the private approach to culture and relief that Americans had always favored. And the government became increasingly committed to the free-flow doctrine of cultural exchange that would keep the world open to Americanizing influences. America's cultural offensive, no less than its postwar economic program, represented a government-directed effort to integrate others into a new pax Americana.

Eleven

★═══★═══★

SPREADING THE DREAM?

THE growth of American power from the 1890s to the 1940s was spectacular. Always restlessly pushing outward, American citizens sought new markets, investments, or converts. In a famous *Life* editorial of 1941 entitled "The American Century," the prominent publisher Henry Luce reflected the views of many twentieth-century policymakers and citizens when he characterized America "as the dynamic center of ever-widening spheres of enterprise, America as the training center of the skillful servants of mankind, America as the Good Samaritan . . . and America as the powerhouse of the ideals of Freedom and Justice." America's expansion, always benign, always uplifting, seemed based not on military force or government design but on the wonders of its private industry, the skill of its experts, the goodness of its philanthropists. Luce's vision of the American dream differed little from that projected at the Columbian Exposition of 1893. But entrapped in misapplied notions of nineteenth-century liberalism and myths of America's exceptional mission, Luce and other apologists for an American imperium only obscured understanding of the process by which Americans expanded their influence.

In the late nineteenth and early twentieth century, except for the flurry of annexationist activity after the Spanish-American War, the most energetic expansionism did come from private citizens, especially missionaries and businessmen. But the government gradually came to assist much of this private expansion, not so much because special interests demanded government support (though many did call for a stronger show of the flag) but because policymakers began to accept expansion as a fundamental condition of "national interest" and international betterment. In the twentieth century, in ever more complex ways, the government helped citizens export American influence, while private businesses and groups, in turn, helped the government fulfill the expansive "national interest." This relationship progressed through three general stages: the promotional state, the cooperative state, and the regulatory state. Throughout, economic and cultural expansion were closely related.

From the Administration of Benjamin Harrison to Woodrow Wilson, most of the framework for the promotional state was hammered into place: a big navy; bargaining tariffs; the open-door policy; attempts to spread the gold standard; legislation allowing monopolistic combinations in the export trade, in foreign investment and in overseas branch banking; many new or improved executive-branch bureaucracies such as the Tariff Commission, the Federal Trade Commission, the Bureau of Foreign and Domestic Commerce, and the consular corps of the State Department; and some coordination of private philanthropy through the Red Cross and the American Relief Administration. All of this new governmental activity in support of cultural and economic expansion remained compatible with America's liberal tradition of limited government. Promotional activities encouraged the growth of the private sector; they presumably liberated, rather than restricted, the free-enterprise system that lay at the heart of a liberal order.

Following World War I, the world experienced an even greater surge of American expansion. Promotional activities continued, especially the effort to make the tariff a tool for expanding the most-favored-nation principle, but government undertook more vigorous steps to shape the international impact of private citizens and groups. Herbert Hoover symbolized the cooperative strategy by which public goals were to be carried out through private means. The hallmarks of the cooperative state were "voluntary" guidelines set for investors by government and the chosen instrument, in which policymakers informally awarded a private group or corporation official blessing or monopolistic privileges in return for carrying out some element of American foreign policy. The chosen-instrument approach developed in every sector the American government considered essential to American expansion—international communications, international investment banking, strategic raw materials. By cooperating with businesses and various kinds of private associations, the government hoped to improve America's competitive position in the world. Through the private approach of the cooperative state, policymakers believed the United States could expand its global influence and yet preserve the liberal tradition of limited government.

With the collapse of the international system after 1929 and the onset of worldwide depression and then war, the cooperative, private emphasis of the 1920s gave way to more direct governmental involvement in the international economic and cultural order. Government officials believed that the difficulties of the 1930s stemmed from inadequate international economic mechanisms (because of the limitations of working through the private sector) and from a lack of military preparedness to halt countries that desired to carve out restricted spheres of influence. According to this view, the road to stability, prosperity, and peace required new governmental mechanisms to guide the world economy, new agencies to disperse American information and relief, and a powerful military presence (enhanced by military-assistance programs and possession of the new atomic weaponry) to prevent the growth of closed spheres of influence. Though government still promoted private expansion and still used cooperative, chosen-instrument relationships (as in resource policy), expansion became an elaborate process directed by a variety of official cultural and economic agencies. Governmental or intergovernmental agencies such as IMF, IBRD, GATT, AID, USIA, and other technical-assistance agencies assumed functions previously conducted by private citizens.

In each of these stages, the realities of American expansion increasingly diverged from the liberal-developmental theories invoked by policymakers. More precisely, policymakers tended to apply their liberal canons selectively—upholding those that would favor American expansion and modifying or ignoring those that might not.

The Americans who guided foreign relations from 1890 to 1945 tried to create an international order based on certain liberal tenets. For commerce, American policymakers sought stable exchange rates based on gold, equal access to markets, and (after 1934) freer trade. All these were to promote wider markets for American exports, greater production and employment at home, and rising levels of world trade. For investment, Americans desired stability, open access, and nonsocialist forms of economic organization that would not threaten American investors' property rights abroad. For various cultural and philanthropic exchanges, policymakers also sought to promote unrestricted access—that is, the doctrine of free flow. In all areas, Americans stressed private ownership and denounced the restrictions or monopolies that foreign governments imposed. This brand of liberalism—emphasizing equal trading opportunity, open access, free flow, and free enterprise—was advanced as a formula for global development, a formula that the Americans liked to think had succeeded in the United States.

There were many problems with liberal-developmentalist goals. First, America's own development did not arise from following these liberal principles but from an expedient mix of individual initiatives and government policies promoting growth. American policymakers did many of the things they cautioned foreigners against. They restrained trade through protective tariffs and, after they began to lower their tariff barriers, used import quotas. They indirectly subsidized the export sector through taxpayer-financed promotional bureaus and lending agencies. During two wars, they effectively nationalized key sectors of the economy and vigorously pursued foreign expansion, taking advantage of the temporary merger of public and private spheres to outmaneuver foreign competitors. They supported American producers' monopolies and price-setting cartels (though, of course, America's cartels were privately owned). They carefully nurtured domestically owned communications and transportation, making sure that foreign companies never dominated the technology or dissemination of information. After World War II, they created many governmental agencies that directly dispersed American loans, relief, and information, thus manipulating to political advantage what might have been an unguided flow of information and capital. By all these means, America's governing elites retained control; they shaped domestic growth and diversification and then guided its expansion into the world.

By pressing free flow, free enterprise, and open access on others, the American government, in effect, was proscribing a developmental process for foreigners quite unlike their own—a "development" dominated by strong American-based structures and organized by American capital and expertise. For weaker states, the influx of foreign ownership and foreign-dominated communications that accompanied policies of open access could ultimately mean a surrender of national control over basic decisions regarding the organization of economic and social life. For twentieth-century American policymakers, international liberalism, a Pax Americana, and global development were synonymous goals. Nationalists, especially in Latin America, Asia, or Africa, increasingly believed that policies promoting free flow, free enterprise, and open access integrated them into a global system dominated by others and were thus incompatible with well-balanced, or nationally controlled, development in their own countries.

Second, America's liberal approach of maximizing the power of private capital and minimizing governmental restrictions did not rid the world of obstacles within the mythical free marketplace but merely made it easier for such obstacles to grow within the private sector. American-dominated private cartels and huge international businesses could practice monopolistic arrangements behind a shield of rhetoric extolling American individualism and free enterprise. And the American government supported them by denouncing restraints by foreign governments as autocratic interference with the freedom of the private sector. Americans, in short, did not really seek a *free* marketplace but a *privately owned* marketplace which they mistakenly labeled "free."

Third was another problem relating to the power of private capital. In order to become more competitive with European enterprises in a global rivalry, American companies—Firestone Rubber, Standard Oil, or Pan American Airways, for example—might carve out a dominant position in an economically weak nation. The United States government, invoking the principle of advancing international competition, might assist that effort as part of an antimonopoly campaign against Europeans. But the private corporation and, behind it, the cooperating hand of government might then exert a monopolistic, or illiberal, control on the smaller nation. Similarly, a joint government-industry effort to increase American information abroad might be justified by the liberal doctrine of free flow. Yet a strong American communications sector could, in weak states, exert a dominance that was positively stifling. Liberalism in the international order, then, could run directly counter to both liberalism and balanced, nationally controlled development in weaker nations. That the advance of international liberalism could generate its polar opposite—entrenched conservatism and a narrow range of options—in many areas of the world was a contradiction that exporters of the American dream persistently refused to acknowledge. In powerless states, archconservative regimes catering to domineering American private interests or agencies often directly resulted from America's expansion within a liberal international order; they were not unfortunate accidents brought about by America's insufficient attention to "human rights" abroad.

Fourth, although American liberal-developmentalists posited an open, global contest between alternative visions of human possibilities, they clearly believed that America's own formula for advancement would inevitably triumph in the global marketplace. The dilemma constantly presented itself: how could foreign countries who resisted American-prescribed "development" (often called "civilization" or later "modernization") be handled without violating their "liberty" to try out competing ideas and techniques? Each generation of liberal-developmentalists found ways around this difficulty by developing theories of America's special mission to uplift the world. Doctrines of racial superiority and evangelical mission prevailed early in the century; a faith in granting prerogatives to new middle-class professionals emerged with turn-of-the-century progressivism and grew stronger between the wars; and a fervent anti-Communism justified much illiberal conduct after World War II. There could, American liberal-expansionists believed, be no truly enlightened dissent against the ultimate acceptance of American ways, and this faith bred an intolerance, a narrowness, that was the very opposite of liberality.

The American dream as represented in the ideal of liberal-developmentalism differed from the reality of America's expanding cultural and economic influence. Americans involved in international affairs could preach and even believe in the basic tenets of free enterprise, open access, and free flow, while they themselves applied them selectively and ignored their contradictions.

★≡★≡★
BIBLIOGRAPHICAL ESSAY

DURING the past fifteen or twenty years, there has been a silent revolution in the writing of American histories of foreign relations. Examining the roots of American expansionism regained its prominence as a theme, especially after the publication of William A. Williams's *Tragedy of American Diplomacy* (1959). Then, taking cues from domestic historians such as Louis Galambos and James Weinstein, scholars also began to explore the implications for foreign relations of the new "organizational synthesis" and the rise of the "corporate state." Interest in expansion and in new organizational structures has taken historians in new directions, broadening the horizons of diplomatic history far beyond the traditional issues of war and peace and official government policy. There is now a rich and growing literature on the development of a foreign-affairs bureaucracy; the role of multinational corporations; issues concerning trade, raw materials, investment, and international exchange; systems of international communications and transportation; and various kinds of cultural expansion. This book is an attempt to synthesize this broad literature, much of which relates to economic and cultural trends and thus still does not fit conveniently into most textbook treatments. It also flows from my own primary research on the period 1914–1929.

The following selective bibliography contains the secondary studies that I have found most helpful and that are available in most college libraries. Although I have also consulted primary materials, I have included these sources only in rare instances.

I: INTRODUCTION

Information on the Columbian Exposition is available in Rossiter Johnson, *A History of the World's Columbian Exposition,* 4 vols. (1897); David F. Burg, *Chicago's White City of 1893* (1976); and Reid Badger, *The Great American Fair: The World's Columbian Exposition and American Culture* (1979). To understand the liberal underpinnings of American foreign relations, good places to start would be Louis Hartz, *The Liberal Tradition in America: An Interpretation of American Political Thought Since the Revolution* (1955); Charles Beard, *The Idea of National Interest* (1934); and N. Gordon Levin, *Woodrow Wilson and World Politics: America's Response to War and Revolution* (1968). Many of the books cited below elaborate on this theme in specific situations.

II: CAPITALISTS, CHRISTIANS, COWBOYS

On economic developments that affected the overseas expansion of the American economy, see Edward C. Kirkland, *Industry Comes of Age: Business, Labor, and Public Policy, 1860–1897* (1961); Fred A. Shannon, *The Farmer's Last Frontier: Agriculture, 1860–1897* (1945); Alfred Chandler, Jr., *The Visible Hand: The Managerial Revolution in American Business* (1977); and Howard P. Schonberger, *Transportation to the Seaboard: The "Communication Revolution" and American Foreign Policy* (1971). The export boom is treated especially well in David E. Novack and Matthew Simon, "Commercial Responses to the American Export Invasion, 1871–1914: An Essay in Attitudinal History," *Explorations in Entrepreneurial History* 3 (1966), 121–47. The standard books on American investments are Cleona Lewis, *America's Stake in International Investments* (1938), and Mira Wilkins, *The Emergence of Multinational Enterprise: American Business Abroad from the Colonial Era to 1914* (1970). Wilkins's bibliography should be consulted for the hundreds of histories on individual companies and entrepreneurs. Robert Bruce Davies, *Peacefully Working to Con-*

quer the World: Singer Sewing Machines in Foreign Markets, 1854–1920 (1976) is an enlightening study of the evolution of one of America's oldest international companies.

Helpful studies of specific geographical areas include John Dunning, *American Investment in British Manufacturing Industry* (1958); Ian Lumsden, ed., *The Americanization of Canada* (1970); Robert S. Schwantes, *Japanese and Americans* (1955); Michael Hunt, "Americans in the China Market," *Business History Review* 51 (1977), 277–307; Sherman Cochran, *Big Business in China: Sino-Foreign Rivalry in the Cigarette Industry, 1890–1930* (1980); David M. Pletcher, *Mines and Progress: Seven American Promoters in Mexico, 1867–1911* (1958); Clarence Clendenen et al., *Americans in Africa, 1865–1900* (1966). Both economic and cultural outreach before 1890 is treated in Milton Plesur's excellent book, *America's Outward Thrust: Approaches to Foreign Affairs, 1865–1890* (1971).

On the American missionary movement in China and the Middle East, see Paul Varg, *Missionaries, Chinese, and Diplomats, 1890–1952* (1958), and John De Novo, *American Interests and Policies in the Middle East, 1900–1939* (1963). Valentin H. Rabe, *The Home Base of American China Missions, 1880–1920* (1978) brings the "organizational synthesis" to the study of missionary activities. The activities of the YMCA's Student Volunteers are dealt with in the fine study by Charles H. Hopkins, *History of the Y.M.C.A. in North America* (1951); in William H. Morgan, *Student Religion during Fifty Years* (1935); and the fascinating study by Shirley S. Garrett, *Social Reformers in Urban China: The Chinese Y.M.C.A., 1895–1926* (1970).

Works dealing with other types of cultural contact include Henry Blumenthal, *American and French Culture, 1800–1900: Interchanges in Art, Science, Literature, and Society* (1977); Richard H. Heindel, *The American Impact on Great Britain, 1898–1914* (1968); John Burke, *Buffalo Bill* (1973). Two of the most important books for this and subsequent chapters are Merle Curti, *American Philanthropy Abroad* (1963), and Merle Curti and Kendall Birr, *Prelude to Point Four: American Technical Missions Overseas, 1838–1938* (1954).

III: THE PROMOTIONAL STATE

General works dealing with American expansion include Charles Beard, *The Idea of National Interest* (1934); Benjamin H. Williams, *Economic Foreign Policy of the United States* (1929) and *American Diplomacy* (1936); Albert K. Weinberg, *Manifest Destiny: A Study of Nationalist Expansionism in American History* (1935); William A. Williams, *The Tragedy of American Diplomacy* (1959), *The Roots of the Modern American Empire: A Study of the Growth and Shaping of Social Consciousness in a Marketplace Economy* (1969), and *Empire as a Way of Life* (1980); Walter LaFeber, *The New Empire: An Interpretation of American Expansion, 1860–1898* (1963); David Healy, *United States Expansion: The Imperialist Urge in the 1890s* (1970); Charles S. Campbell, *The Transformation of American Foreign Relations, 1865–1900* (1976); Akira Iriye, *From Nationalism to Internationalism: U.S. Foreign Policy to 1914* (1977); and Richard Drinnon, *Facing West* (1980). Tom E. Terrill, *The Tariff, Politics, and American Foreign Policy, 1874–1901* (1973) deals with an important aspect of economic policy.

For development of the structures of a promotional state, see, for general background, Robert H. Wiebe, *The Search for Order, 1877–1920* (1967); James Weinstein, *The Corporate Ideal in the Liberal State, 1900–1918* (1969); Jerry Israel, ed., *Building the Organizational Society: Essays on Associational Activities in Modern America* (1972); Louis P. Galambos, "The Emerging Organizational Synthesis in Modern American History," *Business History Review* 44 (1970), 279–90; Burton I. Kaufman, "The Organizational Dimension of United States Economic Foreign Policy, 1900–1920," *Business History Review* 46 (1972), 17–44; Ellis Hawley, "The Discovery and Study of a 'Corporate Liberalism,' " *Business History Review* 52 (1978), 309–20; and Richard H. Werking, *The Master Architects: Building the United States Foreign Service, 1890–1913* (1977). Two useful histories of business associations developed during this period include George L. Ridgeway, *Merchants of Peace: The History of the International Chamber of Commerce* (1959), and Albert K. Steigerwalt, *The National Association of Manufacturers: A Study in Business Leadership, 1895–1914*

(1964). John A. S. Grenville and George B. Young, *Politics, Strategy, and American Diplomacy: Studies in Foreign Policy, 1873–1917* (1966), and Richard D. Challener, *Admirals, Generals, and American Foreign Policy, 1898–1914* (1973) help place naval policy in a broad perspective.

There are numerous histories with a focus on Presidential policies. On Harrison, Cleveland, and McKinley, see Ernest R. May, *Imperial Democracy: The Emergence of America as a Great Power* (1961); Walter LaFeber, *The New Empire* (1963); H. Wayne Morgan, *America's Road to Empire: The War with Spain and Overseas Expansion* (1965); Paolo E. Coletta, ed., *Threshold to American Internationalism: Essays on the Foreign Policies of William McKinley* (1970); and Charles S. Campbell, *The Transformation of American Foreign Relations* (1976). On Theodore Roosevelt, see Howard Beale, *Theodore Roosevelt and the Rise of America to World Power* (1956); David H. Burton, *Theodore Roosevelt: Confident Imperialist* (1968); Raymond Esthus, *Theodore Roosevelt and the International Rivalries* (1970); and Frederick W. Marks III, *Velvet on Iron: The Diplomacy of Theodore Roosevelt* (1979). On William Howard Taft, see Walter and Marie Scholes, *The Foreign Policies of the Taft Administration* (1970); Donald F. Anderson, *William Howard Taft: A Conservative's Conception of the Presidency* (1973); Paolo E. Coletta, *The Presidency of William Howard Taft* (1973); and Ralph S. Minger, *William Howard Taft and United States Foreign Policy: The Apprenticeship Years, 1900–1908* (1975). Influential imperialists and anti-imperialists are treated in David Healy, *United States Expansion* (1970); Robert Beisner, *Twelve Against Empire, 1898–1900* (1968); E. Berkeley Tompkins, *Anti-Imperialism in the United States: The Great Debate, 1890–1920* (1970); John Braeman, *Albert J. Beveridge: American Nationalist* (1971); Kenton Clymer, *John Hay: The Gentleman as Diplomat* (1975); William C. Widenor, *Henry Cabot Lodge and the Search for an American Foreign Policy* (1980); Robert Seager II, *Alfred Thayer Mahan: The Man and His Letters* (1977); and Gerald Eggert, *Richard Olney: Evolution of a Statesman* (1974).

Many works examine United States relations with specific regions. For England, see Charles S. Campbell, *Anglo-American*

Understanding, 1898–1903 (1957). For Asia, see Frederick Field, *American Participation in the China Consortiums* (1931); Fred Harvey Harrington, *God, Mammon, and the Japanese: Dr. Horace N. Allen and Korean-American Relations, 1884–1905* (1944); Charles Vevier, *The United States and China, 1906–1913* (1955); Thomas McCormick, *China Market: America's Quest for Informal Empire, 1893–1901* (1967), a book that is also especially valuable for its discussion of currency policies; Akira Iriye, *Across the Pacific: An Inner History of American–East Asian Relations* (1967); Paul A. Varg, *The Making of a Myth: The United States and China, 1897–1912* (1968); Marilyn B. Young, *The Rhetoric of Empire: American China Policy, 1895–1901* (1968); Jerry Israel, *Progressivism and the Open Door: America and China, 1905–1921* (1971); Michael Hunt, *Frontier Defense and the Open Door: Manchuria in Chinese-American Relations, 1895–1911* (1973). On the Philippines, consult William J. Pomeroy, *American Neocolonialism: Its Emergence in the Philippines and Asia* (1970); Daniel B. Schirmer, *Republic or Empire: American Resistance to the Philippine War* (1972); Richard E. Welch, *Response to Imperialism: The United States and the Philippine-American War* (1979). Glenn A. May, *Social Engineering in the Philippines: The Aims, Execution, and Impact of American Colonial Policy, 1900–1913* (1980) stresses the incoherence and limited nature of attempts at Americanization.

Works on United States relations with countries in the Western Hemisphere include Dana G. Munro, *Intervention and Dollar Diplomacy in the Caribbean, 1900–1921* (1964); Lester Langley, *United States and the Caribbean, 1900–1970* (1980); P. Edward Haley, *Revolution and Intervention: The Diplomacy of Taft and Wilson in Mexico, 1910–1917* (1970); Philip Foner, *The Spanish-American-Cuban War and the Birth of American Imperialism*, 2 vols. (1972); Allan R. Millett, *The Politics of Intervention: The Military Occupation of Cuba, 1906–1909* (1968); James H. Hitchman, *Leonard Wood and Cuban Independence, 1898–1902* (1971); Jules R. Benjamin, *The United States and Cuba, 1880–1934* (1974); Robert E. Hannigan, "Reciprocity 1911: Continentalism and American Weltpolitik," *Diplomatic History* 4 (1980), 1–18 (on Canada).

IV: WORLD WAR I AND THE TRIUMPH OF THE
PROMOTIONAL STATE

General studies of Woodrow Wilson's diplomacy include those
by Arthur S. Link, *Woodrow Wilson,* vols. II–V (1960–1965); N.
Gordon Levin, *Woodrow Wilson and World Politics* (1968); Arno
Mayer, *Wilson versus Lenin: The Political Origins of the New Diplomacy, 1917–1918* (1964). Noel H. Pugach, *Paul S. Reinsch: Open
Door Diplomat in Action* (1979); Lawrence Gelfand, *The Inquiry*
(1963); and Mark T. Gilderhus, *Diplomacy and Revolution: U.S.-
Mexican Relations under Wilson and Carranza* (1977) all provide
further insight into the Wilsonian world view.

On economic organization and expansion, see Burton I. Kaufman, *Efficiency and Expansion: Foreign Trade Organization in the
Wilson Administration, 1913–1921* (1974); Grosvenor B. Clarkson,
*Industrial America in the World War: The Strategy Behind the
Lines, 1917–1918* (1923); Paul P. Abrahams, *The Foreign Expansion of American Finance and Its Relationship to the Foreign Economic Policies of the United States, 1907–1921* (1976); and Paul
Koistinen, *The Military-Industrial Complex: A Historical Perspective (1980). Works by Carl P. Parrini, Heir to Empire: United States
Economic Diplomacy, 1916–1923* (1969); Roberta A. Dayer,
"Strange Bedfellows: J. P. Morgan and Co., Whitehall and the
Wilson Administration during World War I," *Business History* 18
(1976), 127–51; Emily S. Rosenberg, "Economic Pressures in Anglo-American Diplomacy in Mexico, 1917–1981," *Journal of Interamerican Studies and World Affairs* 17 (1975), 123–51 and "Anglo-American Economic Rivalry in Brazil during World War I,"
Diplomatic History 2 (1978), 131–52; and John De Novo, "The
Movement for an Aggressive American Oil Policy Abroad, 1918–
1920," *American Historical Review* 61 (1956), 854–75 all develop
the themes of Anglo-American rivalry, American economic ascendancy, and the importance policymakers placed on economic
power. Many of the works cited in the previous chapter and in
Chapter VIII are also relevant to an understanding of Wilson's
economic and political policies.

On relief efforts during World War I, see Frank M. Surface
and Raymond L. Bland, *American Food in the World War and
Reconstruction Period* (1931); John M. Thompson, *Russia, Bol-*

242 ★ BIBLIOGRAPHY

shevism and the Versailles Peace (1966); George W. Hopkins,
"The Politics of Food: United States and Soviet Hungary,
March–August, 1919," *Mid-America* 55 (1973), 245–70; David
Burner, *Herbert Hoover: A Public Life* (1979); and Benjamin M.
Weissman, *Herbert Hoover and Famine Relief to Soviet Russia
1921-3* (1974).

On the Creel Committee, see George Creel, *How We Advertised
America* (1920); James R. Mock and Cedric Larson, *Words that
Won the War: The Story of the Committee on Public Information,
1917-1919* (1939); Robert C. Hilderbrand, *Power and the People:
Executive Management of Public Opinion in Foreign Affairs, 1897-
1921* (1981). Stephen L. Vaughn, *Holding Fast the Inner Lines:
Democracy, Nationalism, and the Committee on Public Information* (1980) deals only with the Domestic Section but does help
capture the spirit of the CPI.

Labor diplomacy during World War I is covered in Ronald
Radosh, *American Labor and United States Foreign Policy* (1969);
Sinclair Snow, *The Pan-American Federation of Labor* (1964); and
Harvey A. Levenstein, *Labor Organizations in the United States
and Mexico* (1971).

Three of the most perceptive recent studies of the spread of
professionalism and expertise and of the social impact of these
trends are Burton J. Bledstein, *The Culture of Professionalism: The
Middle Class and the Development of Higher Education in America*
(1976); David F. Noble, *America by Design: Science, Technology,
and the Rise of Corporate Capitalism* (1977); and Christopher
Lasch, *The Culture of Narcissism: American Life in an Age of
Diminishing Expectations* (1979). The implications of their anal-
yses might well be extended into foreign relations.

V: INTERNATIONAL COMMUNICATIONS

Communications policies from the Wilson Administration
through the 1920s are treated in Joseph Tulchin, *The Aftermath of
War: World War I and U.S. Policy toward Latin America* (1971),
and Michael Hogan, *Informal Entente: The Private Structure of
Cooperation in Anglo-American Economic Diplomacy, 1918-1928*
(1977). Useful older studies include Gleason L. Archer, *History of
Radio to 1926* (1938); Leslie Bennett Tribolet, *The International*

Aspects of Electrical Communications in the Pacific Area (1929);
and George A. Codding, Jr., *The International Telecommunications Union* (1952). On the closely related subject of the expansion
of news services, Kent Cooper's memoir, *Barriers Down* (1942), is
indispensable.

On trends in the export of motion pictures, including material
on foreign restrictions, Robert Sklar, *Movie-Made America* (1975),
and Howard T. Lewis, *The Motion Picture Industry* (1933) are
excellent. See also Lewis Jacobs, *The Rise of the American Film*
(1939); Arthur F. McClure, ed., *The Movies: An American Idiom:
Readings in the Social History of the American Motion Picture*
(1971); David Strauss, "The Rise of Anti-Americanism in France:
French Intellectuals and the American Film Industry, 1927–
1932," *Journal of Popular Culture* 10 (1977), 753–59; Frank
Southard, Jr., *American Industry in Europe* (1931); and Lawrence
Cohen, *Movietone Presents the Twentieth Century* (1976).

On aviation, see Wesley Phillips Newton, *The Perilous Sky: U.S.
Aviation Diplomacy and Latin America, 1919–1931* (1978), and
Matthew Josephson, *Empire of the Air: Juan Trippe and the Struggle for World Airways* (1943).

VI: FORGING A GLOBAL FELLOWSHIP

The peace movement and various internationalist organizations
are examined in Charles Chatfield, *For Peace and Justice: Pacifism
in America, 1914–1941* (1971); Charles DeBenedetti, *Origins of the
Modern American Peace Movement, 1915–1929* (1978) and *The
Peace Reform in American History* (1980). Harold Josephson,
James T. Shotwell and the Rise of Internationalism in America
(1975) examines a noted liberal-internationalist, and Robert Ferrell, *Peace in Their Time* (1952) examines the Kellogg–Briand
Pact. Merle Curti, *Peace or War: The American Struggle* (1936);
D. F. Fleming, *The United States and World Organization, 1920–
1933* (1938); Sondra R. Herman, *Eleven against War: Studies in
American Internationalist Thought, 1898–1921* (1969) are also useful.

Specific organizations or people dealing with cultural relations
during the 1930s are examined in Merle Curti, *American Philanthropy* (1963); Charles Hopkins, *History of the Y.M.C.A.* (1951);

Raymond Fosdick, *The Story of the Rockefeller Foundation* (1952); Waldemar Nielsen, *The Big Foundations* (1972); Peter Collier and David Horowitz, *The Rockefellers: An American Dynasty* (1976); Charles F. Marden, *Rotary and Its Brothers: An Analysis and Interpretation of the Men's Service Club* (1935); Arnold H. Taylor, *American Diplomacy and the Narcotics Traffic, 1900–1939* (1969); Warren I. Cohen, *The Chinese Connection: Roger S. Greene, Thomas W. Lamont, George E. Sokolsky and American-East Asian Relations* (1978); George W. Gray, *Education on an International Scale* (1941); and Laurence H. Shoup, *Imperial Brain Trust: The Council on Foreign Relations and United States Foreign Policy* (1977).

VII: ECONOMIC EXPANSION

Post-World War I expansion of American business is thoroughly treated in Mira Wilkins, *Maturing of Multinational Enterprise, 1914–1970* (1974). Consult her bibliography for specific companies and industries. Lewis, *America's Stake in International Investments;* Clyde Phelps, *The Foreign Expansion of American Banks* (1927); Robert Dunn, *American Foreign Investments* (1926) are useful. The movement of American business into South America is treated in Dudley Phelps, *Migration of Industry to South America* (1936), and J. F. Normano, *The Struggle for South America: Economy and Ideology* (1931). For business relations with the Soviet Union, see Joan Hoff Wilson, *Ideology and Economics: U.S. Relations with the Soviet Union, 1918–1933* (1974); Anthony Sutton, *Western Technology and Soviet Economic Development, 1917–1930* (1968); William A. Williams, *American-Russian Relations, 1781–1947* (1952); H. John Lewis Gaddis, *Russia, the Soviet Union, and the United States: An Interpretative History* (1978); and Peter Filene, *Americans and the Soviet Experiment, 1917–1933* (1967). On Canada, see Irving Brecher and S. S. Reisman, *Canada–U.S. Economic Relations* (1957); and Hugh G. Aitken et al., *The American Economic Impact on Canada* (1959). John Dunning, *American Investment in British Manufacturing Industry* (1958); Frank Southard, Jr., *American Industry in Europe* (1931); and Donald T. Brash, *American Investment in Australian Industry* (1966) examine other regions. John Lorant, *The Role of Capital*

Improving Innovations in American Manufacturing during the 1920s (1975) examines the tremendous growth of American productivity, and the National Industrial Conference Board, Inc., *Trends in the Foreign Trade of the United States* (1930) presents data on the growth of American export trade.

Policies toward raw materials are covered in Alfred E. Eckes, Jr., *The United States and the Global Struggle for Minerals* (1979); Stephen D. Krasner, *Defending the National Interest: Raw Materials Investments and U.S. Foreign Policy* (1978). Benjamin Williams, *Economic Foreign Policy of the United States* (1929) is especially good on Hoover's fight against state-controlled foreign monopolies. On oil policy and the cartel agreements, see John Blair, *The Control of Oil* (1978), and Anthony Sampson, *Seven Sisters: The Great Oil Companies and the World They Shaped* (1975). Many of the works cited in the next chapter provide information on trade, investment, and raw-materials policies for specific countries.

VIII: THE COOPERATIVE STATE OF THE 1920S

There are many excellent books on economic foreign policy and the attitudes of policymakers of the 1920s. Among the best are Melvin Leffler, *The Elusive Quest: America's Pursuit of European Stability and French Security, 1919–1933* (1979); Michael Hogan, *Informal Entente* (1977); Robert D. Schulzinger, *The Making of the Diplomatic Mind* (1975); and Joseph Tulchin, *Aftermath of War* (1971). Joan Hoff Wilson, *American Business and Foreign Policy, 1920–1933* (1971) dissects the split between business "nationalists" and "internationalists." Herbert Hoover's role is examined in David Burner, *Herbert Hoover: A Public Life* (1979); Lawrence Gelfand, ed., *Herbert Hoover: The Great War and Its Aftermath, 1914–1923* (1979); Joan Hoff Wilson, *Herbert Hoover: Forgotten Progressive* (1975); Ellis Hawley, "Herbert Hoover, the Commerce Secretariat and the Vision of an 'Associative State,' 1921–1928," *Journal of American History* 61 (1974), 116–40; Lloyd Craig, *Aggressive Introvert: Herbert Hoover and Public Relations Management, 1912–1932* (1972); and Joseph Brandes, *Herbert Hoover and Economic Diplomacy* (1962). The many articles by Robert D. Cuff provide thoughtful analysis of policymaking structures; especially valuable are his "Herbert Hoover: The Ideology of Voluntarism," *Journal of American History* 64 (1977), 358–72, and "An Organizational Perspective on the Military-Industrial Complex," *Business History Review* 52 (1978), 250–72. Three exceptionally useful studies on international economic stabilization are Lester Chandler, *Benjamin Strong, Central Banker* (1958); Stephen V. O. Clarke, *Central Bank Cooperation, 1924–31* (1967); and Richard H. Meyer, *Banker's Diplomacy: Monetary Stabilization in the Twenties* (1970). On government policies toward trade and investment, see Herbert Feis, *The Diplomacy of the Dollar: First Era, 1919–1932* (1950), and the books by Benjamin Williams.

On economic diplomacy toward Asia, see Roberta A. Dayer, *Bankers and Diplomats in China, 1917–1925: The Anglo-American Relationship* (1981), and Warren I. Cohen, *The Chinese Connection* (1978), the section on Lamont. Arthur N. Young, *China's Nation-Building Effort, 1927–1937: The Financial and Economic Record* (1971) provides an exceedingly important account of his financial mission in that country. Middle Eastern involvement can be followed in John De Novo, *American Interests and Policies in the Middle East, 1900–1939* (1963); Phillip J. Baram, *The Department of State in the Middle East, 1919–1945* (1978); and Benjamin Shwadran, *The Middle East, Oil, and the Great Powers* (1955). Arthur C. Millspaugh, *Americans in Persia* (1946) recounts the experience of that author's financial mission.

For Europe, see Melvin Leffler, *Elusive Quest* (1979), and Stephen A. Schuker, *The End of French Predominance in Europe* (1976) on the Dawes Plan. Frank Costigliola, "The United States and the Reconstruction of Germany," *Business History Review* 50 (1976), 477–502 and "American Foreign Policy in the 'Nutcracker': The United States and Poland," *Pacific Historical Review* 48 (1979), 85–105 are excellent. Piotr S. Wandycz, *The United States and Poland* (1980) has a fine chapter on economic relations during the 1920s.

Economic concerns with Latin-American countries are covered in Robert F. Smith, *The United States and Revolutionary Nationalism in Mexico, 1916–1932* (1972); Lorenzo Meyer, *Mexico and the United States in the Oil Controversy, 1917–1942* (1977); N. Stephen Kane, "Bankers and Diplomats: The Diplomacy of the Dollar in

Mexico, 1921–1924," *Business History Review* 43 (1973), 335–52; Dana Munro, *United States and the Caribbean Republics, 1921–1933* (1974); Robert F. Smith, *The United States and Cuba: Business and Diplomacy, 1917–1960* (1960); Jules Benjamin, *The United States and Cuba, 1880–1934* (1974); Stephen Rabe, "Anglo-American Rivalry for Venezuelan Oil, 1919–1929," *Mid-America* 58 (1976), 97–109; Carl E. Solberg, *Oil and Nationalism in Argentina: A History* (1979); and Stephen J. Randall, *The Diplomacy of Modernization: Colombian-American Relations, 1920–1940* (1977). Kenneth Grieb, *The Latin American Policy of Warren G. Harding* (1976) is also useful.

IX: DEPRESSION AND WAR

On international conditions and Franklin Roosevelt's diplomacy during the 1930s, the most helpful books include Robert Dalleck, *Franklin D. Roosevelt and American Foreign Policy* (1979); Frederick Adams, *Economic Diplomacy: The Export-Import Bank and American Foreign Policy, 1934–1939* (1976); John Morton Blum, *V Was for Victory* (1976); Arnold Offner, *The Origins of the Second World War* (1975); Mira Wilkins, *Maturing of Multinational Enterprise, 1914–1970* (1974); Norman D. Markowitz, *The Rise and Fall of the People's Century: Henry A. Wallace and American Liberalism* (1973); Charles P. Kindleberger, *The World in Depression, 1929–1939* (1973); Gabriel Kolko, *The Politics of War* (1968); Lloyd Gardner, *Economic Aspects of New Deal Diplomacy* (1964); and Max Winkler, *Foreign Bonds, an Autopsy: A Study of Defaults and Repudiations of Government Obligations* (1933). Wartime and postwar economic policies are covered in Fred Block, *The Origins of International Economic Disorder: A Study of United States International Monetary Policy from World War II to the Present* (1977); Alfred Eckes, Jr., *A Search for Solvency: Bretton Woods and the International Monetary System, 1941–71* (1975); Daniel Yergin, *Shattered Peace: the Origins of the Cold War and the National Security State* (1977); John Gimbel, *The Origins of the Marshall Plan* (1976); George C. Herring, Jr., *Aid to Russia, 1941–1946: Strategy, Diplomacy, the Origins of the Cold War* (1973); Thomas Campbell, *Masquerade Peace: America's U.N. Policy* (1973); and the most indispensable book, Richard N. Gardner, *Sterling–Dollar Diplomacy: The Origins and Prospects of Our International Economic Order* (1969).

Relations with Asia are dealt with in Akira Iriye, *Power and Culture, The Japanese-American War, 1941–1945* (1981); Michael Schaller, *The U.S. Crusade in China, 1938–1945* (1979); Christopher Thorne, *Allies of a Kind: The United States, Britain, and the War against Japan, 1941–1945* (1978); Robert A. Hart, *The Eccentric Tradition: American Diplomacy in the Far East* (1976); Irvine H. Anderson, Jr., *The Standard-Vacuum Oil Company and United States-East Asian Policy, 1933–1941* (1975); Charles E. Neu, *The Troubled Encounter* (1975); Warren I. Cohen, *America's Response to China* (1971); Edward Friedman and Mark Selden, eds., *America's Asia* (1971); Waldo H. Heinrichs, *American Ambassador: Joseph C. Grew and the Development of the United States Diplomatic Tradition* (1966); and Dorothy Borg, *The United States and the Far Eastern Crisis of 1933–1938* (1964). On the Near and Middle East, see Bruce R. Kuniholm, *The Origins of the Cold War in the Near East* (1980); Phillip J. Baram, *The Department of State in the Middle East, 1919–1945* (1978); Benjamin Shwadran, *The Middle East, Oil, and the Great Powers* (1955).

The most helpful works on Latin America include Irwin F. Gellman, *Good Neighbor Diplomacy: United States Policies in Latin America, 1933–1945* (1979); Stephen G. Rabe, "The Elusive Conference: United States Economic Relations with Latin America, 1945–1952," *Diplomatic History* 3 (1979), 279–94; Randall B. Woods, *The Roosevelt Foreign-Policy Establishment and the "Good Neighbor": The United States and Argentina, 1941–1945* (1979); Dick Steward, *Trade and Hemisphere* (1975); Frank McCann, *The Brazilian-American Alliance, 1937–1945* (1973); Jules R. Benjamin, "The New Deal, Cuba, and the Rise of a Global Foreign Economic Policy," *Business History Review* 51 (1977), 57–78; and Alton Frye, *Nazi Germany and the American Hemisphere, 1933–1941* (1967).

On issues relating to oil, see Michael B. Stoff, *Oil, War and American Security: The Search for a National Policy on Foreign Oil, 1941–1947* (1980); Aaron David Miller, *Search for Security: Saudi Arabian Oil and American Foreign Policy, 1939–1949* (1980); Alfred E. Eckes, Jr., *The United States and the Global Struggle for*

Minerals (1979); Burton I. Kaufman, *The Oil Cartel Case: A Documentary Study of Antitrust Activity in the Cold War Era* (1979); Robert Engler, *Politics of Oil: A Study of Private Power and Democratic Directions* (1976); and Herbert Feis, *Petroleum and American Foreign Policy* (1944). On American policy toward commercial air transport, see James L. Gormly, "Keeping the Door Open in Saudi Arabia: The United States and the Dhahran Airfield, 1945–1946," *Diplomatic History* 4 (1980), 189–206; Matthew Josephson, *Empire of the Air: Juan Trippe and the Struggle for World Airways* (1943); and Burr W. Leyson, *Wings around the World: The Story of American International Air Transport* (1948).

X: THE CULTURAL OFFENSIVE

Frank A. Ninkovich, *The Diplomacy of Ideas: United States Foreign Policy and Cultural Relations, 1938–1950* (1981), which appeared while this book was in press, is an excellent study of this long-neglected subject. His previous articles, especially "The Currents of Cultural Diplomacy: Art and the State Department, 1938–1947," *Diplomatic History* 1 (1977), 215–37, were extremely useful. A good view of the combined impact of cultural offensives for Latin America is provided in Gerald K. Haines, "Under the Eagle's Wing: The Franklin Roosevelt Administration Forges an American Hemisphere," *Diplomatic History* 1 (1977), 373–88. The most valuable works on the OWI are Allan Winkler, *The Politics of Propaganda: The Office of War Information, 1942–1945* (1978); Clayton R. Koopes and Gregory D. Black, "What to Show the World: The Office of War Information and Hollywood, 1942–1945," *Journal of American History,* 64 (1977), 87–105; and John M. Blum, *V Was for Victory* (1976). For an analysis and critical assessment of America's dominance over the means of communication since World War II, see Jeremy Tunstall, *The Media Are American: Anglo-American Media in the World* (1977), and Herbert Schiller, *Mass Communications and American Empire* (1971) and *Communication and Cultural Domination* (1976). On the OSS, see R. Harris Smith, *OSS: The Secret History of America's First Central Intelligence Agency* (1972).

Three government-sponsored studies which are useful, if not highly interpretive, are Wilma Fairbank, *America's Cultural Ex-*

periment in China, 1942–1949 (1976); J. Manuel Espinosa, Inter-American Beginnings of United States Cultural Diplomacy (1977); and Henry J. Kellermann, Cultural Relations as an Instrument of United States Foreign Policy: The Educational Exchange Program between the United States and Germany, 1945–1954 (1978). Several older studies of the "cultural dimension" lack Ninkovich's analytical quality but do provide excellent insights into this new departure in diplomacy: Arthur W. Macmahon, Memorandum on the Post-war International Information Program of the United States (1945); Llewellyn White and Robert D. Leigh, Peoples Speaking to Peoples: A Report on International Mass Communication from the Commission on Freedom of the Press (1946); Ruth McMurry and Muna Lee, The Cultural Approach (1947); Charles A. H. Thomson, Overseas Information Service of the United States Government (1948); Charles A. Thomson and Walter Laves, Cultural Relations and United States Foreign Policy (1963); Philip H. Coombs, The Fourth Dimension of Foreign Policy: Educational and Cultural Affairs (1964); and Merle Curti, American Philanthropy (1963).

Labor diplomacy during and after the war is treated in Ronald Radosh, American Labor and United States Foreign Policy (1969); John P. Windmuller, American Labor and the International Labor Movement, 1940–1953 (1954); Hobart A. Spaulding, Jr., "U.S. and Latin American Labor: The Dynamics of Imperialist Control," Latin American Perspectives 3 (1976), 45–69; and Peter Weiler, "The United States, International Labor, and the Cold War: The Breakup of the World Federation of Trade Unions," Diplomatic History 5 (1981), 1–22.

★═★═★

INDEX